For Carol & Don Roper,
our dear friends,
with best wishes,
Bill Rhoads

CHARLES S. KEEFE

1876–1946

From
the books of
Charles S. Keefe.

200

The Friends of Historic Kingston
presents an exhibit on the topic
of this book from May to October 2018.

www.friendsofhistorickingston.org

CHARLES S. KEEFE

1876–1946

Colonial Revival Architect in Kingston and New York

WILLIAM BERTOLET RHOADS

BLACK·DOME

Published by Black Dome Press Corp.
649 Delaware Ave., Delmar, N.Y. 12054
blackdomepress.com
(518) 439-6512

First Edition 2017
Copyright © 2017 by William Bertolet Rhoads

Hardbound: ISBN: 978-1-883789-90-9
Paperbound: ISBN: 978-1-883789-89-3

Library of Congress Control Number:
2017960088

*Front cover: "Store Building for Granville M. Joslen,
Esq., Hudson, N.Y." Rendering by Charles S. Keefe.
Keefe Archive, Friends of Historic Kingston.*

*Back cover: "Catskill Country Club." Rendering by
Charles S. Keefe. Keefe Archive, Friends of Historic
Kingston.*

*Half-title: "From the books of Charles S. Keefe."
Sketch by Keefe for his bookplate. Keefe Archive,
Friends of Historic Kingston.*

*Title page: "Plans for an Attractive Bungalow."
Design by Keefe, New York Press, Feb. 8, 1914.*

Design: Abigail Sturges of Sturges Design

Printed in the USA

10 9 8 7 6 5 4 3 2 1

Note: Places are in New York State
unless otherwise identified.

Contents

Foreword

The answer to the question "What is American architecture?" can be very complicated. When looking at the built environment from coast-to-coast, or simply driving through any modern American city, one is confronted with many different images and styles. But no matter one's personal preference—whether mid-century modern or Victorian gingerbread—houses that can be identified as Colonial Revival can be found in almost every residential section across the country. The house is, after all, the heart of America, one of our distinguishing features, and one of its prominent styles is the "Colonial."

What is "Colonial Revival?" It can be diverse and range from small white Cape Cod houses with long slanting roofs, to an imposing red brick structure with columns and a pediment across the front, or even to an imitation of Washington's Mount Vernon with a long two-story porch held up by thin wooden piers. Houses such as these can be found everywhere in America. But then, in addition, one can also sight a dwelling with light-colored thick stucco walls and red tile roof that resembles the Spanish era, or perhaps even a Creole-inspired house with two-story porch. They, too, are "Colonial." Also very much a part of the Colonial Revival are furniture, interiors, and garden designs harking back to America's early days, and paintings, prints, and photos depicting America's seventeenth- and eighteenth-century history. Further, the Colonial Revival was not just for houses, but was also employed in commercial and public buildings. Novels, too, can be part of the Colonial Revival, such as Kenneth Roberts's *Rabble in Arms* (1933) set on the Hudson River. Colonial Revival is a very broad category that is not really a style but an association with early American history both prior to and soon after Independence. The Colonial Revival is at the heart of American architecture.

The story of the Colonial Revival and how it came into being can also be long and complicated. Historic preservation plays a role. While Washington's Mount Vernon is usually cited as the first to be historically preserved, the saving and restoring of Washington's headquarters—the Hasbrouck house at Newburgh, New York—in 1850 was actually the first state-sponsored achievement. Worthy of note as well is Washington Irving's mid–1830s fictional Dutch Colonial house farther down the Hudson River at Tarrytown.

However, it wasn't until the 1870s with the Centennial and its patriotic celebration of American history that the Colonial Revival in architecture rose to great popularity, eventually to become dominant in the decades between the 1890s and the Great Depression. The 1930s witnessed a dramatic decline in building, but look at post offices constructed during the New Deal and one will find the Colonial Revival as the dominant image. The standard story of American architecture is that Modernism arrived after World War II and the Colonial Revival was consigned to the graveyard. But, as noted earlier, a drive through almost any residential section across the U.S. will reveal that the Colonial lives on today. It will not die!

Although the reasons for the revival of the Colonial are manifold and complicated, one of the major causes was a search for a genuine American style. And this is where Charles Keefe fits in. He wrote in 1930 that, while he had studied many of the original houses of the thirteen colonies, "I have found no sort of house that has engaged my affections and aroused my sympathy and enthusiasm more than the unpretentious and lovely type known as the Cape Cod cottage."

Charles Keefe is an excellent example of the forgotten star. Except for the odd bibliomaniacal scholar who might have come across some of his publications, Keefe has all but vanished from architectural history. But now, in William Rhoads's excellent study, Keefe reemerges as a major figure. Keefe's career and writings illuminate some of the issues of the Colonial Revival and also of architectural practice in the period of the later nineteenth century and the first half of the twentieth century. Although he designed some rather expensive houses, much of his work was more modest. Yes, he did have a New York office for some time, but the real impact of this work was seen in smaller towns and through the many publications in which he was involved. The old saw, "Does a building exist if it isn't photographed?" can be expanded to, "architects don't exist unless they are published." As this study of Keefe shows, even small-town architects can make an impact. Thank goodness Keefe has been rediscovered.

RICHARD GUY WILSON

Richard Guy Wilson is the Commonwealth Professor at the University of Virginia where he teaches the history of architecture and design. His research and publications include articles, books, and exhibitions. Among them are: *The American Renaissance*, *The Machine Age in America*, *Thomas Jefferson's Academical Village*, *Edith Wharton at Home*, and *The Colonial Revival House*.

Introduction

Why write a book about Charles Keefe, an architect whose life and career were in many ways perfectly ordinary, who designed mostly small Colonial Revival houses (for middle-class clients) and outbuildings on large estates (for the wealthy), who achieved only a limited national reputation in his lifetime, and who is almost forgotten today? Some readers may be drawn to the story of a boy from a family of modest means and standing in Kingston, who went to the big city and, with no formal training outside architectural offices, no spark of genius, but some talent, a good deal of hard work, and the ability to make friends, did well enough as a Colonial Revival architect, author of *The American House*, and compiler of a new edition of *The Georgian Period* to have his obituary published in *The New York Times* under the subheading, "Expert on Colonial Homes and Farm Buildings," and in the *Architectural Record* where he was identified as a "widely known house architect and an authority on Colonial American houses."[1]

I have devoted much of my career as a researcher and writer to the Colonial Revival (beginning with a 1975 doctoral dissertation at Princeton). Keefe's Colonial houses, built from New England to California, were often published in leading architectural journals and in popular magazines, and he was a prime advocate for the Colonial in the battle with modernism. (Keefe, however, remains in the shadow of Royal Barry Wills [1895–1962], the younger and better-known Colonial propagandist in the 30s and 40s.[2]) Finally, there is the happy circumstance that many of Keefe's drawings, some of his office correspondence, and a few of his personal papers and family photos survive seventy years after his death. This survival allows a remarkably full reconstruction of his outlook and career from his rise in New York in the 1910s, to the peak of his practice in the 1920s when it extended to Ecuador, to the Depression of the 1930s when he was forced to retreat from New York and work out of his home in Kingston while still attracting Lowell Thomas and Thomas Dewey as clients.

Charles Keefe at his drafting board, February 1905.

The person primarily responsible for the preservation of material from Keefe's office was his widow, Grace. In her 1954 will, she called upon her executors to "publish a book consisting of the photographs and plans of the houses designed by my late husband; said book to be entitled 'Houses, by Charles S. Keefe, A.I.A.'" At her death in 1971 her estate did not have the funds to publish this book, and Keefe's drawings, photos, and office files were dispersed. Fortunately many of these were purchased by Robert H. Palmatier (1939–2009) of Thumbprint Antiques in Stone Ridge, where they were discovered by my wife, Sally Rhoads, and then bought by us in November and December 1975. In 2004 we donated most of our Keefe material to the Friends of Historic Kingston, which, thanks to its executive director, Jane Kellar, has offered a long-term home for Kingston-related architectural archives. The present book is not exactly the book Grace Keefe had in mind, but I hope it does serve as a permanent record of an American architect dedicated to his profession and traditional architecture in the first half of the twentieth century.

CHAPTER ONE

The Early Years in Kingston, 1876–1907

The Family

Three Keefe boys. Left to right: Charles, Andrew, and Augustus. (T. D. Lewis photo)

Charles Schoonmaker Keefe was born October 12, 1876, in Kingston, New York, the son of Andrew J. and Celestina Keefe. His birth year was propitious for an architect known for reviving the Colonial era, since 1876 saw the celebration of the centennial of American independence and increasing enthusiasm for preserving landmarks from Colonial and Revolutionary times, as well as drawing upon their forms in new construction.

Keefe's origins were modest. His father, Andrew J. Keefe (1842–1935), was of Irish Catholic heritage and was born and raised in rural Vermont in and near the Town of Richmond, not far from Burlington. Andrew's father and mother, Charles (1811–73) and Mary McByrne Keefe (died 1896), are buried in St. Mary Cemetery outside the village of Richmond. Their tombstone records that Charles was "Native of County of Fermanagh, Ireland," and his grandson Charles was always conscious of his Irish heritage.

By 1872 Andrew was employed as a clerk and living in Kingston. For over fifty years he was associated with L. S. Winne & Co., hardware merchants, on Kingston's Wall Street, and as a young man he was an active member of Wiltwyck Hose Co. Andrew married Celestina Priscilla Schoonmaker (1848–91), the daughter of Augustus and Jane Elting Schoonmaker. (Celestina had been married previously, in 1870, to George Winter.) Charles Schoonmaker Keefe was the oldest of Andrew and Celestina's four children; Charles's siblings were Augustus (1879–1934), Andrew (1887–1961), and Celeste (1891–1982). After Celestina's death in 1891, Charles's father remarried in 1894, and with his second wife, Mattie B. Pultz Keefe (1865–1949), had three sons and a daughter (Robert, Eileen, James, and John) who survived at her death in 1949. In 1932, Keefe noted wryly

Left to right: Andrew Keefe and his sons, Charles, Robert, and Augustus, at 291 Washington Avenue, Kingston.

that he had found a number of photos of himself as a child: "Maybe the pictures were taken to keep things straight as I was the first child of eight and some records were necessary."[1]

In Kingston, Andrew J. Keefe was a member of St. Joseph's Catholic Church and was buried in St. Mary's Cemetery. Celestina Schoonmaker, with Dutch Reformed roots, was a Catholic at her death, while Mattie Pultz Keefe was a Methodist, though buried with her husband at St. Mary's Cemetery. (The Andrew Keefe monument at St. Mary's Cemetery is inscribed with Celestina's name and dates below Andrew's, while Mattie's are inscribed on the back of the monument.) Charles was brought up Catholic, but eventually joined St. James Methodist Church and was a member of its Official Board. Still, religion seems not have had a central place in his life, and he designed no churches. Charles's wife Grace was the more active member of St. James where her father was a long-time member.[2]

Charles—known as Charlie or Charley to family and friends—maintained ties with his father's family in Vermont, and New England (including its architecture) would always appeal more strongly to him than other parts of the country with the possible exception of his native Hudson Valley. He and Grace motored to Vermont for the first time in their Overland automobile in August 1919. Later trips to Vermont included one to attend an uncle's funeral in 1932 and another for ten days in 1939 accompanied by Dr. Christopher Keefe, an uncle residing in Kingston. In July 1925 he drew plans for altering a plain, one-story, frame house, apparently on the family farm in Vermont. The plans did not call for an indoor bathroom. Vermont vernacular architecture—familiar to his grandparents—certainly influenced Keefe's mature "Cape Cod" designs.[3]

Charles and Grace on their first trip to Vermont with Overland automobile, August 1919.

Little is known about his relations with his mother and his mother's family. However, his obituary (probably reflecting information from his widow Grace, who had Huguenot ancestors) failed to mention his father's Irish ancestry, while it emphasized that, from his mother, a Schoonmaker, he was "a member of the old Dutch family connected with the early history of Kingston. He was also descended from the Eltynge family famous in Ulster County annals."[4] When Keefe assisted with making measured drawings of the Bevier-Elting house in New Paltz in 1934 for the Historic American Buildings Survey, he may have been moved in part by family sentiment, since he was no admirer of the New Deal that sponsored the survey.

Keefe's younger sister, Celeste, joined the Daughters of the American Revolution in 1935 and she appears in Colonial costume as retiring regent of the local D.A.R. chapter in a photo of festivities celebrating the 350th birthday of Kingston. But Charles Keefe made no public avowal of his old Dutch ancestry. This was in contrast to his friend and sometime rival, Myron S. Teller (1875–1959), who was of purer early Hudson Valley Dutch ancestry and, as a member of the Holland Society, expressed pride in that ancestry. Keefe was not eligible for Holland Society membership, as it was open only to men who could trace their ancestry to New Netherland in the direct male line. In fact Keefe seems to have delighted in his character traits traceable to Irish progenitors more than whatever traits might derive from his Dutch ancestors. In 1933, when neighbors of his clients, the MacMurpheys—both of Irish blood—dared come to Keefe's office to complain about the siting of the MacMurphey house, Keefe told Ann MacMurphey that he wanted to "ask . . . in my best Irish way, 'Who in hell did they think they were.'"[5]

*Andrew F. Mason house and office. (*Art Work of Ulster County, *1893)*

Schooling and Architectural Training,
Service in the Spanish-American War

Keefe's formal education was limited to Kingston schools, culminating at the Kingston Academy (by Keefe's time, the city's public high school) located on Academy Green in a building designed in the 1830s by Albany architect Henry Rector, with a large addition in 1883 by Charles W. Romeyn, a Kingston native who, like Keefe later, became a prominent New York City architect.[6] According to a detailed profile of Keefe written in 1936 for Kingston readers, young Keefe "did not wait to graduate [from the Academy] but left to study architecture with Andrew Mason in this city."[7]

Like many young men with architectural ambitions but little money in the 1890s, Keefe did not attend college or receive formal training in architecture, but instead received on-the-job training as a draftsman. Donna Keefe, Charles's niece, explained that "there were eight in the family & no money those days for education." The 1895 Kingston directory lists him as an "architect apprentice." Keefe in later years cited his training for some three years (probably 1895–98) in the Kingston office of Andrew F. Mason (1844–?) at 15 Downs Street. Mason's office was located in his residence, built about 1893. Its Queen Anne façade was a complex arrangement of projecting gables and porches, the central motif being a circular, spindled, conical-roofed belvedere. Wall surfaces began at the rough-textured stone basement proceeding upward to alternating layers of wood clapboards and shingles, while stained-glass panels topped first-story windows. Mason's design for the first stage of George Jay Gould's Furlough Lodge

(1890–91) in the remote wilds of the Town of Hardenburgh was a rustic "palace of logs." His New Paltz Savings Bank (1891–92) had some of the weighty stonework favored by Boston architect Henry Hobson Richardson and also evident in the monument over the grave of Mason's wife, Melissa J. Benedict (1840–1901), in Wiltwyck Rural Cemetery.[8] Soon Keefe would reject this busy complexity of forms, materials, and historic sources for the simplicity and calm order of the Colonial Revival. While Mason achieved success in local terms, his designs were not published in prestigious professional journals and he did not attain membership in the American Institute of Architects, both signs of a national reputation which Keefe eventually acquired.

In 1898, while a young architect-in-training, Keefe served in the Spanish-American War as a private in Company M, 1st New York Volunteer Infantry. He appears dimly in a group photo taken by photographers Lorillard & Bratt of San Rafael, California, which may have been his most distant posting. He remained proud of his military service as a life member of the 8th Army Corps Veteran Association and as designer of the American Legion's Kingston quarters.[9]

Early Career in Kingston

Unfortunately very little is known about Keefe as a young architect in Kingston. He was first listed as "architect" in the 1898 city directory. However, in 1902, 1905, and 1906 he is identified as a "draughtsman" employed by Myron S. Teller, another young Kingston architect on the way to a notable career, while in 1904 Keefe's employer was the Peckham Company, manufacturers of railway car trucks and wheels.

30 Lafayette Avenue with Donna Keefe and T. Jay Rifenbary. (Author's photo, 1984)

The only building designed by Keefe during this early period that has come to light is a house at **30 Lafayette Avenue**, built about 1900 as an investment-rental property by Keefe's father, whose 291 Washington Avenue home backed into the Lafayette Avenue property. Keefe, trained in Mason's office and working with a very limited budget, designed an economical Queen Anne house much simpler than Mason's own. The Lafayette Avenue house was long occupied by Charles's younger brother Andrew, Superintendent of the Ulster County Highway Department. After his death in 1961, it became the home of Andrew's daughter Donna J. Keefe, in 1944 a stenographer for the Ulster County Agricultural Conservation office. Donna Keefe (1914–90), the last of the family who had been close to Charles, gave me very helpful personal reminiscences of her Uncle Charlie.[10]

A photo showing Keefe at his drafting board with a February 1905 calendar on the wall behind him is the best portrait we have of the architect (see page 9), yet exactly what he was designing that year remains a mystery. Keefe presents himself as a handsome young professional man neatly attired in suit and vest, high starched collar and necktie, with carefully trimmed moustache and dark hair parted in the middle. He is a pipe smoker—two hang on the wall. Rolled plans and drafting tools are close by, ready to be picked up once he doffs his jacket and raises his idle right arm. He gazes out the window at his left, still a key source of daylight for the right-handed designer despite the electric light hanging above his board. The office is most likely in Kingston as the calendar is from H. W. Palen's Sons, Kingston purveyors of lumber and woodwork. Drawings behind Keefe indicate his preference for the picturesque Shingle Style house and the Richardsonian Romanesque commercial building—still of the sort designed by Mason—not the classical designs of the leading offices in New York City nor the Colonial that would soon dominate Keefe's practice.[11]

Another photo taken at the same time of the same office again shows Keefe at his drafting board while to the left, behind a partition, two young men are seated with plans in a darker space presided over by a cat on the drafting table. While all three men are dressed similarly, Keefe appears to have a superior place in the office, better lit and by himself. Still, it may be that the office is headed not by Keefe but by Myron Teller, since Keefe was listed in 1905 as a draftsman in Teller's office.[12] A bust-length photo of Keefe from around the same time suggests a romantic artist acutely aware of his appearance, with broad bow tie and collar reaching his jaw, face half obscured in shadow but large eyes peering intently, moustache thick and black as is the hair curving precisely over both sides of his forehead.

Before his marriage, Keefe generally resided with his father Andrew and family at 291 Washington Avenue, a house built about 1895 and still standing with Eastlake spindle-work in the front and side gables, while otherwise much altered. However, in 1902 he was both a draughtsman in Myron Teller's office and residing at The Kirkland, a half-timbered boarding house recently designed by Teller.[13] By 1904 he was back in the parental home.

Grace de la Montanye Keefe

On his twenty-ninth birthday, October 12, 1905, Keefe married a younger Kingstonian, Grace de la Montanye (1885–1971). The de la Montanyes were an old Hudson Valley Huguenot family. Grace was the granddaughter of John D. L. Montanye (1808–68), elected Ulster County clerk in 1854, and daughter of John DeWitt de la Montanye (1848–1931), a boot and shoe salesman or "commercial traveler," and Elizabeth Traver de la Montanye (1853–1923). Charles was closer to Grace's parents than to his stepmother, and in his 1922 will Charles named them as sole beneficiaries of a trust fund if Grace were deceased. John de la Montanye celebrated his eightieth birthday in 1928 at the Keefe home, and the *Freeman* reported that John was "widely known as the veteran salesman" and "always jovial and ready to tell a good story of incidents 'while on the road.'" About 1938 Charles and Grace chose as the picture for their Christmas card a daguerreotype of John and his dog taken, Charles believed, when John was three. "A swell fella, I say," wrote Charles in explaining the image.[14]

Grace had studied at the Kingston Academy and Miss Kathryn I. Hewitt's training school for teachers, also in Kingston.[15] She was a spirited young woman; in a photo of the women of the Olympian Club, founded in Kingston in 1910, Grace presented herself as a devil, clothed as a man and holding a cigar, despite her Methodist upbringing and herself teaching a Bible class at St. James Methodist Episcopal Church in 1912. Several of the women in the photo are dressed as men and hold a pipe or sport a moustache, yet others are dressed in old-fashioned feminine garb, one as Martha Washington. Other Olympian Club activities in the 1910s and 20s were more conventional; Grace spoke on such topics as "The Unwritten History of Scotland," "As Teacher and Learner," and "political and economic issues." Thanks to her husband's profession, she also gave papers on "The Beauty of Tile and its Place in Architecture" (1916) and "vacation memories" of Cape Cod (1923).[16]

Grace Keefe (lying in front) and the Olympian Club.

With this experience, in 1925 she became local chairman of the lecture course committee of the Federation of Women's Clubs. She was also involved with the Women's Christian Temperance Union and the auxiliaries of Benedictine Hospital and Ulster County Tuberculosis Hospital, which Charles had had a small role in designing.[17]

Not surprisingly, the energetic Grace was by 1919 learning to drive an automobile, taught by her husband, although over the years the *Freeman* reported on her several minor crashes and infractions. She did not limit her driving to Kingston and vicinity; in 1928 while near Flushing "she was in trouble with her car," but with the help of a stranger from Flushing was able to drive home to Kingston.[18]

CHAPTER TWO

New York City, 1907–20

Edward Burnett and Alfred Hopkins

"Sketch of Small Stable for Horse and Cow."

In 1907 the ambitious young architect departed Kingston and set out for New York City and a career at the center of American architectural practice. Keefe was fortunate to find a place with Edward Burnett (1849–1925), a Harvard graduate, son-in-law of the poet James Russell Lowell, and one-term member of Congress who established himself as a "farm expert"—especially for employment by "country gentlemen," notably members of the Vanderbilt family at Biltmore and elsewhere. Burnett had no architectural training but sometimes collaborated with landscape architects Olmsted Brothers, sons of Frederick Law Olmsted. By 1902 Burnett was working with architect Alfred Hopkins (1870–1941), a native of Saratoga Springs who received architectural training at the renowned École des Beaux-Arts in Paris.[1] Thus Keefe achieved a striking transformation from small-town architect to architect in a prestigious New York office where Hopkins would serve as his mentor, the major influence upon Keefe's development as a mature architect.

Keefe apparently found a position with Burnett and Hopkins quickly after his departure from Kingston. He wrote architect and fellow Ulster Countian George Young, December 21, 1926, that "I have been in New York for about twenty years, seven years with one firm, six years with a partner and the balance alone, which, after all, I like best." Since Keefe's partnership with Hopkins ended in 1920, that would indicate 1907 to 1914 with Burnett and Hopkins, then 1914 to 1920 in partnership with Hopkins. In 1920 he noted that he had been specializing in farm and country buildings for twelve years.[2]

Hopkins's book, *Modern Farm Buildings*, was published in April 1913 with the dedication: "TO EDWARD BURNETT AN AUTHORITY ON ALL MATTERS RELATING TO THE FARM, THIS BOOK IS INSCRIBED WITH THE REGARD OF THE AUTHOR." Very soon, however, the Burnett-Hopkins partnership ended. Hopkins announced his removal from 11 East 24th St. to 101 Park Ave. in the *Real Estate Record & Builder's Guide*, June 14, 1913, while Burnett remained on East

FIG. 53—SKETCH OF SMALL STABLE FOR HORSE AND COW

C. S. Keefe, Architect

24th. Hopkins set up his own practice, still specializing in gentlemen's country estates. Keefe became closely associated with Hopkins, but never an equal partner. His professional relationships with Burnett and Hopkins were fluid and subject to various combinations, and sometimes he designed alone, notably when working on Kingston commissions. While associated with Hopkins, Keefe's "Sketch of Small Stable for Horse and Cow" was published by Hopkins in his *Modern Farm Buildings* (p. 167) and credited simply to "C. S. Keefe, Architect."[3]

By 1902 Burnett and Hopkins had completed farm buildings for such wealthy clients as banker Otto H. Kahn in Morristown, New Jersey, and railroad baron Frederick W. Vanderbilt at Hyde Park, New York. Little is known about Keefe's relations with Burnett, although he maintained a business connection with the older man after Keefe and Hopkins had a bitter falling out that resulted in Keefe setting up his own office in 1920. When Burnett died in 1925, Keefe was informed of the funeral plans by Burnett's son-in-law, Stanley Cunningham, who had been a Harvard-trained engineer for Burnett and was Keefe's friend. Cunningham wrote "Charlie" that Burnett "thought very highly . . . of you."[4]

Keefe retained some of Burnett's drawings until May 1933 when the Depression forced him to move to a smaller office and discard the large tubes containing drawings for the Percy R. Pyne farm buildings in Bernardsville, New Jersey, and presumably other Burnett buildings as well.[5] However, a packet marked "Old Burnett films," negatives of farm buildings for several clients including Louis Comfort Tiffany, remains in the Keefe archive, but the negatives are of poor quality. The Tiffany negatives record his farm and stable buildings at Laurelton Hall on Long Island, designed by Hopkins before 1913 in the "vaguely Moorish" style of the main house.[6]

Alfred Hopkins, although only a few years older than Keefe, had the important credential of Beaux-Arts training and so could serve as Keefe's mentor, introducing the forward-looking Kingston Academy dropout to the sophisticated world of New York City architects and architecture. Hopkins sought clients belonging to New York's upper class. In his 1902 essay on "Farm Barns," Hopkins addressed the "Anglo-Saxon branch" of the "human race" and those with the "wealth of the gentleman farmer." While treating the "practical side of the country gentleman's farm," he also demonstrated his wit and charm by closing with a tribute to farm animals and the "sweet grace with which they accept and accustom themselves to what he [the architect] has provided." If they find something awry, "they make no audible comment . . . in this regard they certainly become ideal clients."[7]

While Hopkins designed for elite society, he is not listed in the New York Social Register and never was a member of the Century, the exclusive club for gentlemen practitioners and supporters of the arts. Moreover, while a member of the American Institute of Architects, which acknowledged both professional competence and acceptable social standing, he never was named a Fellow of the A.I.A., and in fact was only a member from 1912 to 1919. Like Hopkins, Keefe would not have a place in the Social Register, become a Centurion, or be advanced to Fellow of the A.I.A., although he was an A.I.A. member almost continuously from 1924 until his death. Both men were associated with the Architectural League of New York, Hopkins from 1906, Keefe from 1919.[8]

European Study Trip

No young New York architect of any sophistication at the turn of the century could consider his education complete without traveling through Europe to study key architectural landmarks. For one like Keefe who lacked formal academic training at an American architectural school, this travel would be even more vital. In 1910 mentor Hopkins, Paris-trained and well-traveled, provided his protégé with funds and a typed "Itinerary" that Keefe followed with few deviations. Hopkins asked Keefe to write him letters once a week reporting on his observations. This exercise would make the traveler "look at things much more carefully . . . and . . . it is very interesting to read your opinions when they become 5 years old or so and you will see how your tastes are changed and why." Hopkins encouraged Keefe to "Have a bully time and learn all you can." Clearly the understanding must have been that what Keefe learned would be put to good use in designs for Hopkins.[9]

Keefe wrote faithfully to Hopkins, and happily the letters survive in the Keefe Archive. On November 30, 1910, Keefe sailed for Liverpool on the *Mauretania*, the Cunard steamship that held the speed record between New York and Britain. Keefe spent two weeks in rainy England, with a clear focus on late-medieval houses, sources to be drawn upon in assisting Hopkins design mansions in the English manner.[10]

From England Keefe reported on his hurried progress from city to city and building to building, often in disagreeably wet weather, with brief assessments of what he observed. In his first letter, written from Oxford five days after landing in Liverpool, Keefe reported that he had had "a very decent voyage over." In line with the itinerary Hopkins provided, Keefe took the train from Liverpool to Rowsley, then walked to Haddon Hall: "the walk was delightful. Haddon Hall surpassed my expectations in every way. It was fine. I went thru every room they would permit and climbed the tower. Afterwards I went thru the gardens and then walked all around it." The next day, in Chester, "I walked around on top of the walls [historic defensive walls around the former medieval town] and then thru the town. I saw a great many good small houses too." Then briefly to Warwick (the exterior of the older part of the Castle was "fine," the interior not so) and Stratford (all enjoyable despite the rain). Walking around Oxford, Keefe "enjoyed Merton College the most; the old Tudor Quad is great; something to remember." But he confessed that trying to go through Oxford's many colleges made him "dizzy."

Hopkins' itinerary had called for Keefe to go to Blackwell's and Parker's book shops in Oxford and make purchases again with a medieval focus—anything on Norman architecture, as well as the original edition of Brandon's *Specimens of Gothic Architecture*. Hopkins was a bibliophile, but he was not a scholar. *Specimens of Gothic Architecture* was published in the 1820s by Augustus Pugin, not Brandon. Raphael and J. Arthur Brandon were responsible for the two-volume *Analysis of Gothic Architecture* (1847). Keefe managed to find Brandon's *Gothic Architecture* at Parker's (although in the end he purchased its two volumes from Batsford in London) and announced he had purchased for himself two volumes of Joseph Nash's *The Mansions of England in the Olden Time* with lithographed plates: "Just to think I'll own some of Nash's drawings."[11] Influenced by Hopkins, Keefe over the years took pleasure in forming his own collection of old books on architectural and other topics. (See Appendix III.)

Writing from London on December 18, Keefe reported that ongoing rain severely limited his photography and, while guardedly admiring its Gothic landmarks, expressed disappointment with London. Its recent classical-style buildings "seem to lack study. I think our people do it better." He could not understand why the London buildings did not follow "the old work" more closely: "In Chester an attempt has been made to keep the new buildings as much like the old as possible; that town appeals to me." A day at the South Kensington museum elicited an enthusiastic response to German ironwork, della Robbia colored terra cottas, and historic architectural woodwork. At Hampton Court he found the garden front "charming" and told Hopkins, apparently in reference to a client, "I don't blame Mrs. Bowen for wanting those windows." Although Keefe gave England mixed reviews, he reassured Hopkins that "I am learning, learning all the while, in fact when I reach home again I will be five years or more ahead of what I was when I left."[12]

Keefe admitted to being "lonesome" in England.[13] On his return to New York, Keefe organized a neat packet, "Notes—European Trip," which reveals little of the pleasures the young man allowed himself after intense sight-seeing days. But he did preserve a colorful program from an evening at London's Palace Theatre of Varieties, "The Handsomest Music Hall in Europe" according to the program and still a London landmark. An alluring dancing girl adorned the program's cover and, within, Keefe penciled his opinions of the acts, using the same terms he applied to buildings noted in his journey—The Great Wieland was "fine," while Anna Held was "Rotten."

It seems that Keefe originally planned on traveling only to England, neglecting Continental architecture, a focus he came to believe was too narrow as he actually experienced buildings across the Channel. In Paris and Versailles he again preferred the old. The Louvre and Petit Trianon were admired, vastly superior to the modern French: "I thought the modern English buildings were bad, but I must say most of the modern or present day French architecture is rotten especially the suburban residences." He seems to have been especially put off by the "poor colors . . . red & yellow brick alternating" of the suburban houses. Such coloration must have reminded Keefe of outdated American buildings of the

1860s; in his own designs, he would avoid the brash coloring of the Victorians. Knowing that Hopkins was a product of the Ecole des Beaux-Arts, Keefe nevertheless concluded regarding recent French building, "No Beaux Arts for me if this is the result."

Hopkins's Itinerary called for a visit to the "Madeline Library," Beaux-Arts source of Charles McKim's renowned Boston Public Library façade. Keefe was obliged to report that there was no Madeline Library—Hopkins doubtless intended him to admire the Bibliothèque Ste. Geneviève—and so Keefe missed studying a masterful work of the Beaux-Arts architect Henri Labrouste. Gothic design, as at Notre Dame, continued to attract Keefe; he found the stained-glass and tracery of the Gothic church of Ste. Chapelle resulted in "a perfect gem." Hopkins's own fondness for the Gothic set him apart from other Beaux-Arts architects like McKim and Stanford White who were devoted to the classical. Hopkins doubtless was pleased to read from Keefe, "The more I see of Gothic the better I like it and the more I want to get a chance at some of it."[14]

After Paris there were shorter stays in Belgium and Germany: Brussels (where he particularly admired the Gothic Hôtel de Ville); Bruges (it was too cold to sketch the many Gothic buildings, but some sunshine permitted taking a dozen photos, which do not survive); Ghent ("very little old stuff left compared with Bruge"); Antwerp ("the cathedral . . . tower is the most beautiful I have yet seen"); and Cologne (the Gothic cathedral with "so much detail"). Keefe expressed surprise that, in Cologne, "some modern German buildings (business buildings) really they don't look as badly as they do in the architectural papers. They use a stone here very much like that used in the 5th Avenue Bank building"—possibly a bank by Hopkins. On the train along the Rhine to Mayence (Mainz), he stood in the corridor to see old castles. From Heidelberg he again complained that it was too cold to do more than a little sketching (including a sketch of a policeman on his hotel bill) and the weather was often poor for photography, but he assured Hopkins that "I make little rough sketches in the [note] book and try to keep a complete record of my trip." This notebook is lost, but some of the letters to Hopkins include thumbnail sketches of buildings observed, and he gathered postcards of picturesque late-medieval structures in Cologne, Dilsberg (near Heidelberg), and Mainz —where, as Keefe wrote, "houses overhang the streets and are all sorts of shapes and sizes." On the train between Freiburg and Basel, "we came to two or three fine old villages, half timber and stucco. They were the best I have seen on the Continent"—but there was no time to stop for careful study. And Swiss architecture, too, was seen from train windows: "The little Swiss cottages just fit their sites, no other style would do as well."[15]

Italy meant quick looks at the architectural landmarks of Milan, Brescia, Verona, and Vicenza; in the latter Keefe found "more good architecture to the square inch" than anywhere else in Italy, thanks to Palladio whose classical buildings Keefe may have known had long been influential in America. However, the American was offended by a recent fresco in Vicenza where "the artist was too realistic. He painted the hair under the arms of his nude figures. If one of his models had had a wart on her—he quite likely would have had that in too." Unseemly depictions of the body called to mind other signs of Italian vulgarity: "Italy is rather dirty to my mind (and nose too). The men over here piss in the most public way I ever saw. I would not be surprised to see a woman put up her leg and let it go against a tree." These derogatory comments were crossed out in Keefe's original letters, undoubtedly by Hopkins, and were not included in the typed copies prepared in Hopkins's office. Still, Keefe had to admit that, "While the Italians do not appeal to me as a people," Italy was everywhere endowed with "architectural monuments," so many monuments that "Some architects in the old days must have been very busy . . . there must have been some C. P. H. G.'s here too. . . ." C. P. H. Gilbert was a prolific and fashionable architect in New York City—the highly selective *AIA Guide to New York City* (2000) lists more than thirty buildings by him.

Then Keefe was on to Venice, which seemed to make little impression, although later Keefe made a beautiful ink drawing, "Venice," of a corner in the

city mingling vernacular housing, a neoclassical church (San Maurizio), and tall campanile (of Santo Stefano). In Italy the weather improved, and he took photos (now lost), including one in Venice of the panels at St. Marks which he believed would appeal to Hopkins. In Bologna he "saw the fine little Palace Bevilacqua with its most beautiful court and the fountain, like the idea you had for the Bourne job." (Hopkins designed farm buildings for Frederick G. Bourne's estate in Oakdale, Long Island.) Keefe rushed through Florence's landmarks. At the Cathedral, "so many colored marbles and so much ornament bewilders me." Next came Fiesole and Siena whose cathedral he preferred to Florence. The tower of the "Plazzo Pubbico" (Palazzo Pubblico) in Siena reminded him of the Armory on 4th Avenue in New York, although the original was "a little better than the copy on the Armory." (The 71st Regiment Armory of 1904–05, later demolished, had been designed by Clinton & Russell.[16]) Then to Orvieto, where Keefe followed Hopkins's itinerary instructions to "See the cathedral and try the wine."

Writing from Rome on January 27 and surrounded by classical architecture, Keefe admitted that his original idea of limiting his study tour to England alone would have given him "a wrong impression." He concluded, "All the other countries

"Girl at Pisa."

are side streams, Italy is the mainstream when it comes to architecture." The Roman Forum attracted him most: "I could spend a week there alone with great profit." On the other hand, his visit to St. Peter's failed to inspire any comment. This budding Colonial Revivalist and man of simple taste had nothing good to say about his introduction to the "Baroque style." Evident at St. Peter's and elsewhere in Rome, it was "too coarse and extravagant to suit me." The last letter from Europe to be preserved is dated Rome, February 3, 1911. Hotel receipts indicate that from Rome Keefe traveled to Pisa (where on February 8 he sketched a young woman, dining and wearing a feathered hat), Genoa, and Naples, and finally a ship for home.[17]

The letters Keefe wrote from Europe were undoubtedly written hastily and according to Hopkins's advice: "Don't try to use any fine or elaborate language, but make it brief and cover everything fairly well." Still, the letters reveal Keefe's limitations as a young architect who never completed his studies at the Kingston Academy and who confessed to Hopkins, "I can not write an interesting letter, nor can I go into great detail without rewriting a couple of times. The only examination I ever failed in at Grammar or High School was in Grammar, it is the weakest point of my several weak ones." (Keefe's letters from later years reveal he overcame this weakness.) Moreover, his architectural training was in Kingston and New York offices where he had little opportunity to study the history and vocabulary of European architecture. He further acknowledged to Hopkins that, "I have found out since coming over that I didn't really understand the styles and periods as I do now. Pictures tell a lot but the buildings tell so much more." Keefe tried to supplement his written record with sketches and photographs, but the poor light and wet weather of Europe in winter often frustrated him.[18] No photos taken by Keefe in Europe are known, and the only surviving architectural sketches are the thumbnails in his letters to Hopkins and another on his bill from the Hotel Stadt Coblenz in Mainz.

Still, Keefe's observation of brickwork on his travels allowed him to write not long after his return about the appeal of the time-weathered brick walls of northern Italy, France, the Low Countries, and England. His article, "The Mellowness of Old Brick, Can It Be Obtained in a New Building?", published in *Architecture*, January 1912 (pp. 18–19), was his first writing to appear in an architectural journal. But his later, mature career would depend primarily upon his study of the early architecture of America, not Europe.

Graphic Art Inspired by Europe and Old New York

The European study trip later inspired Keefe to create works of graphic art, especially representing medieval and picturesque buildings. In 1917 Keefe made a drawing and etching of the towered gateway to Dilsberg, based on a postcard he no doubt acquired there. Another etching dated 1917 depicts picturesque English housing with casement windows and stucco second-story walls overhanging the first. An etching in Keefe's collection, J. André Smith's "Woodstock Fair," (one of the few works of art mentioned in Grace Keefe's will—see Appendix VII) includes an old-fashioned bay window and dormers with casement windows that must have appealed to Keefe given his taste for quaint English houses and villages, which is also apparent in Keefe's undated pen-and-ink drawing, "An English

"Dilsberg."

Picturesque English housing, 1917.

Yard." After the Colonial, the picturesque architecture of late-medieval England would remain Keefe's preferred style in house design, seen, for example, in his Stanley Matthews house. The classical tradition's appeal was always less strong; Keefe began an etching of the circular Temple of Hercules Victor (once known as a temple of Vesta) in Rome, but the etching is unsigned and appears unfinished.

Keefe was part of the decade's enthusiasm for etchings of architectural subjects, often etched by practicing architects. In 1915 a review of *Etching: A Practical Treatise* appeared in the journal, *American Architect & Architecture*, and observed that "Men who, like most architects, have the ability to draw, take naturally to etching processes. The fugitive character of lead pencil drawings .

"Books Bought and Sold."

. . has a tendency to make artists seek some more permanent medium." The reviewer concluded that the book "will be of great service to draftsmen."[19] J. André Smith was one of those architects who connected architecture with the fine art of etching. It is not known when or how Keefe learned to etch, or whether he printed his own etched copper plates, but his archive does include both those plates and a c. 1917 sales catalogue put out by Brooklyn's "M. M. Kelton's Son, manufacturer of steel and copper plate presses."

Framed prints of European architectural landmarks allowed Keefe in New York to connect with the grand traditions of the Old World; he owned a 1923 etching of the Arch of Titus in Rome by Luigi Kasimir and another of the Late Gothic tower of St. Stephen's Cathedral in Vienna. Keefe had been enthusiastic about his study of the Roman Forum during his 1911 visit, and the Arch of Titus stood prominently nearby. Kasimir, a Viennese artist, was a popular and prolific producer of color etchings of both European and American landmarks. Sigmund Freud, a collector of antiquities, hung Kasimir's print of the ruinous Roman Forum in his consulting room in Vienna about the same time Keefe acquired his print of the Arch of Titus. Earlier, Charles McKim had pinned a picture of Bernini's colonnade at St. Peter's above his designing table as inspiration for New York's Pennsylvania Station. However, Keefe never had the opportunity to design using such grand classical sources.[20]

Keefe, while making drawings and etchings based on his European sojourn, also carried out a series of remarkable drawings of old, run-down bits of New

"Murrys Junk Shop."

"Furniture Bought & Sold."

York City. He did not focus on well-known, beautiful Colonial landmarks like St. Paul's Chapel or the Morris-Jumel Mansion, but instead on nineteenth-century housing and shops showing signs of neglect and often covered with crude signage. In "Books Bought and Sold," Keefe, a collector of used books, recorded a Greenwich Village shop that was almost literally a hole in the wall. Its modest sign was surmounted by a billboard portraying Freddie Welsh and Willie Ritchie, boxers fighting March 11, 1915, at Madison Square Garden. Another billboard advertised Van Tassell & Kearney Carriage Repository and (Horse) Auction Mart. This East 13th Street establishment was "where the Belmonts and Vanderbilts . . . transacted their horse affairs."[21] In a companion drawing, Keefe memorialized the cluttered front of Murrys Junk Shop and a soon-to-be-obsolete horseshoeing shop. (Both drawings were probably made in preparation for etchings.) Other drawings juxtapose the mighty girders of the el with decaying wood-frame houses and shops (one announcing "Furniture Bought & Sold") or set a still elegant Greek Revival doorway against the mild disorder of a carpenter-builder's yard whose sign looms in the foreground. On the back of this drawing Keefe noted, "41 St between Lex & 3d."

When Charles took his 1910–11 study tour of Europe, Grace was left behind—perhaps in Leonia, New Jersey, since Charles wrote in 1926 that his wife had taught a class at a church in Leonia fifteen or sixteen years before. Their 1905 marriage had certainly not led to a honeymoon abroad. Hopkins, sophisticated and financially successful, took his bride to England in 1915. He sent Charles a picture postcard of Clovelly, a picturesque village on the southwest coast, and informed him, "This is a very pretty place for a honeymoon."[22] Only in 1930 did Grace visit Europe for the first time, while Charles, in the year of their twenty-fifth wedding anniversary and first year of the Depression, so disastrous for architects, remained at work in New York.

The Keefe House on Lucas Turnpike

Whatever Grace felt about missing the European adventure, she did soon gain, with her husband, a fine new home, designed by Charles in 1911 and furnished and occupied by 1912.[23] The **Keefe house** remains at 258 Lucas Avenue (earlier known as Lucas Turnpike) near the Kingston city limits. In a 1913 snapshot, Grace stands by her bureau, reflected in its mirror, in what she proudly calls "My room, window looks out on Catskills." Her stationery (undated) fondly names the home, "The Little White House-on-the-Hill." However, the name more often attached to the house, Lisnaskea,[24] must have been chosen by Charles to honor the Irish origins of the Keefes. Lisnaskea is a town in County Fermanagh from which Charles's grandfather Charles had emigrated.

The name of the house was Irish, but for the exterior of their house Keefe adopted a simple version of the American Colonial Revival—two stories with gable roof, white clapboards with dark (probably green) shutters, and a symmetrical façade with central doorway. While generally inspired by eighteenth-century Georgian models, there was no effort to be correct in details: double-hung window

Charles and Grace Keefe house. (postcard)

sash had eight panes in the upper but only one in the lower sash; the trellis, pergola, and pair of plain, chunky, stucco-surfaced columns at the front door and similar columns with lattice panels of the side "living porch" were characteristic of up-to-date designs about 1910 and not of the eighteenth century. (Early photos show no lattice panels on the living porch, but they were added by 1920.) The *Daily Freeman* gave the young architect a boost, noting that the "colonial residence . . . erected by Architect Charles S. Keefe for himself has caused quite a bit of comment. It is of an unusual type, having wide, white clapboards, concrete columns, and a pergola at the entrance. . . . [It] promises to be one of Kingston's prettiest houses."[25] Soon the front pergola was enveloped in vines, and flowers in the window box above the door also ornamented the otherwise austere façade. In designing the house, Keefe drew a bird's-eye perspective showing house and

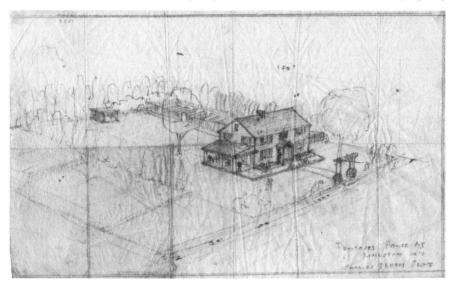

"Proposed House at Kingston."

grounds where he envisioned the pergola not at the front door but as a gateway on Lucas Turnpike, and proposed a formal garden with pavilion and tennis court, neither of which seems to have been carried out. A "Plan of Grounds and Planting Plan" for Keefe by Arthur G. Rotch, a Boston landscape architect sometimes associated with Burnett,[26] called for the tennis court on the east side of the house, a vegetable garden behind the house, and a small laundry yard to the west of the house. There is a pencil list of plants and bushes ordered April 14, no year, including Japanese barberry, spirea, rhododendron, hydrangea, and forsythia, along with clematis and wisteria vines; a receipted bill from The Palisades Nurseries for two Lombardy poplars is dated April 30, 1915.

Keefe designed a one-car garage in 1919–20 for the rear of the property. He wrote George J. Schryver, a Kingston car dealer, in 1919 regarding payment for his purchase of a car and assessing Mrs. Keefe's ability to drive and take care of the car—he thought his wife "competent."[27]

The Keefes' front door with its six panes of glass was more in the Arts and Crafts mode than Colonial, although the brass knocker included an American eagle suggestive of the Federal period of c. 1800. (In 1939 Keefe designed a wooden mailbox for their home; it was ornamented with the silhouette of an eagle painted bright red.) Inside the house the Colonial note was even more muted, the Arts and Crafts more pronounced. Just beyond the front door, a screen of plain balusters shielded the back hall leading to the kitchen. The living room, as seen in 1913 snapshots, featured a fireplace framed with rustic tiles (in 1916 Grace told fellow members of the Olympian Club about "the 'beauty of Tile and its Place in Architecture'"[28]) and plain, stained boards; similar boards com-

posed built-in bookcases on both sides of the hearth. A few pieces of art pottery graced the mantelpiece, while pictures in simple black frames hung from picture moldings. Sturdy oak furniture, of the kind produced by Gustav Stickley, included Morris chairs, a rocker and settle. The 1973 appraisal of Grace Keefe's estate listed, in the living room, a "carved oak desk," "oak desk chair," and "long oak library table."

Still, the Colonial also had a place in the furnishings. Grace noted on a snapshot of the dining room that "the old mahogany table . . . was my great grandmother's and given by grandfather as my wedding gift." In the foreground of this snapshot, a spinning wheel stands in the center hall, good evidence that the Keefes, like other homeowners of the time, saw no conflict between old Colonial and new Arts and Crafts. In her 1954 will, Grace bequeathed her great-grandmother's table and other family heirlooms to family and friends and to the D.A.R. and Senate House Museum. "Old Dutch shelves in Dining Room" were to be "sold or given to a Museum" and

exhibited as "from the collection of Charles S. Keefe, A.I.A." By the time of the appraisal of Grace Keefe's estate, the spinning wheel was "ROUGH" and in the attic.

Bedrooms and a bathroom were upstairs. On a snapshot of the back of the house, Grace identified, poignantly, one second-story window as "in what we planned for a nursery, then a den & now is really a sewing room." On another snapshot from about the same time, Grace described two trees at the front of the house as "precious cedars (our doleful shade trees)." Why the Keefes remained childless is unknown. The unused nursery did not become a den, at least for long, despite Charles's desire for one, articulated in his description of a

Keefe house, living room.

Keefe house, rear.

Colonial Revival den outside Philadelphia in *The American House*: "The room called a den is really a man's own room, being fitted with work bench, cupboards, etc. It is finished in oak and is a real work shop; something that almost every man would like to possess."[29] Similarly, despite his love of books and his frequent inclusion of a library in his house designs, Keefe was unable to have a library in his own home.

Still, Keefe took pride in their Lucas Turnpike home. His fondness for it is perhaps best embodied in his ink and watercolor design for his and Grace's Christmas card (undated) where the house is blanketed with snow, but good cheer projects via a Christmas wreath, red poinsettias, and windows glowing with warm light.

"*A Merry Christmas from Charles & Grace Keefe.*" (Keefe house)

Snapshots of Grace and Charles on their lawn and porch with family, friends, and collie Peggy give hints of happy hours at home. For the childless couple, dogs would be great objects of affection in the teens and twenties. On one 1914 photo, Grace wrote for an unknown recipient, "Hazel Beggs, Peggy and her tongue! To the right of Hazel is my purple rambler & I wish you could see it this spring it has grown so." In another from the same period, Charles stands confidently at his front door in shirtsleeves and with pipe in hand, while Grace places her hand on her "precious dawg" and three women, like Grace in long white dresses, look on cheerfully.[30]

A later photo shows Charles with a chow chow, probably Bingee who was given to the Keefes as a pedigreed puppy by client Clarence McKenzie Lewis.[31] In 1929 Keefe wrote Lewis after returning from Cape Cod: "Bingee was over at Cape Cod on her vacation and had a great time chasing the sea gulls and other new things. However, she does not like salt water bathing." After Bingee was killed by a car in 1932, Keefe penned this tribute and sent it to Lewis: "She was a little lady, black outside but white all the way thru. Bingee was very happy with us and enjoyed all of her eight years of life. She has a sweet disposition was kind & gentle & we know she has gone where all good dogs go. We loved her."[32]

Among the young people shown enjoying themselves on the Keefe lawn is a young woman in white identified by Grace as "Dot." She was probably Miss Dorothy M. Fielding, one of the girls in Grace's class in her church in Leonia, New Jersey, around 1910. In 1926 Dorothy Fielding applied for a position with

Charles and Grace on their side or "living porch," with three friends, Grace and Ray Ebersole and Dot.

Grace and their collie at their front door. (undated photo)

Charles and their chow chow.

the Travelers Aid Society, and Charles was delighted to write a highly favorable recommendation, having known her as a member of Grace's class and continuing to "follow her progress." He recognized the qualities needed in the position and assured Travelers Aid that Dorothy "is approachable and democratic and has good common sense." The word "democratic" very rarely appears in Keefe's correspondence. After completing the recommendation, he wrote Dorothy assuring her (and flattering her) that, "I told all the good things I could about you and they were many. Come to think about it, I did not mention your beauty, but that is so apparent it was probably duly impressed upon them when you made your application; red is such an interesting color one hardly ever passes it without notice. That's that."[33]

For reasons unknown, Keefe placed an advertisement for the sale of his house in the October 1921 issue of *Country Life* (p. 9). Had Charles and/or Grace tired of his spending weekdays in New York, away from home, and decided to move closer to his city office? Along with a photo of the landscaped façade, he listed the advantages of the "small country house . . . 89 miles from New York. An ideal place for summer or year around. Country living with city advantages." Hoping to attract garden lovers, Keefe described the site in more detail than the house: "Over half acre of ground. Lawns, planting, bearing fruit trees, garden, asparagus bed." The ad concluded, "Designed and built by architect for own use."

The Keefes retained their Kingston place, and the architect's handiwork received greater publicity when published not as an ad but in the main content of the June 1923 *House Beautiful* (p. 604). Here it was observed that "the rectangular house without projections is always the inexpensive house to build," but again the appeal of Keefe's place seemed to reside in the plantings, dense bushes and vines "as far removed as possible from the stereotyped evergreen planting." Was this, too, an attempt to lure a buyer?

In 1933, when the Depression forced him to close his New York office, Keefe again put their home up for sale, now with an ad in *The New York Times:* "Colonial 6-room home of architect Charles S. Keefe, Lucas Turnpike, Kingston-on-Hudson; sell; every improvement; furnished; unfurnished; ½ acre, landscaped; garage; excellent schools; view Catskills, Berkshires, Shawangunks."[34] But rather than sell the home, Charles moved his office into the house, and the couple continued to live there until their deaths.

Little is known about daily life in the Keefe home. During the Depression of the 1930s, with little work to occupy him, Keefe designed alterations to the kitchen. When client George Branson told of the hot job of canning the peas and strawberries he and his wife had grown in Maine, Keefe replied, "I know you nearly expire working over a hot stove during canning season for we used to do this at home. My wife still cans fruit and makes jelly. Its [sic] hard work and your wife is probably disgusted with the way her hands look when she gets thru. But, Oh, Boy: next winter how good such things taste."[35]

Bungalow Designs

Charles and Grace's home had Arts and Crafts elements, but Keefe in May 1911 made drawings for a more thoroughly Arts and Crafts bungalow, also in Kingston, at 55 Johnston Avenue. Keefe titled the drawings "**Bungalow for George A. Winter, Esq.**", and that August the *Freeman* reported that Winter was "having a bungalow erected on Johnston Avenue." Winter's family had a long-established music, book, news, and express business in uptown Kingston, and Keefe's mother, before marrying his father, had been married to an earlier George Winter in 1870. George A., like his architect, had served in the Span-ish-American War.[36]

The Winter home was indeed a bungalow—one-story, with a spacious front porch (originally open to receive summer breezes), prominent hipped roof, and broad chimney. Walls were of wide spruce siding, left rough from the saw and stained a reddish brown. Where the exterior of Keefe's own house was clearly Colonial, the Winter house had no obvious historical roots. Only the white dou-ble-hung window sash and shutters gave a hint of Colonial influence. (That influ-ence appears stronger in Keefe's early–1920s design for the Winter garage.) The interior continued the exterior's Arts and Crafts simplicity and lack of pretension: the woodwork of chestnut, stained and waxed (except for the white-enameled bathroom); walls buff-colored up to the picture molding, then white for the upper wall and ceiling. The simply formed light fixtures and hardware gave the appear-ance of "old brass."

The Winter bungalow was the subject of "Bungalow for the Eastern States," an article that Keefe both wrote and illustrated with floor plans and two of his own photographs that appeared in the July 1913 *Country Life* (p. 72). The photos demonstrated the improved appearance resulting from newly planted trees and

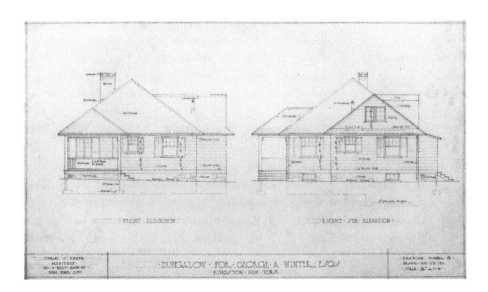

George Winter bungalow.

shrubs. Keefe described how his bungalow design was suited to the eastern climate, in contrast to the standard California bungalow, and how it met the universal desire for privacy. He admired California bungalows for their "comforts, conveniences and picturesque qualities," but found them "totally unfit" for colder climates. California's "beautiful climate permits a rambling plan," whereas in climates such as Kingston's a "compact" plan was required to reduce the cost of heating the house. Further, California's "brilliant sunshine makes a large overhanging roof a necessity," while in the East such a roof would make the interior "dark and cheerless." Moreover, Keefe believed the lack of privacy common in bungalows where bedrooms were grouped around the living room was acceptable in "a summer camp," but not in a "year-round house" where those going from bedroom to bathroom should not be seen by visitors in the living room. Keefe's plan set the bedrooms apart from the living room and added a short hallway for access to them.[37]

Just when Keefe was at work on the Winter bungalow, he published his design for "A Concrete Bungalow" in *Cement Age*. While Keefe was familiar with concrete construction through his work with Hopkins, he usually favored more traditional materials—wood, brick, and stone. The unsigned text accompanying his perspective rendering and floor plans stressed that here "concrete could be used to advantage as the straight and simple lines of the walls without ornament make a good medium for concrete. . . . We are in a new age, where the most plastic, permanent and useful of building materials is helping us build beautiful homes." The walls of Keefe's concrete bungalow would in fact be flatter, more in tune with "modern ideas" than the rough siding of the Winter bungalow. But like that bungalow, the concrete example retained Colonial window sash and shutters. And again Keefe separated first-floor bedrooms from the living room by inserting a hallway. Expressive of the new age, a one-car garage with "man's room" and tool room would also be of concrete, yet a "carriage block" was still to be placed on the drive near the front door.[38]

In 1914 Keefe's drawings for a wooden version of the concrete bungalow received newspaper publication as "Plans for an Attractive Bungalow," with his explanatory text. The perspective rendering shows the house framed by flat patterned trees of the sort favored by Arts and Crafts draftsmen. Separation of the living and sleeping spaces remained Keefe's goal in laying out the plan. He pointed out the convenience of living on one floor—something apartment dwellers had become accustomed to. However, there was, as in the concrete bungalow, a second-story bedroom and sleeping porch, but no bathroom on that floor. (A second-story bedroom in the Winter bungalow was designated for the maid.) The higher roof and front gable differed from the Winter bungalow and, combined with the shutters and double-hung, eight-over-eight window sash, brought the design close to the Colonial cottage that would become Keefe's standard house type. He specified that the exterior walls of split cypress shingles could be left unpainted to weather—in the Arts and Crafts manner—or painted white—

·PERSPECTIVE·

A BUNGALOW DESIGNED BY CHARLES S. KEEFE, ARCHITECT, NEW YORK.

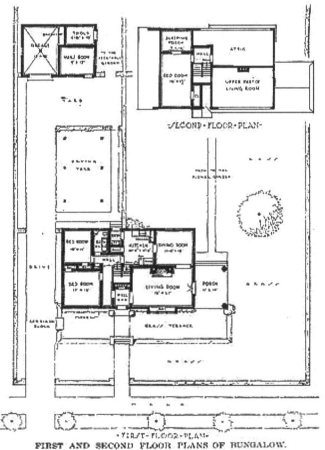

·SECOND·FLOOR·PLAN·

·FIRST·FLOOR·PLAN·

FIRST AND SECOND FLOOR PLANS OF BUNGALOW.

A CONCRETE BUNGALOW

Charles S. Keefe, a New York architect, has developed some interesting ideas in bungalow design, as the accompanying plans and perspective show. The first floor arrangement is very effective. The two bedrooms and bath are *en suite*. The one chimney serves both the fireplace in the living room and the kitchen range. The high ceiling living room, with a fireplace, and opening onto a side porch, should be very livable.

Upstairs, the one bedroom, sleeping porch and attic complete the house. A garage, providing sleeping quarters for one person, is also included. The modern ideas in design make for simplicity. Hallways are omitted where possible, and all space is utilized to the highest degree possible.

In the construction of this bungalow, concrete could be used to advantage as the straight and simple lines of the walls without ornament, make a good medium for concrete. All exterior work, such as porch floors, walks, garden fixtures, etc., would be in concrete. We are in a new age, where the most plastic, permanent and useful of building materials is helping us build beautiful homes.

[71]

"A Concrete Bungalow."

-PERSPECTIVE-

"Plans for an Attractive Bungalow."

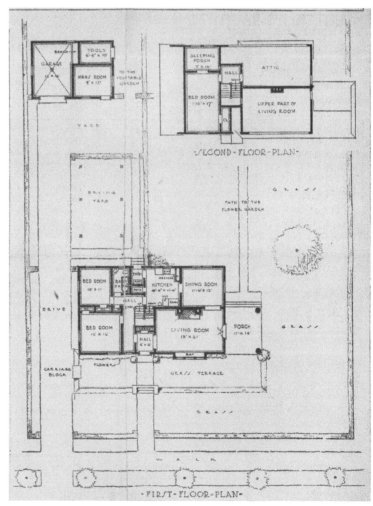

-FIRST-FLOOR-PLAN-more in the Colonial Revival taste. If the shingled walls were unpainted, the window casings and shutters ("blinds") were to be white; if the walls were painted white, so would be the window casings, while the shutters would be green. As at his own house, porch columns were of stucco on wood forms. The interior retained Arts and Crafts elements; the living room ceiling "finished with beams and . . . run up into the roof space," and the room's woodwork was "chestnut, stained a dark brown." Dining-room woodwork might be similarly stained or painted white. A horseless carriage sheltered in the garage still required a carriage block along the drive.[39]

While Keefe never abandoned his preference for simple forms found in both his own home and the bungalows, he did, like many Americans, after about 1915 reject the essentially original forms of Arts and Crafts architecture and furnishings in favor of more fully Colonial-inspired designs.

The Knights of Columbus

Kingston's **Knights of Columbus Building** at 389 Broadway was designed in 1913 by Keefe on his own without Hopkins. It is his earliest-known building of a semi-public or civic nature.[40] Publicity for the new Knights' building identified it as "of the colonial style of architecture . . . most appropriate for a club building in Kingston, a city that occupied a leading place when colonial architecture was at its best." In 1913 the Kingston Council of the Knights was also at its best, flourishing with a large and influential membership of Roman Catholic men.[40] A prominent site was chosen on Broadway at Andrew Street so that "the home will be one of a group of public buildings which now adorn the central part of

Knights of Columbus Building (Curt Teich postcard, c. 1916)

this city, viz: The City Hall, the Public Library, the Kingston City Hospital, the State Armory, the U. S. Post Office and the new Central High School which is soon to be erected." Hopkins and Keefe had entered the competition to design the High School, but in April 1913 lost to Arthur Curtis Longyear of Kingston and New York, who had designed several Kingston schools. A year earlier Longyear had submitted sketches to the Knights' building committee. Longyear must have taken satisfaction that, while he failed to receive the Knights' commission, he defeated Hopkins and Keefe and nine other firms in the competition for the larger High School project.[41]

Keefe described the Knights' building as a "club house," and it included a "recreation room" with card, billiard, and pool tables, as well as other rooms for ceremonial and social purposes. The large, second-floor council chamber was dignified with classical pilasters and could be arranged for plays and "moving picture machines."

The architect designed the exterior in the American Georgian style. Its somewhat severe, dour appearance is relieved by the arched window and wrought-iron balcony supported by Renaissance brackets over the central doorway. And Keefe did insert a play of colors, light limestone trim against what he called "Harvard brick laid Flemish bond with black headers and red stretchers." He assured Kingstonians that "This bond was much used by the masons of Holland and introduced by them into America." (Harvard brick refers to a type of brick associated with Georgian Revival structures on the Harvard campus and at the Harvard Club in New York. Flemish bond is a pattern of bricks where the long [stretcher] and short [header] faces of the brick alternate in each row of bricks.) In his 1912 article on the virtues of old brickwork, Keefe had advised against using new, smooth-surfaced "pressed brick" and narrow mortar joints while favoring bricks in a variety of colors—advice which he himself took at the Knights of Columbus.[42]

It was the hipped roof, however, that improbably sparked an architectural debate between a member of the building committee, Rondout businessman James F. Dwyer, and the architect. It seems that some Knights ridiculed the appearance of their new home, especially the slope of the roof. Keefe responded to Dwyer: "as to the design . . . I feel that I am more competent to judge this than you are. . . . Your building when complete will be a fine home for the K. of C. and one of which you can be proud. If, as you say, anyone laughs at it they only show their ignorance. Do you remember Congress Hall, part of the Independence Hall Group in Philadelphia? It is one of the best pieces of Colonial Architecture in Philadelphia and has the same sloping roof you say people laugh at." Dwyer also had criticized Keefe for neglecting supervision of construction, as he was in New York during the week. Keefe refuted these criticisms,[43] but bad feeling lingered between client and architect. Even at the time of the burning of the mortgage in 1921, Joseph F. Sullivan, a former Grand Knight, diminished Keefe's role in the successful completion of the building:

The architect, Charles Keefe, accompanied the committee on their many trips [to inspect club houses in other cities], and while it is proper to give him his full credit for work performed, yet in the interest of truth and accuracy, it should be stated that the designer of this building was the chairman of the committee, Bro. William D. Cashin, who drew the rough sketches, showing the committee's ideas, and the architect then drew the plans and specifications to conform with such design. Bro. Cashin also acted as the superintendent of construction of the building and in this way saved the Council much money. . . ."[44]

Both the roof and the façade with its balcony were loosely based on Congress Hall, a Georgian building erected between 1787 and 1789, where Congress met in the 1790s. Congress Hall underwent a restoration in 1911–12 and was in the news when rededicated by President Woodrow Wilson in October 1913. Selecting a patriotic landmark as inspiration for the design—probably Keefe's idea—would help demonstrate to the public that the Knights of Columbus was altogether American. At the laying of the cornerstone—a ceremony attended by some 5,000 people, including 2,000 knights from around the region—Ulster County District Attorney Cunningham, a member of the K of C, exhorted the crowd to dedicate the organization and themselves "to the best civic and patriotic purposes." At this event and the 1914 dedication, calls for patriotism were joined with attacks on corruption and socialism. This was a period when some Protestants, especially those having early American ancestry, were suspicious of the Catholic Church as the faith of ignorant, venal, and dangerous immigrants, a foreign, un-American faith dominated by the pope in Rome. Keefe, with both old American Protestant and Irish Catholic family origins, would have understood the desirability of designing a home for the Knights of Columbus that looked American, not Italian or Irish or German. In 1915 the new building was the setting for the celebration of Washington's Birthday by the Knights of Columbus; Joseph Sullivan assured the assembly that a "man could be loyal to his church and still be a true patriot." The Knights were "as loyal Americans and as true to their country as the pioneer settlers of the country."[45]

"The Development of the American Doorway"

Kingston was not only Keefe's home and location of some of his earliest buildings, but its historic doorways were the subject of Keefe's second important publication in an architectural journal. "The Development of the American Doorway," an article illustrated with photographs of doorways in Kingston and nearby Hurley (with a few others from Annapolis and Philadelphia), appeared in 1918 in *The American Architect*, a leading professional journal. The article helped establish Keefe's credentials as an expect on Colonial architecture. He convincingly outlined the development of the locality's doorways from early heavy, two-part (Dutch) doors in plain frames, as found at the Nash house (better known as

The Development of the American Doorway

By Charles S. Keefe

WHILE the doorways of most of our old houses reflect the good or bad taste of their builders, the greatest factors in determining their forms were the conditions under which they were built. As the conditions in the homes changed, so changed the doorways, and a study of the different phases of the American home from Colonial days to the present time gives one a clear idea of the reasons for the different types that have survived.

The development of these doorways can best be traced by securing from one locality examples of all the different periods into which they naturally fall and by studying the history of that locality we can find the causes that effected the changes that are so apparent. Although local conditions will affect

DOORWAY OF THE NASH HOUSE
Note Heavy Wood Frame with Wooden Pins. Date at Side Placed by Present Owner. A Batten Door Without Transom

DOORWAY OF ELMENDORF HOUSE
Frame and Doorway Similar to Nash House, but a Transom Has Been Added

some of these doorways, the different stages of development follow each other more naturally than if the examples were selected from widely scattered places. If the dates for the different periods do not agree by many years with similar ones in other localities it must be remembered the ways of communication were very slow in those days and that changes did not take place very rapidly.

For purposes of illustration the doorways of Kingston, New York, were selected. This town was prominent in Colonial days, being situated on the Hudson River, one of the great early thoroughfares, subject to all the influences that have left their marks on our architecture and may be considered typical of many of the early towns in

the Van Deusen House) in Hurley, to paneled and molded doors with transoms above, as at the post–1777 Van Steenburgh house in Kingston. Later, "skilled mechanics" with access to architectural books and working for more prosperous owners designed doorways with "good design, the side lights and transoms of leaded glass and note the careful workmanship, the good taste of the owners." These doorways, inspired by classical taste, were Kingston's finest, thought Keefe, and ranged from the simple "Suydam-Van Lueven House" (or Sudam House, dated c. 1790 by Keefe but now dated c. 1812 and preserved by the Friends of Historic Kingston) to the richer treatment of the Judge Lucas Elmendorf and General Sharpe Houses and the Ulster County Court House, all predating 1830. He recognized some merit in the subsequent "Grecian" doorways of the Plass, Fitch (actually Finch, at 17 Pearl Street), and Van Anden houses (the latter at 78 Main Street), but "some of the mouldings are clumsy and heavy and . . . lack the grace and beauty of the preceding period."

Keefe followed informed architectural opinion of the time, holding that periods after the Greek Revival were marked by "utter bad taste" in "the so-called Gothic period, the ginger-bread and zig-saw age." However, even from this benighted period, one could still find "good mouldings" when carpenters used old moulding planes. Keefe concluded that "today . . . we have again awakened to the fact that the doorway reflects the taste of the house owner and tells each passerby the sort of man that dwells therein." Implied was the hope that clients and architects would come together in reviving the doorways that were in best taste.

Myron S. Teller, with whom Keefe had a long and usually friendly connection, far surpassed Keefe in dedication to studying the historic buildings of the region, especially its early stone houses. Teller contributed information to Helen W. Reynolds for her *Dutch Houses in the Hudson Valley before 1776* (Payson & Clark, 1929) and at the end of his life wrote *The Early Stone Houses of Ulster County* (Ulster County Historical Society, 1959). But Keefe was always interested in local history, for example placing in his files information about the history of local roads and bridges compiled by Henry S. Myer (1851–1938). Myer sent Keefe information about mill machinery for use in the Thornburgs' projected water-powered gristmill in Pawling, and Keefe also clipped and filed Myer's obituary. Myer had been born into an old Palatine family in a stone house in the Town of Ulster and was considered an authority on old Dutch lore and customs, including their stone houses, ovens, and early highways. Myer, like Keefe, practiced architecture in both New York and Kingston.[46]

Farm Buildings with Hopkins

While designing the occasional building in Kingston on his own, Keefe in the 1910s was engaged primarily in the larger arena of Hopkins's practice, especially in the planning of farm buildings on upper-class estates, one of Hopkins's specialties. As a rule the owner's residence was designed by another architect, while Hopkins, with his detailed knowledge of the practicalities of farm buildings for gentlemen, would design those buildings in a style harmonious with the main residence. Robert B. MacKay, in his encyclopedic study of Long Island country houses, describes Hopkins as "the unquestioned dean of farm group architecture," yet the implication is that the farm group expert occupied a lower place in the architectural hierarchy than the designer of mansions.[47]

About 1905, before Keefe's time with Hopkins, Louis Comfort Tiffany had Hopkins design Moorish-style farm buildings, generally in harmony with the residence the artist had himself designed at Laurelton Hall. By 1915 Keefe played a subordinate but significant role in Hopkins's creations of handsome farm structures. While Hopkins's Beaux-Arts training meant that architectural style remained key in designing farm buildings, so too were practical matters involving the care of animals and the handling of crops. Hopkins's focus on barn and stable sanitation—especially when producing milk—was then a topic welcomed in architectural journals, and Keefe followed his partner's lead in, for example, filing away for future reference a sanitary engineer's 1918 blueprint and notes for "a liquid manure line" for **Percy Straus's** stable in Middletown, New Jersey. Straus, a Harvard graduate and polo player, was connected with R. H. Macy & Co.[48]

In an undated and probably unpublished nine-page typescript, "Farm Buildings for the Small Place," Keefe advocated planning farm buildings (including the farmer's cottage and motorcar housing) for the convenience of the "help," while noting that "the housing of cows and the production of clean milk require more attention than do other portions of the farm group." Practical advice ranged from "the barn must be clean" to "the cow must be brushed and the udder should be washed and the long hairs on the udder should be clipped." Little was said about the historic styles, although Keefe held to the common principle that "to have the farm buildings follow the architectural style of residence helps the place as a whole."

Hopkins in the 1920 edition of his *Modern Farm Buildings* added a Chapter X to present his understanding of how best to design these structures.[49] Keefe's ideas regarding farm buildings closely followed Hopkins's: Keefe never disavowed his mentor's architectural influence in this area or others, despite the breach in their partnership that occurred in 1920.

For both Hopkins and Keefe, farm buildings were best built of wood—shingles or siding for walls, shingles for roofs—and with Colonial details. Hopkins described walls of white-painted shingles or clapboard siding as practical, inexpensive, and visually attractive—and sanctioned by Colonial tradition in New England and on Long Island. He opposed elaborate ornament: "The farm buildings of our ancestors were entirely free from any attempt at ornament, and even in the house the moldings were simply designed and sparingly used, a habit of building our modern architects have taken a long time to acquire." Hopkins did allow a grape arbor, or bits of trellis- or lattice-work, to enliven plain walls as long as they were not "overdone." Some Colonial details were recommended, "especially the elliptical arches, a distinctive and a beautiful feature of the old Colonial designers," as well as leaded glass at the sides and in the transoms of entrance doorways. He also favored covered passageways and flower or plant boxes. All of these Keefe would incorporate in his designs, some already in his Kingston home, but as Hopkins insisted, always "sparingly."

For Hopkins, "the farmer's cottage" was "not the least interesting part of the farm group," and for a precedent, "nothing could be more satisfactory than the designs of the home builders of our colonial period, and the author here confesses his perpetual wonderment and admiration for the little white clapboarded or shingle buildings which one sees nestling among the trees of our old and sometimes abandoned farms." These buildings were created by carpenters having few if any architectural books, yet comparing their work "with the work of our modern architects," one "realize[s] that a training at the Beaux Arts has done much more harm than good when it comes to revising the simple Colonial forms of the Colonial period." Keefe certainly had heard these words from Hopkins and must have felt better about his lack of Parisian training.

Keefe in his travel letters revealed his disgust for the vulgar habits of Italians. Hopkins, in writing about housing for farm workers, advised providing "separate bedrooms" for "foreign labor" to diminish the risk of the men cutting and stabbing each other. He was happy that farmers—presumably native-born men who supervised the foreign-born workers—seemed "immune from the contagion of such disturbing philosophies" as "socialism," and so Hopkins attempted to "reward" them with a "comfortable" home: well-placed bathrooms, a pleasant and functionally designed kitchen for the farmer's wife.[50] Although there is no record of Keefe's political views until the 1930s when he opposed the New Deal, it seems reasonable to suppose that earlier Keefe shared Hopkins's antipathy towards socialism.

While Keefe's part in the design of Hopkins's farm buildings before the 1920 breach cannot be precisely defined, Keefe undoubtedly played a significant role in the creation of farm groups for these rich families on Long Island:

Mortimer L. Schiff (1877–1931), very wealthy son of the German Jewish banker Jacob Schiff, was a partner in the financial firm of Kuhn, Loeb & Co. The mansion at Northwood, his Oyster Bay estate on Long Island's Gold Coast, was designed by the prolific C. P. H. Gilbert about 1905 in the picturesque Tudor half-timbered manner. Northwood's farm buildings, including a "herdsman's house" and "place for the storage of hydrangeas for the winter," were planned to be in harmony with the mansion, though with more stucco and less half-timbering, and were credited to Hopkins alone in the *Architectural Forum*. However, another source, the *Real Estate Record & Builders' Guide*, named Hopkins & Keefe as architects for an addition containing a horse stable, cow barn, hay barn, and living quarters.[51]

J. Adolph Mollenhauer (?–1926) was a Brooklyn sugar refiner whose marriage to Anna Dick (c.1860–1935) joined the fortunes of two German-American families who, along with the Havemeyers, organized the American sugar industry. The Mollenhauers' estate at Bay Shore, Long Island, included white-shingled Colonial farm buildings and a "farmer's cottage." *The Architectural Record* and *Architectural Forum* credited Hopkins alone with their design, and the *Forum* identified their style as that "of Long Island farm buildings . . . the tower reminiscent of

Gardener's cottage for Adolph Mollenhauer.

some of the old windmills which may still be seen in West Hampton and Southampton." Hopkins, in the 1920 edition of *Modern Farm Buildings*, illustrated the Mollenhauer farm buildings without naming Keefe. He was identified as "Associate" to Hopkins when the *Architectural Review* published the Mollenhauer buildings and noted that the architects designed with such "appreciation and knowledge of the old work that they might easily be taken for old buildings." Keefe, one suspects, was not happy when his role was ignored, and he pointedly captioned the Mollenhauer's gardener's cottage by "Alfred Hopkins & Charles S. Keefe, Architects" in his book, *The American House*.[52]

Anna Dick Mollenhauer's niece was Mrs. Horace Havemeyer. Hopkins and Keefe planned farm buildings for **Horace Havemeyer, Jr.**, in Islip, Long Island. The English Tudor mansion was by Harrie T. Lindeberg in 1918, and Keefe included a clipping of Lindeberg's preliminary sketch in his blank-page binding of *The American House*.[53]

For **Anson Wood Burchard**, Hopkins laid out white-shingled Colonial farm buildings, including farmer's cottage and dairy, at Birchwood, his Locust Valley estate. Burchard, a General Electric official who eventually became vice chairman of the board, married a colorful widow, Allene (Mrs. Theodore) Hostetter in London in 1912. She would go on to marry Prince Henry XXXIII of Reuss and then an Estonian count, dying in 1955 as Countess Allene De Kotzebue with a fortune of some $15 million.[54]

Glenn Stewart, of a Pittsburgh family, and a 1908 Yale graduate, was second secretary of the American legation in Havana in 1914 when he married **Greta Hostetter**, whose mother Allene presided over Birchwood. Greta had made her debut at the Court of St. James in London, and she was identified as the client or

owner of the Locust Valley estate whose farm buildings Hopkins and Keefe designed. Keefe pictured the Stewarts' superintendent's cottage in *The American House*, named Hopkins and himself as its architects, and described it as "a true Dutch Colonial type as developed near New York. The long sloping roof, the tall slender columns and the plain wall surface under the porch are all suggestive of this charming style. The absence of dormers is quite usual in these houses." This last point would have surprised many who were familiar with the commonplace Dutch Colonials of c. 1920 with their extended dormers on gambrel roofs. Again, when the cottage was published in the *Architectural Record*, *Architectural Forum*, and the 1920 edition of *Modern Farm Buildings*, Keefe's role was not acknowledged.[55]

John Klaber, writing in the *Architectural Record*, proposed that the Stewart cottage, "slightly more ambitious" than Hopkins's other farm cottages, "should be capable of furnishing a useful suggestion to the builders of small country houses."[56] In years to come, several Keefe farm or estate cottages (e.g., the Farrell gardener's cottage) would be similarly recommended for standard middle-class use.

A Bank, a House, and Two Prisons with Hopkins

While associated with Hopkins, Keefe played a significant role in designing three major buildings, the **Adirondack Trust Company** in Saratoga Springs, the Court-House and Prison of Inferior Jurisdiction in Manhattan, and the Westchester County Penitentiary at Eastview. Hopkins was a native of Saratoga Springs, and the bank directors chose, on February 26, 1916, his firm's design over those submitted by eight other architects. The bank building was completed rapidly and was open for public inspection New Year's Day, 1917. It remains today a beautiful and immaculately maintained landmark on Broadway in the center of Saratoga Springs.

Hopkins wrote for publication "The Story" of building the Saratoga bank. This architect who abhorred socialism began with his belief that in America "the bank is the backbone of the body politic," and so bank architects should aim for "noble architecture." The architects used "the Greek architecture of Athens, the type of the Parthenon," admittedly with a number of modifications, to express that nobility. Like a Greek temple, the exterior walls are white marble, and Hopkins indicated "the cornice is pure Greek." No Roman arches are present, but some Roman details were allowed—Roman garlands in the side pylons and, like a Roman triumphal arch, an attic level above the cornice, with, over the entrance façade, a panel inscribed with the bank's significant dates. Above that, a shield was surmounted by a stag's head, emblematic of the Adirondacks. Other stag heads graced the chandeliers within, and Adirondack scenes were modeled in bronze panels on the main doors. Hopkins and today's visitors are especially pleased with the interior's great open space, lit from three sides and defined by walls of marble and caen stone, and originally with a light bronze screen separating customers and tellers. Franklin heads worked into the bronze brackets supporting wall check desks were intended to be instructive "of honesty, industry and thrift."[57]

Hopkins did not name his partners in writing the story of the bank, although Keefe and John H. Scarff were named along with Hopkins in publicity put out by the bank. An etching of the bank exterior in the Keefe archive, with fashionable Saratoga pedestrians and an auto, is unsigned but certainly by Keefe, and a 1937 *Freeman* article about Keefe, based on an interview with the architect, credits Keefe with the bank design. No doubt the design was a actually a collab-

Adirondack Trust Company.
(etching by Keefe)

Charles C. Van Deusen house before and after alteration.

orative effort between Hopkins, Keefe, and Scarff. Keefe's etching omits much of the ornament Hopkins mentioned in his story, instead focusing on the geometry of the marble surfaces. Hopkins himself would stress that "both the exterior and interior are of dignified and restrained architecture; . . . nowhere is there the frequent meaningless jumble of architectural forms."[58]

Shortly after the completion of the bank, Hopkins and Keefe in 1918–19 carried out the thorough alteration of a Victorian-era house on North Broadway for **Charles C. Van Deusen**, a bank vice president who would become president in 1924. Keefe alone authored an article identifying the problem—a house with "a very bad exterior." It had been "built about 1880 . . . of the usual Queen Anne type of brick house, with bands and mouldings, round porches and an odd-shaped and inartistic tower." The solution, cheaper and quicker than tearing down and completely rebuilding—"All the excrescences were removed and a two-story porch was built on the side."[59] The well-preserved house stands today at 658 North Broadway, set back a few yards from the sidewalk, like other great houses of similar vintage on this stretch of North Broadway. While the exterior details are classical, the façade is asymmetrical, a consequence of the building's Victorian origins. The off-center entrance was made Colonial or Federal with sidelights and fanlight and sheltered by a small porch supported by twin columns with pediment broken by an arch. A tall, six-column porch with floors on both first and second stories looks out upon a broad lawn on the south side of the house.

Banks and jails would both, according to conventional wisdom, express protection or isolation of their contents by means of formidable exterior walls. The bank exterior looks to be a dignified and substantial storehouse of wealth, and Hopkins's brick and terra-cotta municipal **Court-House and Prison of Inferior**

Jurisdiction (also known as the Manhattan Third District Magistrate's Court-house), on Second Street at Second Avenue in Manhattan, puts forward a comparable solidity with revived Renaissance forms reminiscent of Charles McKim's Boston Public Library and the Bibliothèque Ste. Geneviève that Keefe had missed in Paris. In September 1914, before construction of what was then called the "million-dollar building" began, the *Times* hailed Hopkins's design, victor in a competition, as the "first New York prison to provide roof space where prisoners may take exercise." Hopkins had visited modern jails in England, Holland, and Germany, where he found that American jails with "inside cells" lacking direct access to outdoor light and air were considered zoo-like, inhumane, and so he designed as many "outside cells" as possible. Drawings for the court-house and prison were published in the March 1916 *Architectural Review* and credited to "Alfred Hopkins, Architect; Charles S. Keefe." The drawings call for a façade of large stone blocks with ornamental cartouches in the Beaux-Arts manner, but the building actually constructed, which began functioning in 1919, was much simpler. The Second Street and Second Avenue walls were of red brick with touches of black, again it seems inspired by old Italian brickwork. The prominent cornice was fashioned of terra cotta, as was the frame of the main, arched entrance. There the terra cotta was molded with low-relief images of foxes and hounds and of chain links, presumably referring to the pursuit of lawbreakers and their incarceration.[60]

Court-House and Prison of Inferior Jurisdiction. (1938 photo, courtesy NYC Municipal Archives)

Keefe was also associated with Hopkins in designing the **Westchester County Penitentiary and Workhous**e (1915–17) on farmland at Eastview, and in later years Keefe enjoyed telling a story about one little-known detail. The Westchester institution reflected Hopkins's progressive belief that conventional prison architecture was outmoded, that new prisons need not have massive walls to prevent escape since very few inmates attempted escape, and that the life for the inmate should be as close to that of a free person as possible. Hopkins had studied nineteenth and twentieth-century prisons in both the United States and Europe, and while he disliked the radiating arrangement of cells in Philadelphia's Eastern State Penitentiary (1829, by John Haviland), Hopkins did admire its main front, "a fine and appropriate type of Gothic architecture." So it was surely Hopkins who chose Gothic for the exterior of the Westchester Penitentiary, but not the fortified Gothic-castle type of Eastern State. Instead the façade of the administration building at Eastview resembled a Tudor country house (or college) with its central motif of entrance archway with bay window above. The façade implied that this was not a dark place of grim punishment, but an enlightened institution where the malefactor would be treated humanely and might be rehabilitated. Prisoners occupied individual cells, not as punitive solitary confinement, but to allow some privacy. (The toilet in each cell was partially screened from view by guards, and the cells were designed with the comfort of the inmate in mind.) Four schoolrooms demonstrated a commitment to education and rehabilitation.[61]

Not everyone thought prisoners should reside in such pleasant quarters. *The New York Times* reported in February 1918 that Westchester prison officials were looking to fill vacant cells, and that "invitations have been sent by the prison de luxe to Rockland, Orange, and Dutchess Counties to try the new penology. The penitentiary renowned for its table linen, marble shower baths, scented soap, patriotic exercises, and an individual cow for every convict, still has accommodation for 100 guests."[62]

Westchester County Penitentiary and Workhouse.

Keefe played a part in the design of the penitentiary, having the opportunity to put his on-site study of English Gothic houses to good use. But no drawing or print in his papers can be identified relating to the penitentiary, and there is no evidence that Keefe was interested in social reform of any kind. Still, in later years Keefe liked to tell a story about his intimate knowledge of the Westchester prison: "I told a man once, and he still looks upon me as a potential jail-breaker, that I designed a secret passage for myself alone. Not much of a hole, but it's there, and if they ever put me in, watch me get out, I told him. He seemed more impressed by that hypothetical hole than the whole institution together." The writer of Keefe's obituary in the *Freeman* believed that the tale confirmed his reputation in his hometown, that "stories about his keen humor and kindly disposition are legion." In any case, the hypothetical hole is no more. A new penitentiary opened in Valhalla in 2004, and the Hopkins-Keefe buildings were demolished.[63]

CHAPTER THREE

Independent Practice in New York, the 1920s

Departure from Hopkins

Beckley National Bank.

Keefe announced in March 1920 that "he has severed his connection with the firm of Alfred Hopkins and Charles S. Keefe and is opening an independent office for the practice of architecture at 368 Lexington avenue, New York, N.Y." Soon Keefe and Hopkins were running rival advertisements as architects for farm buildings and all kinds of country work on the same page of a magazine, *The Field Illustrated*, which catered to gentleman farmers—Keefe noting that he had specialized in this work for twelve years.[1]

The decision to depart must have been difficult, given Hopkins's earlier role as Keefe's kindly mentor; in December 1917, when Keefe had a concussion from a fall and was hospitalized, it appears that Hopkins paid the St. Vincent's Hospital bill, including day and night nurses, of $79. A month after announcing the split, Keefe wrote Hopkins, "I acknowledge the receipt of a great deal of advice from you and so will anyone that has worked in the office." But, angry, Keefe spelled out why he was determined to sever relations with Hopkins: "I left because you did not keep the promises made over a period of seven years. The consummation was always in the future. Scarff I believe also knows how your promises are kept after his experience on his return." John H. Scarff, who had been at the prestigious American Academy in Rome in 1913–14 and then had a role in the design of the Adirondack Trust Company, left Hopkins in 1918, presumably because he, like Keefe, felt aggrieved about Hopkins's failure to carry out a partnership agreement.[2]

While Keefe broke with Hopkins, he remained on friendly terms with Scarff, Stanley Cunningham, an engineer in the Burnett-Hopkins office, and Burnett himself. Keefe's 1921 office statement includes receipts from E. A. Burnett for jobs 75 to 78. In 1925 Keefe took some pleasure in telling Cunningham, then in Boston, that "All the men in Hopkins's [office] but one left him this winter. These

FOVNDED A·D·1872

·THE·BECKLEY·NATIONAL·BANK·

PROPOSED BUILDING FOR
THE BECKLEY NATIONAL BANK
BECKLEY W.VA

CHARLES O. KEEBE ARCHITECT
368 LEXINGTON AVE.
NEW YORK

men were the ones that did the bank work for him, so I do not know how the 'Bank Specialist' can specialize now."[3]

Early in 1926 Keefe was still writing bitterly about Hopkins, assuring landscape architect Hallam Movius that, in dealing with a client they shared, he was not "trying any Hopkins stuff. . . . I would rather go out of business than lose the respect of my associates." A few months later Hopkins tried to mend relations after Keefe wrote a condolence note to Hopkins on the death of his brother, Walter L. Hopkins, an architect with the prominent firm of Warren & Wetmore. Hopkins replied to Keefe: "I was always genuinely sorry that after so many years of work together we couldn't be friends. Let's forget that whatever it was." Keefe replied politely, "I am willing to forget anything in the past for after all life is too short to hold grudges. I too have missed our old association." Still, there is no evidence that the friendship was restored on anything like its former level.[4]

When Keefe broke away from Hopkins in 1920, his professional standing in New York was high; W. H. Crocker, editor of *The American Architect*, wrote him that "men like yourself . . . will do more to give the touch of refinement to our suburban localities than anyone working in that field, and with the shortage of housing and the probability of an early resumption of building, I feel all sorts of prosperity ahead for you."[5] And it would be as a designer of country and suburban houses in the 1920s that Keefe would become best known.

On his own, Keefe tried but failed to continue as a designer of banks and prisons. For the **Beckley (West Virginia) National Bank**, Keefe proposed a classical building comparable to the Saratoga bank, but more modest in scale, materials, and ornament, befitting a small city in the coal-mining region of southern West Virginia. In his color rendering (with Keefe at 368 Lexington Avenue, c. 1920–21), the figures resemble those in his etching of the Saratoga bank, although skirts tend to be a little shorter than a few years earlier and a black woman appears holding a bundle. Keefe did not obtain the Beckley commission,[6] and he seems to have then abandoned bank design.

Keefe also turned away from prison design after a failed attempt to design additions to the **Nassau County Jail** in 1920 in collaboration with Charles M. Hart as "Hart and Keefe." In 1923 Keefe's office opened off Hart's office at 247 Park Avenue. Keefe included the house Hart designed for himself in Pelham Manor in *The American House*, and in 1938 Keefe wrote a letter recommending Hart to the National Council of Architectural Registration Boards, which favored college graduates in architecture: "My feeling is that Mr. Hart is fully equal to most college graduates in culture and technical knowledge and I may say superior to many I have known."[7]

In the early 20s, when Keefe was still hoping to obtain large-scale commissions, he contemplated entering the celebrated competition for the **Chicago Tribune Administration Building**. In his application to compete, he cited his design of two prisons and the Adirondack Trust Company, and this was sufficient to be judged "qualified." Howells & Hood's Gothic design ultimately defeated the more progressive proposal of Eliel Saarinen and the boldly modern one of Walter Gropius, as well as other Gothic submissions, including one by James Gamble Rogers, soon to be famous for his Gothic buildings at Yale.[8] In the end, Keefe probably did not submit a design in the competition, realizing that skyscraper design required experience beyond his own.

Collaboration with Burnett, Rogers, Movius, and Teller

In 1921 Keefe collaborated with Edward Burnett and James Gamble Rogers ("Burnett, Keefe & Rogers") on a calf barn and cottage boardinghouse for greenhouse men at the **Hamilton McKown Twombly** estate, known as Florham, at Convent Station, New Jersey. From 1892 to 1900, Burnett had been employed as general manager of Florham, which included a great park, elaborate greenhouses, and model farm. Twombly, Harvard Class of 1871, had married Florence, daughter of William H. Vanderbilt, in 1877. Vanderbilt died in 1910, and his pallbearers included J. Pierpont Morgan and Edward Burnett.[9]

Twombly farm cottage.

The Florham mansion—reminiscent of Christopher Wren's brick Hampton Court Palace, visited by Keefe a decade earlier—had been designed in the1890s by McKim, Mead & White with landscape advice from Frederick Law Olmsted. Historian Richard Guy Wilson has described the estate as "one of the most elaborate ever constructed in the United States." A pencil rendering, signed Charles S. Keefe and Edward Burnett Architects, 331 Madison Avenue, from the early 1920s and probably drawn by Keefe, represents the Twombly farm cottage as a Colonial Revival brick building. Brick was unusual for a Keefe cottage, but it was in harmony with the mansion and other buildings on the estate.[10]

In the twenties Keefe shared office space in New York with Hallam L. Movius (1880–1942), a Harvard-trained Boston landscape architect who had worked briefly for Burnett. Movius and Keefe frequently collaborated, especially on farm and garage groups. (In 1914 Movius and Arthur G. Rotch, another Harvard graduate with Burnett connections who had planned Keefe's own garden, formed a landscape architecture partnership with offices in Boston and New York.) Correspondence between Keefe and Movius suggests Keefe felt deferential to Movius, perhaps due to his Harvard education and memberships in the Dedham Polo Club and Norfolk and Middlesex Hunt Clubs in Massachusetts, signs of his superior social standing but also helpful in getting clients from that social set. Keefe, when trying to convince William Rice to engage him to design his residence, wrote Rice, "You know Movius' standing and ability and . . . you must know that he would not associate with me in work unless he knew that I could do good work."[11]

As a young man Keefe had worked in Myron Teller's office and while Teller, unlike Keefe, belonged to the prestigious Holland Society, the two near-contemporaries remained friendly rivals and occasional collaborators. Drawings made in 1924 for an Ulster County Tuberculosis Hospital name Myron Teller as architect and Charles Keefe as associate. These plans were not carried out. In 1927 a site with a fine view on Golden Hill was chosen, and the hospital was built in 1930-31 according to plans "in the Colonial spirit" (including a classical portico and cupola) by Teller and his younger partner Harry Halverson, with Keefe associate. When interviewed in 1984, Harry Halverson stated that he was the designer of the hospital, that Keefe had made no contribution to the building as completed, but that it was proper for Keefe to be credited as associate given his work with Teller in the 1924 proposal for another site.[12]

Keefe's friendship with Myron Teller apparently led to cordial relations with his young partner, Halverson, who received book-collecting advice from Keefe (see Appendix III). Halverson reciprocated in 1931 by congratulating Keefe on the publication of one of his cottages in the *Herald Tribune*. The next year Halverson sent Keefe a clipping from the Middletown newspaper, and in his note of thanks Keefe relayed his struggle to find work: "Have a couple of jobs so am able to get started for the season. Nothing startling but something to do."[13]

In the 1920s Keefe had prospered as a designer of a wide range of buildings, from a one-story brick building in Manhattan for the storage of cement at the southeast corner of 12th Avenue and 50th Street to ongoing commissions for country places. He informed an English acquaintance, James D. Taylor, in 1926: "The building rush is still on here in the city and in all the suburban towns. I have been very busy all winter which is quite unusual as January and February are generally quite slow. The reduction of income taxes has caused more work on the country estates and I am getting more of this type of building." More and more his practice centered on moderate-sized houses for middle-class clients, as well as cottages, garages, and servants' quarters on the country estates of the wealthy. In 1925 he wrote Stanley Cunningham, formerly in Burnett's office, "There are not so many farm buildings these days, as I am busy with houses."

That same year Keefe and Hallam Movius were angling for a house commission from William Rice, and Movius reminded Keefe to avoid telling Rice that they primarily did farm buildings.[14] In the midst of this busy period, Keefe found time to prepare books for publication.

The American House

Hopkins provided a model for Keefe of the architect who solidified his reputation by publishing a book, in Hopkins's case, *Modern Farm Buildings* (1913 and later editions). In November 1920, Keefe, on the way to defining himself as a house designer, began soliciting architects, including leading architects Bertram Goodhue and John Russell Pope, for photographs of their residential designs for publication in *The American House*, which was published in 1922 by the U.P.C. Book Company ("Book Publishers for the Companies of the United Publishers Corporation"). U. P. C. mostly put out books on technical subjects, for example, *The Automobile Repairman's Helper* and *Designing Heating & Ventilating Systems*, but in 1921 it had published *Homes of Moderate Size* by Kenneth W. Dalzell (trained in architecture at Columbia) and in 1922 *Northern Italian Details* by Walter Grant Thomas (trained at Harvard and in Paris and Rome) and John T. Fallon.

In his foreword, Keefe noted that the book, primarily a "collection of illustrations," was directed to both "architect and layman," whereas Dalzell aimed to instruct laymen.[15] Architects would have been familiar with many of the houses illustrated, as Keefe drew from houses published in *The American Architect*, *Architectural Forum*, *Architectural Record*, and *Architectural Review*. His aim was to "present . . . the best types of American houses," and he was convinced that these recent examples represented "progress" over houses published fifteen years

The American House.

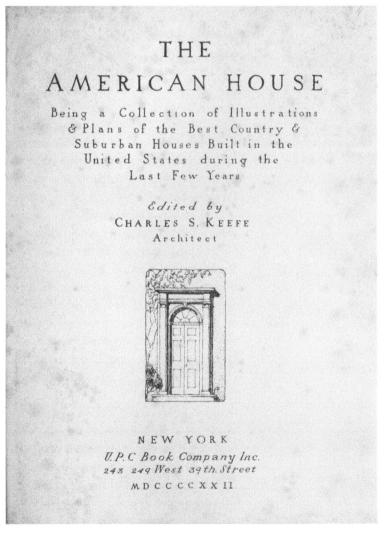

THE
AMERICAN HOUSE

Being a Collection of Illustrations
& Plans of the Best Country &
Suburban Houses Built in the
United States during the
Last Few Years

Edited by
CHARLES S. KEEFE
Architect

NEW YORK
U. P. C. Book Company Inc.
243 249 West 39th Street
MDCCCCXXII

earlier. And while Dalzell focused on "moderate size," Keefe included houses of various sizes and expense. "Whether our house is large or small, it can be beautiful and a pleasure to ourselves, our friends and to the passerby. While our wants and our pocketbooks determine the size of the houses; our own good taste determines its character. . . . houses, such as these, will grow better as age adds its softening touch and they will be good houses as long as they endure."

Again in contrast to Dalzell, whose practice was centered in Maplewood, New Jersey, and whose book included only his own designs, Keefe played down his own accomplishments and selected houses by leading architects from a number of cities. His publisher's publicity assured architects: "Men you know—whose work you admire—made this new book. Pope—Bottomley—Mellor & Meigs and Myron Hunt have contributed."[16] While Keefe primarily sought out work by architects practicing in New York City—John Russell Pope and William Lawrence Bottomley, as well as Delano & Aldrich, Peabody, Wilson & Brown, Murphy & Dana, Walter D. Blair, James W. O'Connor, Dwight James Baum, Mott Schmidt, Lewis Colt Albro, Andrew J. Thomas, Julius Gregory, Howard Major, H. G. Morse, Charles M. Hart, Parker Morse Hooper, Hopkins & Keefe—all of whom were represented in the book, he did approach and finally include well-known firms around the country including Mellor & Meigs in Philadelphia, Myron Hunt in Los Angeles. Also represented were architects in Kingston (Myron Teller) and Utica (Bagg & Newkirk) in New York State, Boston (Parker, Thomas & Rice), Providence (Hilton & Jackson), Farmington, Connecticut (Theodate Pope), Philadelphia (John Graham, Jr.), Baltimore (Lawrence Hall Fowler), Los Angeles (Walter S. Davis), Pasadena (Reginald Johnson), and Santa Barbara (George Washington Smith).

The house illustrations were organized by style, which Keefe hoped laymen would find helpful, with appended sections devoted to interiors and doorways.[17] He included "examples of the various styles suitable for the living conditions in different parts of the country"—Colonial, Georgian, Italian, French, and English. (Dalzell had organized his examples according to "Colonial, Italian and English architectural styles," as listed on his title page.) Keefe noted that "the Colonial style seems to predominate"—with twenty-three houses vs. ten Georgian, three Italian, four Spanish, two French, and nine English in the main section of the book, while in the doorways section all but one was Colonial, the exception being Georgian. He justified the Colonial's dominance "by the fact that more houses of this style have been erected." Keefe did not admit that the Colonial was in fact his own preferred style. Moreover, while the four Spanish houses were in California, where one of them was built for a descendant of a noble Spanish family and "among the old olive trees," hence "eminently fitted to its environment," he chose not to suggest how Italian houses were suited to Kentucky, Long Island, and New York City.

In his preface to the descriptive notes for each house, Keefe, the plain speaker averse to pretense and elaborate theory, warned that the descriptions would be "simple and concise, because . . . it is so easy to wander into generalities that mean nothing." Still, he did feel obliged to state the case for free adaptation of the historical sources for the several styles:

> The term style as applied to the designs in this book must be taken in rather an elastic way. Good designers never slavishly copy a design, but, use in their own way certain forms that determine the style. This gives individuality to a building, that otherwise, it would not have. Also, our buildings are made to fulfill certain wants that did not exist when the various styles were developed. For example: porches and sun rooms must now be incorporated in most plans. All this means a reasonable amount of freedom in following a precedent but does not permit a jumbling of motives from various sources. [In one case, the Ladew house, Brookville, Long Island, by James W. O'Connor, Keefe allowed that while the Colonial exterior cladding an English interior was "well done in this instance, it is not a thing to be recommended."][18]

The first house in the first, Colonial, section was Delano & Aldrich's J. A. Burden House in Syosset, Long Island. This large, formal, brick house by a distinguished firm may well have been first in Keefe's personal ranking of the houses in the book, as he began its description: "The design of this house is refined and has unusual distinction. A pleasing type of Southern Colonial embodying its best traditions both in exterior and plan." Keefe characterized Southern Colonial as using brick and marked by a central building, often with bold interior details as at

Delano & Aldrich's Burden house.

Mount Vernon. The second house in the section, the Lathrop Brown House, St. James, Long Island, by Peabody, Wilson & Brown, was also very large and Southern Colonial in style, though spare in exterior ornament. Keefe considered it "one of the best houses in America." It followed his (and many others') belief that adaptation was better than strict copying: "While the design was undoubtedly inspired by Westover in Virginia, there has been no attempt to make the new house a copy of the older one." Neither of these revivals of Southern Colonial was located in the South, but William L. Bottomley's Wise residence in Henrico County, Virginia, did refer back to Virginia's Colonial tradition.[19]

Keefe separated New England Colonial from Southern Colonial. New England was often less formal in exterior and plan. Both could be "rambling," as in the case of Dwight James Baum's Lewis House in Hartsdale. But a symmetrical brick façade could also be New England Colonial, such as Murphy & Dana's Phelps House in New Haven, Connecticut, "that takes its place naturally among its olden time neighbors"[20]

Long Island presented for Keefe a type of Dutch Colonial marked by gambrel roofs, gables without overhangs, porches with slender columns, and walls of white-painted, hand-split cypress shingles. For examples, Keefe simply turned to his own work done in partnership with Hopkins—the farmer's cottage on the George S. Brewster estate in Brookville and superintendent's cottage on the Glenn Stewart estate, Locust Valley.[21]

Pennsylvania, Keefe wisely noted, had its own brand of Colonial, dubbed "Germantown Colonial." Keefe selected houses by Philadelphia architects erected in the eastern part of the state, usually of local stone, sometimes whitewashed, as at John Graham, Jr.'s Wetherill residence in Laverock whose "prototype" was "Wyck" in Germantown, or not whitewashed as in Mellor & Meigs's Brown residence in Downingtown.[22]

Left out of the Colonial categories was Hudson Valley Dutch, for which Myron Teller was best known. Rather than include an exterior by Teller, Keefe chose Teller interiors whose regional character was less explicit, although in the hallway of the artist Julia Dillon's house in Kingston, Dutch tiles with blue figures faced the fireplace, and exposed beams and floorboards overhead were "in the spirit of the old Dutch builders at Kingston, New York."[23]

Keefe's first example in the Georgian category was John Russell Pope's grand Ogden Mills country house in Woodbury, Long Island. It resembled the plan of Southern Colonial houses with a central main block and lower wings, but on a larger scale. Its classical details stemmed from the Adam Brothers, and its interiors were more stately and formal—more upper-class British—than in American examples. But for Keefe as for others, "Georgian" could encompass a very wide range of design. He acknowledged that semi-detached housing by Hilton & Jackson for workers at the Glenlyon Dye Works in Providence, Rhode Island, were only "somewhat influenced by Georgian work"; their plain brick elevations might better be called "Colonial." During World War I, workers' housing had emerged as a major opportunity for architects, and Keefe, in the spirit of the times, opined that "the streets of many American towns [are] such dreary affairs. We are understanding more and more the effect of a man's environment upon his character and the best way to start social improvement is in the houses of the workers."[24] Keefe never had the opportunity to design housing for industrial workers, instead planning cottages for country estate employees.

Italian, Spanish, and French categories were of limited interest to Keefe, as they were to American clients and architects generally. (Keefe, however, did propose a book compiling Spanish work for publication by the U.P.C. Book Company, which had published a comparable book, *Northern Italian Details*. Nothing came of this.) Italian houses had stucco walls and tile roofs, as did Spanish houses, but while the Italian examples were dispersed in Kentucky and New York, the Spanish examples were concentrated in California and influenced by the region's rediscovery of its Spanish missions. As for French houses, Keefe was clear that "our ways of living are so different from the French that this style is rarely used in America." He chose only two examples, one inspired by the Petit Trianon at Versailles, yet "a very livable house," the other, as simple as the first was glorious, "was inspired by the farm cottages of France where the architect [Walter S. Davis] served during the war."[25]

More English houses were included than Italian, Spanish, or French. Keefe felt that "English ways of living" resembled American ways, and the English countryside resembled the landscape in the East, making English country houses especially fitting there. The English house—including Tudor, Elizabethan, and modern English—displayed half-timbering, a variety of wall materials, verge boards, complex roof slopes, and casement windows. Keefe again acknowledged John Russell Pope's high standing in the profession by placing his Lehman residence in Tarrytown at the head of the English section, while also featuring houses by Mellor, Meigs & Howe and Lewis Colt Albro. Julius Gregory's studio home of Charles E. Chambers in Riverdale fit into the modern English category, but Keefe recognized "early German" influence as well, the only example of such influence noted in his book.[26]

John Russell Pope's Lehman house.

Theodate Pope was the one woman architect whose work Keefe represented— the Chamberlain House (English) in Middlebury, Connecticut, and a cottage (said to be Georgian but actually from seventeenth-century Dutch or English sources) on the Gates estate, Locust Valley, Long Island. Like Keefe, she was a member of the Architectural League and A.I.A. Unlike Keefe, she had the disadvantage of being an upper-class woman whose architectural talents were consequently sometimes overlooked.

In introducing the section on interiors, Keefe pointed to the "range from formal country mansions, to . . . simple farm house interiors; some are intended for high heeled slippers and silken gowns, and in others we can see, in our mind's eye, a group, clad in tweeds, gathered about the hospitable fire place, after a day in the open."[27] None related to the working or lower-middle classes.

Keefe's surviving correspondence with the well-known architects whose houses he wanted to include in the book suggests that, while they were pleased to have their work published, they were not among his close colleagues in the profession. Myron Teller was the principal exception; he was clearly touched to have his work included "among the many more interesting work[s] I am sure you have." He sent Keefe a poem he had been handed celebrating friendship: "God put us all upon this earth/That we might serve His ends./And then, to give the world some worth,/He made some of us—friends." Dwight James Baum was more cordial than others in suggesting, "I . . . meet you some day in my car and show you various things which might interest you."[28]

Two of Keefe's former colleagues were not included in the book, but received a copy from the author. James Gamble Rogers wrote: "My dear Keefe: I received your book 'The American House.' I thank you very much for sending it and also for the inscription to it." John Scarff, who had departed unhappily from Hopkins in 1918, was more generous. Now a partner in the Baltimore firm of Wyatt & Nolting, Scarff, along with congratulations, offered "a good write-up" if a review copy came to the *Baltimore Evening Sun*. The review was better than good: "Mr. Keefe has put together an unrivaled collection. With rare taste and discrimination he has avoided all that is bizarre, and his book shows triumphantly the American use of precedent. A stimulation to one who loves a good house and to [the] architect who loves to build one."[29]

In 1926 George Young, Jr., a boyhood acquaintance of Keefe who was a Cornell-trained architect and professor of architecture at Cornell, left a penciled note at Keefe's office expressing admiration for his published designs and hoping to renew their acquaintance. Keefe subsequently inscribed a copy of *The American House* to Young, but he, coauthor of a book, *Mechanics of Materials* (with H. E. Baxter, published by MacMillan, 1927), was forthright in admitting it was his wife, Helen Binkerd Young, who was more appreciative of Keefe's book: "She is an architect herself and has done some rather good small houses and is particularly interested in the sort of thing you have put into your book."[30]

Helen Binkerd Young (1877–1959) had an architectural degree from Cornell, but as a woman her opportunities to teach or design were severely limited. Using her stationery with a print of their Tudor-style home in Ithaca, Helen Young wrote Keefe that his book "is full of good work and I am enjoying it so much. I never tire of leafing over and browsing thru books on houses—because that is the thing I am more interested in than anything else in the world—from the designer's viewpoint. There are many thoughtful features about your book—its organization for one thing enables one to find precisely what one wants. And I like the cover. I took the paper one off immediately and enjoy the naked book." She invited Keefe to come see "Hiddenhome," the house and garden she and her husband had "composed," but there is no record that he ever did.[31]

As a designer and book collector himself, Keefe took a keen interest in the design of the book. While it is not known whether Keefe owned any incunabula, in the file relating to his book is a typed description of a volume (Gregorius IX, Compilatio nova decretalium domini Gregorii pape noni) printed in Speyer in 1492, along with Keefe's pencil notes about type. Keefe probably lettered his book's title page, and the vignette of a Colonial doorway was surely drawn by him, although it is not a doorway pictured in his "Development of the American Doorway." The cloth binding was distinguished by a leather label with gilt lettering on the front cover and on the spine, probably influenced by Alfred Hopkins's taste for old leather and gilt bindings (see Appendix III). Keefe's own copy of the book is bound in leather with marbled endpapers and gilt edges of the pages adding to its beauty.

Given the care he had taken with the book's design, the proud author was distressed to learn from architect Verna Cook Salomonsky that Richard F. Bach, Associate in Industrial Arts at the Metropolitan Museum of Art and recipient of a review copy at Keefe's request, had voiced criticisms. Keefe wrote Bach that Salomonsky left him with "the impression that you thought the printing rather poorly done. Will you please tell me just what you had in mind? . . . Nearly all of the plates were made for the book and I went to a great deal of trouble to get what I thought was good type, paper, and ink. I shall be glad to have your criticism."[32]

Bach responded with good cheer: "You must not take things so seriously. When I spoke to Mrs. Salomonsky I was talking, not reviewing. However, if you want me to have my say it ought to be this: the book is too heavy, the paper is too thick and a number of the plates are fuzzy. This I say in a friendly spirit. Perhaps it is all personal, for I do not like heavy books. Bindings can be lighter without loss of solidity and good coated paper can also be less cumbersome than that usually used. Of course, on the other side is the bookselling end of it, of which I know nothing at all; which may explain my willingness to rush in where angels, etc., etc. '*The American House*' is a good book. So there!"[33]

Keefe's book received short but favorable notices in newspapers and architectural journals. (A penciled list is in the notebook, "For Publishing Book of Houses designed by Charles S. Keefe.") The most thoughtful review arrived in the form of a letter from William A. Boring, Director of Columbia's School of Architecture. Although Keefe gave a copy of the book to Columbia's library soon after publication, it was misplaced, and so Boring composed his letter March 5, 1925, with apologies for his lateness: "The book is an excellent publication of work done in the vicinity of 1920. I trust that you will get out another one in 1930 for our domestic architecture is changing, and I should like to see from you a description of the styles as they are then developed. In the present book it seems not quite possible to describe the style in all cases, and in ten years more I hope the melting pot will have fused them even more, so that it will not be possible to say this is English style, and this is early Colonial, but I hope to see a distinctly American style come out of all these ideas." Keefe responded: "I really believe that your hope of seeing an American style develop is really coming to pass for I have observed in the last year or two a number of houses that seem to be the forerunners of just such a thing. With so many good architects and the general public showing better taste each year I believe we are in a fair way to do better."[34] Unfortunately Keefe did not identify the characteristics of the forerunners.

Boring also observed in his letter: "The illustrations are excellent and well selected. Some of our best men are left out, but we have so many now that one book could not contain them all." In fact, Chicago and the Midwest were conspicuously absent, evidence of Keefe's aversion to architecture free of the historical revivals—modernism as practiced by Frank Lloyd Wright and the Prairie School. Surviving correspondence reveals that a number of tradition-minded architects whom Keefe invited to appear in the book—New Yorkers Bertam Goodhue, Philip L. Goodwin, Electus Litchfield, and Trowbridge & Ackerman, Adden & Parker of Boston, Edmund Gilchrist of Philadelphia, Pittsburghers Henry Gilchrist and Ingraham & Boyd, Hentz, Reid & Adler of Atlanta, and Willis Polk & Company of San Francisco—for a variety of reasons were not in the end represented. In the cloth binding of *The American House* with blank pages, Keefe pasted illustrations of work by architects not included in the book, among them Duhring, Okie & Ziegler of Philadelphia and Harrie T. Lindeberg of New York. The Philadelphians' Colonial designs were inspired by the early architecture of their region, while Lindeberg's mansions for Tracy Dows in Rhinebeck and Gerard Lambert in Princeton were fitted with Mount Vernon-inspired porches of the sort Keefe would apply to some of his grander houses.

Boring went on to suggest that "Georgian examples seem to point a way to a stronger style as the next phase. The Colonial style is fine, but a bit rarified for those who will follow us. We are so rushed that we must not be held to the restrictions of Colonial days. We lack their good taste, of course, but we have more material wealth and this is bound to come out in our architecture sooner or later. It is scholarly to build archaeologically correct houses of given styles, but it is not necessarily an artistic expression. We are sure to modify the Colonial style even if we do not improve it." Keefe never believed in strict copying of the Colonial, but would always turn to freely adapted Colonial as the best approach to an American style.

Book sales at $10 a copy were moderately successful. Between June 1922 and October 1923, 779 copies were sold, most to architects, although Keefe had expected that the book would appeal primarily to laymen.[35] A year later a second edition was planned, to sell at $7.50 a copy.[36] This edition appeared early in 1925; Keefe was pleased that while the contents were unchanged, the paper and ink had been improved. The journal *Architecture* gave this second edition a short but favorable review, calling the chosen houses "attractive" and their architects "of reputation." In sum, the book was "a useful and helpful reference work for any one interested especially in residential work."[37]

To demonstrate his standing in the profession, Keefe presented a copy of his book to a prospective client, William Rice. Rice remained hesitant to commit to Keefe's design for his house, and so Keefe reluctantly decided "to toot my own horn" and describe the book's reception; requiring a second edition was "something rare for an architectural book. Of the first edition 1000 copies were sold at ten dollars each and the second edition is about half gone. The American and English Press have commented favorably upon it and I believe the selection of subjects shows at least that I have good taste."[38]

Evidence of how the book was used by other architects is provided by a copy Walter T. Arnold, a Meriden, Connecticut, architect, gave a client in 1929.

Arnold suggested that two plates of Colonial houses could be adapted for the client's house.[39]

Some eighty years after the original publication, Dover in 2005 reprinted *The American House* as a large paperback and with a new title, *Elegant Country and Suburban Houses of the Twenties*, even though most if not all of the houses were completed in the teens.

Where Keefe's *American House* was represented as an improvement upon Dalzell's *Homes of Moderate Size*, Augusta Owen Patterson's *American Homes of Today* (New York: Macmillan, 1924) was undoubtedly intended to supersede the Keefe volume. While she enumerated the styles from Colonial through Italian more or less as Keefe did, and included works by several of the architects Keefe had featured, she was able to include more works by star architects like McKim, Mead & White and Carrere & Hastings. Moreover, she wrote chapters rather than brief entries and added topics such as "Historical Background," "The Garden," and "The City House" absent in Keefe. The *Times* critic T. S. Bosworth called it "a sumptuous record," and the book's design, binding, and paper are superior to Keefe's—as they should have been, given the $15.00 cost of the book. Patterson was art editor of *Town & Country* magazine, catering to elite society, and her sophistication shone forth in the Latin dedication she composed to her husband and in her arch manner of writing ("For fear that it may slip the attention, let me point out that we were a British colony until 1776." [p. 1]), in contrast to Keefe's plain English.

While Keefe's opinion of Patterson's book is not known, he did refuse to provide photos of his houses for inclusion in another rival volume, *American Country Houses of Today*, 1935. Its publisher, Architectural Book Publishing Company, nevertheless told him, "we were determined to have you represented, and have included two pages of your prize winning house of John J. Farrell."[40]

The Georgian Period

The Georgian Period, a large gathering of measured drawings, photos, and text relating to early American architecture, constituted an essential source for Colonial Revival architects and had originally appeared in issues of the *American Architect & Building News*. The plates and text were brought together in twelve parts published by the magazine's editor, William Rotch Ware, and copyrighted 1898 to 1901. Two decades later, in 1922, Keefe prepared a new edition of *The Georgian Period* with logically rearranged plates and added indexes, put out in three weighty volumes, by the U. P. C. Book Company. Keefe designed a new title page without his name, and he explained in the preface that his aim was to make this standard work more useful for architects and draftsmen by organizing the plates by building type and location. He noted that a few illustrations and drawings had been added, and he acknowledged contributions by two of his own contemporaries, Dwight James Baum and Baum's sometime designer,

Verna Cook Salomonsky, although it is unclear what the two contributed.[41] Both the *American Architect* and *Architectural Record* gave the new edition enthusiastic reviews.[42] However, architects looking for Hudson Valley Colonial data would be disappointed that neither Ware nor Keefe included plates of any buildings in the Mid-Hudson region.

"Book Material"

Keefe gathered in an envelope marked "Book Material" tracings by various hands on irregular sheets of tracing paper that recorded Colonial details found in architectural books and magazines. Most tracings identify the building where the detail was located and the publication from which the tracing was made. These included *The Georgian Period*, *White Pine Series*, *Colonial Interiors*, J. Frederick Kelly's *Early Domestic Architecture of Connecticut* (1924), and Lewis A. Coffin, Jr., and Arthur C. Holden's *Brick Architecture of the Colonial Period in Maryland and Virginia* (1919), as well as *Architectural Record*, *Architectural Forum*, and *Architectural Review*. The tracings were organized by type of detail, e.g., "Door Architrave" and "Fan Lights." Apparently Keefe had in mind publishing a book of these Colonial details, authentic sources for Colonial Revival draftsmen.

Rationale for the Colonial House in Wood

In 1926 Keefe was one of sixteen architects solicited for an endorsement of wood and Colonial design in constructing new houses. He was approached by West Coast lumber manufacturers, such as Weyerhaeuser, via their West Coast Lumber Trade Extension Bureau and its advertising firm, Botsford-Constantine Company of Seattle. Keefe and the other architects had been recommended by editors of architectural publications, and their endorsements, it was suggested, might appear in advertisements in popular magazines like the *Saturday Evening Post*, *Literary Digest*, and *House Beautiful*, along with photos of Colonial-style wooden houses they had designed.[43]

Keefe, no doubt welcoming the chance to publicize his work, responded with, "several good reasons for the survival of this type of house and for its continuance. First, it is typically American, being developed by the conditions and needs of our climate and our ways of living. Its inspiration came from the Georgian work in England—yet it is as distinct from the English as our ways are from theirs. Lack of certain materials and means of securing them, together with the necessity of working out mouldings by hand, caused a certain restraint that gives the charm often lacking in some modern examples. The real beauty in the old houses lies in their good proportions, delicate detail and their simplicity. We easily grow accustomed to the simple things and live in more comfort with them."

While he had included Italian- and French-inspired houses in *The American House*, and had himself occasionally turned to continental Europe for inspiration, he emphasized that, "Practically, all the other styles have to be adapted to our ways of living, which are so different from the ways of other folks and other climates." Keefe, in proclaiming that the Colonial was "typically American," distinct from foreign design and best suited to American life, was reinforcing a belief long held by American Colonial Revival architects and architectural critics.[44]

Then, too, turning to practical arguments, "the very simplicity of the Colonial house, as to form and ornament, makes for economy in building and maintenance. They look well anywhere, in the country or when crowded by their neighbors in less open places. The style is very adaptable, for in the old New England towns we see the large mansions standing among their smaller neighbors, each one as charming as the other. They are equally suitable for the rich as those of less means and they last if given ordinary good care and even sometimes without it. It seems to me the logical type of house for those who want beauty and utility combined, for the Colonial wood house has both."

While Keefe occasionally designed brick and stone buildings, wood was in fact his preferred material, and New England, not New York, his preferred source of historic forms. Keefe submitted photos of two small buildings he had designed, one with walls of painted shingles (the garden house of Edith Harkness on Long Island) and the other with unpainted shingle walls left to weather (the garage entrance of E. Hope Norton in Connecticut). There was no requirement that West Coast woods had been used, although Keefe also suggested that his California client, Elizabeth Tyng of Palo Alto, be contacted for photos of her "little house . . . of the simple New England type."[45]

Professional Recognition

In 1919 Keefe was elected a resident associate member of the Architectural League of New York and was advanced to resident active member status in 1928. The League, quartered in the American Fine Arts Society building on West 57th Street, held competitions and an annual exhibition with a substantial catalogue. League membership was a useful credential, and Keefe cited it when applying to enter the competition for the Chicago Tribune building in 1922.[46]

More importantly, in 1924 he was elected to membership in the American Institute of Architects.[47] Membership in the A.I.A., with its national organization and high ethical standards, provided clients with evidence of Keefe's good professional standing. None of his predecessors or contemporaries among Kingston architects had been elected to membership in the A.I.A.

Publicity

The gentlemen-architects of the A.I.A. set strict ethical standards that ruled against architects directly advertising their practice, but many architects, including Keefe, took advantage of gray areas. One such gray area that Keefe entered involved writing a testimonial letter for publication with a building material advertisement that often included a picture of a building by the architect. He not only wrote on behalf of lumber manufacturers but also for the American Radiator Company. His letter, signed with great flourish and recommending American Radiator Company's A type heater, was reproduced in an advertisement created by the leading advertising firm, Barton, Durstine & Osborn. Photos of his residential work were used in advertising for Creo-Dipt stained shingles (the Harkness cottage) and Boston's James Lumber Co. (the Hutchins house).[48]

The A.I.A. naturally had no objection to members publishing their work in the editorial (as opposed to advertising) pages of professional and household magazines, which Keefe pursued with great success. Of the professional magazines, the *American Architect* and *Architecture* were especially receptive, as were *The House Beautiful* and Y*our Home* among the household magazines. (See Appendix II.) When listing his credentials to client William Rice, Keefe cited "the design of a small house for *The House Beautiful*. This was undertaken at their request. . . . they said that my houses were among those about which they received the largest number of inquiries."[49] This "stock house," designed in January 1926, appeared in the January 1927 *House Beautiful*.

Travels to New England and Cape Cod

Keefe's first trip abroad in 1910–11 would also be his last, although in the prosperous 1920s a second trip was certainly possible. In 1925 an acquaintance, James Taylor of Wellington, "an old world village" in Herefordshire, offered to show Keefe "some old half timbered houses" on his next visit to England. Keefe surely was fond of such villages, responding that "It is good to know that you are settled in a good old village, where life goes along as it should without the terrible rush and bustle of most of our towns." The following year Keefe wrote fellow architect George Young that he had made one trip to Europe, "but hope to go over again shortly and get some more inspiration." But he did not go over, despite being drawn to old Britain and referring to Taylor's home in 1935 (when he could no longer afford extensive travel) as "what most folks consider the best place in the world to live." In this letter Keefe described the terrible winter weather in Kingston, "with the thermometer going well below zero most of the time." This may have temporarily soured him on Kingston, although he did enclose a photo of his home having a special kind of beauty after a winter storm.[50]

Keefe in the twenties continued to divide his time between Kingston and New York, with Grace as a rule remaining in Kingston. (An exception was the winter of 1925-26 when Grace was ill and in New York for ten weeks, including a few days in the hospital.) As he wrote George Young in 1926, "I still live at Kingston and spend the week in New York, going home Fridays for the week ends."[51] On the July 4th holiday weekend in 1921, Charles and Grace visited the famous old Catskill Mountain House in Greene County.

Instead of European travel, which required both time and money, neither of which Keefe had in abundance, Charles enjoyed vacations driving with Grace through New England with an eye out for its picturesque Colonial buildings. He had a car at least by 1919 when he and Grace visited Keefe family in Vermont. In the Fall of 1920, the couple went on a ten-day automobile trip into the Berkshires and Vermont, using the *Automobile Blue Book* as a guide to hotels. Poor service and accommodations at the Williams Inn at Williamstown, Massachusetts, led him to complain to the publisher, since "in touring I always use the hotels noted in the blue book." Vermont had a strong appeal, and not only the family homestead. Keefe wrote client C. McK. Lewis in September 1922: "For nearly three months I have been trying to get a few days off and have never seemed to be able to find the time. Mrs. Keefe wants to run up to Manchester, Vermont, for a few days, so I am going to take a week's vacation and go along." In 1925 Keefe was too busy to take a week off in the summer, but managed ten days away from work at Christmas, possibly in Vermont but more likely in Kingston, since he reported getting "in some skating in addition to eating too much."[52]

Charles (holding hat and cigar) and Grace at the Catskill Mountain House.

It was Cape Cod that came to be the Keefes' favorite vacation destination, thanks in large part to its distinctive houses, which provided models for several of his own designs of the 1920s. In August 1923 he wrote the *New York Evening Post* inquiring about motor camping to Cape Cod: "We would like to start on an auto trip across Massachusetts ending up at Cape Cod, and would like to know if we will have any difficulty securing places to camp overnight." The reply suggested that while New York State forests were open to campers, the same was not true of Connecticut and Massachusetts. In any event they did succeed in making their way to Cape Cod: that September, Grace spoke to the Olympian Club about her Cape Cod vacation memories.[53]

The date of their next Cape Cod excursion is not known, but in August 1929 Keefe wrote client Robert Bruce that the sketch of his house would be delayed, "as I am going up to Cape Cod for a few days. . . . I have been trying for three years to get a few days off and this year Mrs. Keefe's patience ran out so I am going anyhow. You and Mrs. Bruce would like it up there for they have the nicest little white houses one ever saw. Then when you want clams you go out and get them. I'll never tell how many we eat." In this same period he designed a Christmas greeting card, "Cape Cod Entrance," with its characteristic doorway and shutters, and a woman in old-fashioned costume.[54]

The restoration of Colonial Williamsburg began to take form in 1926, although it was 1932 before the first restored building was opened to the public.

"Cape Cod Entrance."

Keefe's papers do not mention a visit to Virginia or elsewhere in the South. He did, however, travel to New Castle, Delaware, probably in 1929, writing William Rice in 1930: "I went down to New Castle . . . a year or so ago on the day the houses and gardens were both open to the public. It was well worth the trip."[55]

It also appears that Keefe never traveled to the West after 1900. However, when client C. McK. Lewis told him that he was taking his mother to Arizona for a short stay, Keefe asked, "If you happen to have your camera along and see any good old houses, try and get some pictures."[56]

Keefe traveled to and studied old houses to obtain motifs for his own designs, but also to acquire a sense of how they had been lived in, even to immerse himself in the feeling or spirit of a bygone age, no doubt romanticized. Keefe was not given to poetic musings, but probably in the twenties he penciled some thoughts about experiencing old (and new) houses: "Perhaps you have noticed it too when walking or driving through the country. It is what I call the lonesome house, that is a house sitting by itself on its suburban lot or by the country roadside without dependants. . . . In the country yet not of it. . . . I like to see a place with its out buildings. . . . It may be a tool house, a garage, a barn, a shed or about anything. But there it is to tell us of the interests of the occupants of the place."[57] Of course this interest in outbuildings makes good sense since much of his practice was devoted to their design.

"Just What Is a Cape Cod House?"

In an interview published in the popular magazine *Your Home* in 1930, Keefe explained that, while he had made "a special first-hand study of certain old and beautiful architectural types" in the thirteen original colonies, "among them all I have found no sort of house that has engaged my affections and aroused my sympathy and enthusiasm more than the unpretentious and lovely type known as the Cape Cod cottage." Why? "I recommend it without reservation to anyone who wants a small, convenient, economical house whose lines and whose sturdy beauty and common sense will thrill him every time he looks at it."

Keefe, however, warned against loose interpretations of the Cape Cod model: "build the real thing—not one of the shoddy imitations . . . [that] ruin the subtle beauty . . . characteristic of these little houses." Inferior versions "rob the owner of the sense that he has put his roots down deep into the past . . . that he has in some deep spiritual fashion identified himself with it [the past]. This feel for history is an important thing in the culture of a nation or of an individual. . . . We are a new country, and we need it." Writing at the beginning of the tumultuous Great Depression, Keefe understood the old Cape Cods to be "eminently sane and beautiful creations of a race of men and women who lived their lives in close touch with hard realities and produced something lovely out of conditions . . . many would have thought sordid and fatal to such beauty."

His enthusiasm for Cape Cod cottages led him to acquire expert knowledge of authentic early examples, which he recorded in photographs, notes, and drawings. These provided information for his own house designs, but he also understood them as preserving an historical record of buildings constantly threatened with alteration or removal. From his first-hand study, Keefe identified the design characteristics of a Cape Cod house or cottage, which, while originating, he thought, on Cape Cod, Keefe found in many parts of New England.

Reacting against the picturesque, vertical lines employed by Andrew Mason in Kingston, he stressed the "low lines" of the Cape Cod cottage of one or one-and-a-half stories. "The roof is so low that it comes down close over the windows and doors." The roof also projected very little over the walls, being especially close at the gables. Chimneys were low and rose from the middle of the roof. Walls were wood-shingled or sided, and corner boards were common. The entrance door was low, with pilasters at the sides and transom above. There were no porches—"people in that region worked very hard, and they had little time to sit down," and the cool climate was not conducive to porch life. Keefe was curious to observe that often one big, flat stone would be laid in front of the doorway but not touching it, so that "the house seemed to hang in air above the stone."

Internally, "the house was practically built around a great central chimney. . . . The cold climate made this sensible. The chimney had four sides, with a fireplace in each side, one for each room. . . . that whole mass of masonry became heated like a big stove . . . like some central heating plant." Entering the front door, one came upon "a little hall from which ascended a very short, steep, narrow staircase. . . . Battened doors were the rule, with hand wrought hinges. . . . The fireplace end of each room was paneled. Sometimes a kitchen would be boarded vertically. Wainscots were boarded horizontally. . . . The ceilings were rather uniformly seven feet high." Windows had twelve panes in each of the two sashes, although Keefe found few original sashes. A typical dimension for the house would be thirty-nine feet long by thirty feet deep; additions were kept progressively lower as they extended from the main house.

Keefe of course recognized that it would be foolish to exactly duplicate an early Cape Cod—kitchens and bathrooms, plumbing and heating needed to be up-to-date. And he allowed that the architect might even create a "modern version . . . even better and more beautiful than the old."[58]

CHAPTER FOUR

Buildings of the Prosperous Twenties

Harkness garden house.

When associated with Hopkins in the 1910s, Keefe routinely worked on cottages and farm buildings for wealthy clients. This practice continued into the next decade, independent of Hopkins.

The Harkness Estate and Offspring from the Harkness Cottage

William L. Harkness (1858–1919) was a multimillionaire thanks to his father's early investment in John D. Rockefeller's Standard Oil. In 1913 Harkness commissioned James Gamble Rogers to design a 40-room stucco Neoclassical mansion with portico at Dosoris, his Glen Cove, Long Island, estate on the Sound. The estate had earlier been formed by Charles Dana, and a Dana building was incorporated into the Harkness mansion as its servants wing. (The mansion, with the exception of the servants wing, was demolished in the 1930s.) After Harkness's death, a fraction of his fortune went to his alma mater, Yale, to construct William L. Harkness Hall, a collegiate Gothic building by William A. Delano.[1]

Thanks to Rogers's recommendation, Keefe secured commissions from Harkness's widow, **Edith Hale Harkness,** to plan a cottage and garden house for the estate. Edith Harkness (?–1947), like her husband, was originally from Ohio, but could claim descent from Samuel Hale, an original proprietor of Hartford, Connecticut. Her benefactions included the New York Genealogical and Biographical Society, and she belonged to the National Society of Colonial Dames and the highly selective Colony Club in New York. Her interests would seem to make her receptive to the Colonial Revival practiced by Keefe. Still, some of her wealth was directed more adventurously to the founding of Time Inc. in 1923. Keefe corresponded frequently and in detail with Mrs. Harkness both about new work he had designed and maintenance and repairs to existing structures. In his letters Keefe appears especially deferential in an effort to avoid annoying his

Harkness cottage. (ad for CREO-DIPT shingles)

important client. Her own letters, mostly handwritten, related to the business at hand and were formal but cordial.[2]

The Harkness cottage was designed in 1922 and completed in 1923 as the estate superintendent's residence. It stood 200 feet from an inlet off Long Island Sound, but could have been in any middle-class American neighborhood. It was built on the site of a Revolutionary-era house Keefe deemed "not good enough to keep."[3] With its one-and-a-half stories, gable roof with dormers, and walls of white-painted hand-split cypress shingles with dark green shutters, it resembled the Hopkins-Keefe cottages on Long Island of the previous decade, but the façade was distinctive with its projecting cross gable to one side above the doorway and small porch. The porch was a delicate Federal-style composition of slender columns, an elliptical arch, and a pair of benches flanking the paneled door. Having the door only a step or so above ground level enhanced the easy charm of the cottage. Keefe acknowledged the water view from the rear of the house and connected the living room with a broad porch facing the inlet.

The cottage was published in the November 1923 *House Beautiful* with photos by Antoinette Perrett, leading to an inquiry from an eighth-grade art student in Grand Rapids. Keefe, childless, appears to have been fond of children and responded in some detail about the cottage's historical inspiration: "It is Colonial in style following the type of Colonial houses that were developed by the early builders residing in this vicinity. It is very simple and whatever charm it may possess is because of this fact. Remember the early builders had to work out all the mouldings by hand and consequently they were very careful in their use of them. Also, they had a few good books from which they adapted their various ornamental parts. . . . Local conditions and lack of certain facilities often caused them to make changes in the design of their columns, doorways, etc. and this gave the work its individuality and charm." He noted that the hand-split cypress shingles were "the same as used in the old houses. These shingles having slightly rough surfaces are much more effective than a sawed shingle. The roof is of shingles left to weather the very nice soft grey they get near the sea shore."[4] The CREO-DIPT Company furnished 24-inch "Dixie White" shingles for the exterior walls and 18-inch "Weathered Gray" for the roof; the company pictured the Harkness cottage in its advertising, including the *Saturday Evening Post* of February 16, 1924 (p. 155).

Keefe's garden house for Mrs. Harkness, designed in 1925 as a workroom replacing an earlier workroom attached to a greenhouse, was of a more rarefied order, expressive of the sophistication and wealth of the client. When Keefe presented her with construction bids, he assured her that "the building will be worth while showing to your friends. When this building is completed all the buildings will be in conformity and completely cover your needs." Keefe wanted his garden house to be in harmony with Rogers's main house and its classical portico, and he wanted discordant outbuildings surviving from before Rogers's intervention to disappear. The garden house's Federal-style porch was a diminutive temple portico with four attenuated columns and a pediment graced with low relief swags in plaster and a shield-shaped window with inserted linear leading. Writing in *House Beautiful*, Keefe's colleague Verna Cook Salomonsky identified the portico's source as Homewood, a Federal period masterpiece in red brick begun in 1801 and today on the Johns Hopkins campus, but the "delicacy" and "playfulness" of Mrs. Harkness's portico related to its columns being just over half the height of Homewood's.[5]

In photos published in *The Architect*, two Windsor chairs accompany potted plants on the porch. Keefe had ordered the Windsors from William Leavens & Co. in Boston, explaining to them that "I want to use a couple of these chairs on the porch of a Colonial House (as I have done before) so I will get the proper effect. I do this rather than let the owner or tenant put out some funny looking chairs."[6] Architects from Frank Lloyd Wright to Charles A. Platt were fortunate to have clients who allowed them to design or select furniture in harmony with the house design. Keefe rarely seems to have had this privilege.

Keefe sent Mrs. Harkness a copy of *The Architect* with its photos of her garden house and assured her that "Mr. Rogers is Chairman of the Board of this magazine and that is a guarantee of its character and standing." Writing "On board Cythera," her 600-ton yacht, Mrs. Harkness acknowledged that "the illustration of the cottage is lovely."[7] Keefe also alerted James Gamble Rogers that the garden house, "a little building I erected for Mrs. Harkness," had been published in *The Architect*. "I tried to keep this in character with your work on the place, and trust it meets with your approval. Through your kindness I secured this work and I want you to feel that I do everything possible to merit your recommendation." Rogers replied: "Let me congratulate you on the success of the little building for Mrs. William L. Harkness. It is a pleasure to recommend a person who makes good." While congratulatory, the message clearly established that Rogers was the great architect and Keefe the minor one.[8]

Keefe was mortified when a paint manufacturer named Keefe as the architect of the Harkness mansion pictured on a blotter distributed as advertising. In fact Keefe had merely overseen the painting of the exterior. He was further embarrassed that the advertising text identified Mrs. Harkness as a "millionaire." Keefe asked that distribution of the blotter be stopped "so no more harm may be done. An architect's life is hard enough with all its details without some one getting him in trouble [with] a client, which would be the case if the owner happened to see the blotter."[9]

Both before and during the Depression, Keefe welcomed the income from handling even minor assignments from Mrs. Harkness for the Glen Cove estate involving repairs, painting, and equipment, including an electric range and elevator at the main house. When she questioned a plumber's bill, he reminded her that there were eleven bathrooms in the master's portion of the house, not including the servants' quarters. In 1931 Keefe heard "from an acquaintance in Cleveland" that Mrs. Harkness's daughter, Mrs. David S. (Louise)

Elizabeth Tyng house.

Ingalls contemplated building a country house near Cleveland. Keefe sought the job, citing a number of his polo-playing and equestrian clients (Crane, Rice, Farrell, and Haight) whom Mrs. Ingalls and her husband may have known. But Mrs. Harkness wrote Keefe that the Ingalls "had given up all idea of building."[10]

Miss Elizabeth McJ. Tyng saw illustrations of the Harkness cottage, probably in the November 1923 *House Beautiful*. In 1924 she had Keefe design an externally similar home for her in Palo Alto, California, which received an honorable mention in a *House Beautiful* competition. Wide redwood siding painted white substituted for the cypress shingles, and dormers were omitted since the owner's and guest bedrooms were on the first floor. (The three bedrooms of the Harkness cottage, intended for occupation by a family, were all on the second floor.) Miss Tyng's living room opened onto a sun porch and terrace at the rear of the house, reminiscent of the rear porch of the Harkness cottage.[11]

Miss Tyng was vice-principal of Castilleja School, a private school for girls in Palo Alto, but had been a New Englander. *House Beautiful* noted that her home was "logically patterned after early New England houses, both because its owner came from there and because its setting suggests a New England landscape." In

1927 Keefe designed a second house for Miss Tyng in Palo Alto, a two-story Colonial described as "owned" by her, but apparently not her residence, although a photo of the living room shows it finely furnished with Colonial Revival pieces.[12]

The Harkness cottage as published in *House Beautiful* also attracted a Midwestern couple from Troy, Ohio, a small city in the western part of the state. **Dr. Lauren Norton Lindenberger** (1886–1963) and his wife **Harriet Elise Howland Lindenberger** (1892–1971) commissioned their story-and-a-half clapboarded Colonial house, which Keefe designed in January 1924. Drawings for the house include a carefully designed letter "L", two of which would grace the front door head and identify the owner.[13] Later Keefe sent a Christmas greeting to the couple, which inspired Elise Lindenberger to pen a gracious note complimenting the architect on the success of his house: "The longer we live in this small house of yours, the greater our appreciation of its countless good points. It has been an exceedingly comfortable house and the source of much pride. The comments of our small-town Public have been more than gratifying to us—and I'm sure, to you—could they directly reach your ears. We were much interested in your house in January's *House Beautiful*, liking it almost as well as our own."[14] Keefe's design for "A New House Beautiful House" resembled the Tyng House and appeared in the January 1927 issue. Working drawings and specifications for the "story-and-a-half type cottage of Colonial antecedents" could be purchased from the magazine for $50.

The Lindenberger family in their living room.

The Lindenbergers were susceptible to the appeal of a Colonial Revival house since both were drawn to history, he as a member of the General Society of Mayflower Descendants and General Society of Colonial Wars, while she was her church's historian, charter member of the Troy Historical Society, and creator of genealogical files. Not only were they attracted to a Colonial house design, but they also chose wallpaper with eighteenth-century scenes and placed an antique clock on the living-room mantle.

The Lindenberger house still stands at 111 South Plum Street and must always have been a small Colonial outpost amid non-Colonial neighbors. Dr. Lindenberger was a long-time member of the Troy City Planning Commission, beginning in the 1930s; one wonders how his home fit into his concept of a well-planned small city.[15]

A third offspring of the Harkness superintendent's cottage known to have sprung from *House Beautiful* was built for **Robert L. Bruce** (1893–1983) and his

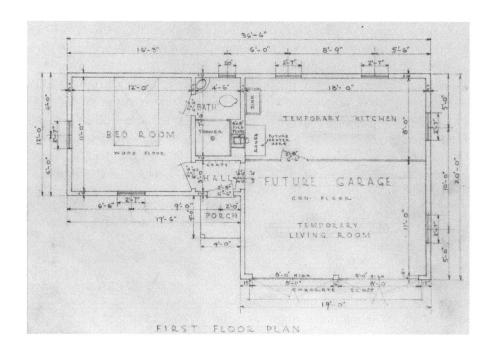

Bruce house, first floor plan.

wife **Kathryn Duerr Bruce** (born c. 1895) of New Martinsville, West Virginia, a small city on the Ohio River. He was an agent for Standard Oil of New Jersey and later mayor of New Martinsville from 1941 to 1967. The Bruces, who had two sons, tried to be good clients. They were eager to have the New York architect's advice on large and small practical details as they planned a version of the Harkness cottage. Financially responsible, they only built what they could afford. Keefe assured the couple that house building was a "serious affair," yet "we can make a good home for you and have some fun doing it too."[16] The voluminous and cheerful correspondence between clients and architect—dozens of letters between December 13, 1923, and November 19, 1932—indicates that, despite Keefe's never traveling to New Martinsville or meeting his clients, and the clients never having the money to build the home Keefe originally designed for them, both sides maintained hope that somehow the Bruces would occupy a new Colonial home.

Keefe's April 1925 drawings for a reworked Harkness Cottage were enthusiastically received, as Robert Bruce wrote the architect: "To say that we are delighted with your work would be expressing our feelings too mildly. We only hope that some day we may have the pleasure of having you visit us in the little home in which you have had a big part."[17] But, to cut costs, Keefe in July planned a garage that would function as house with one bedroom and, in the future two-car garage space, a temporary living room and temporary kitchen. It resembled Keefe's shingled cottages with Colonial windows and shutters, but its most prominent feature was a pair of garage doors. In 1928 Keefe drew plans for a sun room

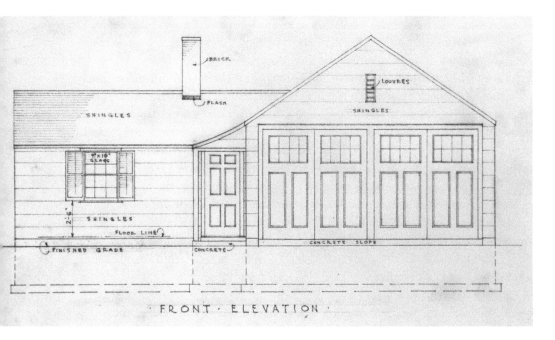

FRONT · ELEVATION ·

Bruce house, front elevation.

addition to the garage, and in 1930 extensive additions and alterations to the "garage" that would completely transform it into a Colonial cottage, though plainer than the April 1925 plans.

Robert Bruce also wondered whether Keefe ever did "any 'camouflaging' of business buildings?" Specifically he hoped to have Keefe design Colonial fronts for two "ungainly" buildings used for auto sales and service. Keefe expressed interest, but Bruce did not pursue the idea.[18]

Finally, in 1931 the Bruces did go ahead and build their home, using a local contractor and Keefe's plans for the transformed garage. Mrs. Bruce trusted that Keefe would provide a Colonial home, but as construction wound down, she was a bit troubled: "What style would you call our house? The man from whom we got our lumber called it 'English,' but I hardly think it is that. We started out to have everything Colonial, and our furniture is all along that line, yet I don't believe the house is strictly that style. Whatever it is, though, I'm sure it will be attractive when we get it all done." Were her friends saying that her home did not resemble pictures of the restoration of Colonial Williamsburg? Keefe tried to be reassuring: "Your house is Colonial of a simple type used more in the North than in the South. Buildings like it were erected in New England and always look homelike and simple."[19]

Keefe was so impressed with the content and style of her letters that he suggested she write an article about her personal experience as a home builder and submit it to Harry J. Walsh, the editor of *Your Home*, who told Keefe he was looking for such pieces. "Just how much they will pay I do not know, but it probably would be enough for a small hooked rug, a lamp or something extra that you wanted." She did write to Walsh, only to be informed that the magazine was discontinuing publication, a victim of the Depression.[20]

Robert M. Anderson (1861/1862–1940) was a client who did succeed in publishing the story of building a Keefe house in America's heartland. Anderson commissioned a standard Keefe story-and-a-half Colonial with cross-gable-to-side façade just as the twenties ended and the Depression began—working drawings are dated January 6, 1930. Unusual among the clients, Anderson was a bachelor and an engineer. Trained at the University of Notre Dame and the Stevens Institute of Technology, Anderson taught mechanical engineering at the Hoboken, New Jersey, school until his retirement in 1930.[21] Circleville, Ohio, was his hometown, and there he returned in retirement. Circleville was some twenty-two miles south of Columbus, and Anderson drew a map indicating that his home on a small lot north of the center of town was a block away from the electric interurban line to Columbus.

Robert Anderson house.

In the *Pictorial Review* article Anderson wrote about his house, he did not reveal how he came to select Keefe as his architect, but he did declare that, "I have always been partial to the New England type of house, and although mine was built in Ohio I selected that style for my home." As an engineer he paid particular attention to heating and cooling, and he selected Johns-Manville rock wool for superior insulation. He also insisted on abundant light fixtures throughout the house. The plan called for four bedrooms, generous for a bachelor, with two on the first floor separated from kitchen, living and dining rooms, while guest and maid's rooms were on the second.

Anderson's active role in planning the house is indicated by his small pencil sketch repeating Keefe's design. Independent of Keefe, Anderson also drew in pen and ink the designs for an iron grill enclosing the small terrace at the rear of the house and for an "antiqued oak library table," the latter in an outdated Arts and Crafts style.

While Keefe provided working drawings and specifications, he did not supervise construction—he did not travel to Circleville. Still, he was pleased with construction photos dated June 30, 1930, and photos of the finished house a year later: "After looking over the pictures very carefully I should say you have a most comfortable and homelike place. The little house seems to settle right down on its lot and looks as if it belonged there." The architect hoped Anderson would write occasionally about how client and home were getting along, and suggested, "If you come this way let me know so we can have lunch at the Architectural League."[22] This is the only surviving reference to Keefe spending time at the League on 57th Street.

Anderson remained proud of his home and wrote, "I Got the House I Wanted," published in the May 1934 *Pictorial Review* (p. 38). Keefe acknowledged that, "Your house created quite a lot of interest and I received about 250 letters from interested people. Managed to get a couple of small jobs . . .

I GOT THE HOUSE I WANTED

By

ROBERT M. ANDERSON

Charles S. Keefe, A.I.A.,
Architect

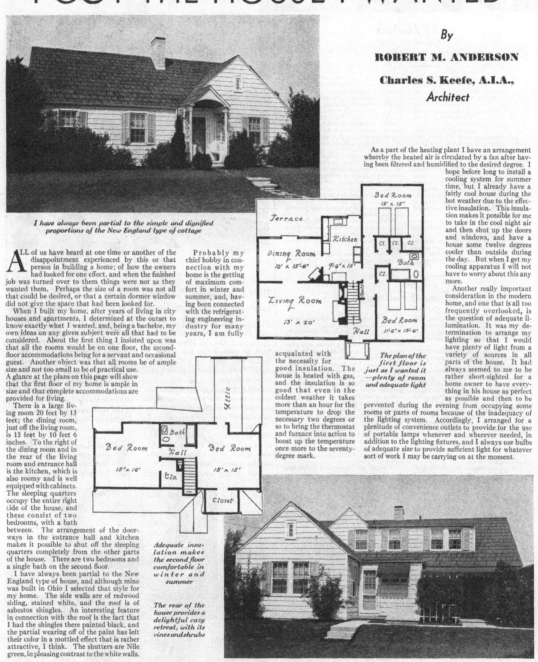

I have always been partial to the simple and dignified proportions of the New England type of cottage

The plan of the first floor is just as I wanted it —plenty of room and adequate light

Adequate insulation makes the second floor comfortable in winter and summer

The rear of the house provides a delightful cozy retreat, with its vines and shrubs

ALL of us have heard at one time or another of the disappointment experienced by this or that person in building a home; of how the owners had looked for one effect, and when the finished job was turned over to them things were not as they wanted them. Perhaps the size of a room was not all that could be desired, or that a certain dormer window did not give the space that had been looked for.

When I built my home, after years of living in city houses and apartments, I determined at the outset to know exactly what I wanted, and, being a bachelor, my own ideas on any given subject were all that had to be considered. About the first thing I insisted upon was that all the rooms would be on one floor, the second-floor accommodations being for a servant and occasional guest. Another object was that all rooms be of ample size and not too small to be of practical use. A glance at the plans on this page will show that the first floor of my home is ample in size and that complete accommodations are provided for living.

There is a large living room 20 feet by 13 feet; the dining room, just off the living room, is 15 feet by 10 feet 6 inches. To the right of the dining room and in the rear of the living room and entrance hall is the kitchen, which is also roomy and is well equipped with cabinets. The sleeping quarters occupy the entire right side of the house, and these consist of two bedrooms, with a bath between. The arrangement of the doorways in the entrance hall and kitchen makes it possible to shut off the sleeping quarters completely from the other parts of the house. There are two bedrooms and a single bath on the second floor.

I have always been partial to the New England type of house, and although mine was built in Ohio I selected that style for my home. The side walls are of redwood siding, stained white, and the roof is of asbestos shingles. An interesting feature in connection with the roof is the fact that I had the shingles there painted black, and the partial wearing off of the paint has left their color in a mottled effect that is rather attractive, I think. The shutters are Nile green, in pleasing contrast to the white walls.

Probably my chief hobby in connection with my home is the getting of maximum comfort in winter and summer, and, having been connected with the refrigerating engineering industry for many years, I am fully acquainted with the necessity for good insulation. The house is heated with gas, and the insulation is so good that even in the coldest weather it takes more than an hour for the temperature to drop the necessary two degrees or so to bring the thermostat and furnace into action to boost up the temperature once more to the seventy-degree mark.

As a part of the heating plant I have an arrangement whereby the heated air is circulated by a fan after having been filtered and humidified to the desired degree. I hope before long to install a cooling system for summer time, but I already have a fairly cool house during the hot weather due to the effective insulation. This insulation makes it possible for me to take in the cool night air and then shut up the doors and windows, and have a house some twelve degrees cooler than outside during the day. But when I get my cooling apparatus I will not have to worry about this any more.

Another really important consideration in the modern home, and one that is all too frequently overlooked, is the question of adequate illumination. It was my determination to arrange my lighting so that I would have plenty of light from a variety of sources in all parts of the house. It had always seemed to me to be rather short-sighted for a home owner to have everything in his house as perfect as possible and then to be prevented during the evening from occupying some rooms or parts of rooms because of the inadequacy of the lighting system. Accordingly, I arranged for a plenitude of convenience outlets to provide for the use of portable lamps whenever and wherever needed, in addition to the lighting fixtures, and I always use bulbs of adequate size to provide sufficient light for whatever sort of work I may be carrying on at the moment.

THE HOME BUREAU

A House of Colonial Type

Long Branch New Jersey

Louis H. Dreyer

THIS HOUSE OF COLONIAL TYPE IS CHARACTERISTIC OF MR. KEEFE'S WORK AND SHOWS THE DELICATE
AND PLEASING DETAIL BY WHICH HIS HOUSES CAN USUALLY BE IDENTIFIED. THE PLAN IS COMPACT
AND SHOWS A WELL-ARRANGED KITCHEN AND A LIVING-ROOM THAT IS MADE TO SEEM MORE AMPLE
BECAUSE OF THE DINING ALCOVE AND THE SUNROOM. A GRADE ENTRANCE LEADS TO THE CELLAR,
WITH WHICH THE STAIRS FROM THE KITCHEN CONNECT

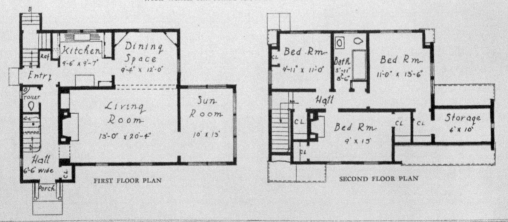

THE HOUSE OF WILLIAM E. CATE, ESQ.   CHARLES S. KEEFE, ARCHITECT [from the publicity]. I hope all my clients are as happy in their homes as you seem to be in yours."[23]

While not derived from the Harkness cottage, the Cate house at Long Branch, New Jersey, was of similar scale and simple Colonial aspect. **William Ervin Cate** (1869–?) was a member of the Harvard College class of 1895, while his wife, **Florence Gertrude Spring Cate** (1876–?), was an 1897 Wellesley College graduate. In the 1920s William Cate was principal of the Long Branch (New Jersey) High School, and Florence Cate a teacher or school librarian. Keefe acquired the Cates as clients thanks to their friendship with Miss Ethel M. Pultz, who was the niece of Charles's stepmother and had been raised in the home of Andrew and Mattie Pultz Keefe.[24]

In 1923 Keefe planned a shingled but formally composed Colonial house for the the Cates, but his 1926 design for the "Cate Cottage" was completed on Brighton Avenue as a less formal Colonial, the asymmetrical façade having at the left a small gabled front entry, a broad cross gable for a second-story bedroom, and at the right a sun room. First published in *The Architect* (September 1927), the Cate house then appeared in *House Beautiful* (February 1928) and *Your Home* (March 1931). *House Beautiful* (p. 176) appreciated "this house of Colonial type [that] is characteristic of Mr. Keefe's work and shows the delicate and pleasing detail by which his houses can usually be identified." Notable in this regard were the radiating slats in the arch over the front door and the seats of the roofless porch or stoop. (A recent Google photo shows neither of these features remains.)

William and Florence Cate house.

While the Cate house had three bedrooms, they were not spacious. *Your Home* called it "The Little House That Never Quite Grew Up," and went on in this vein: "'Let's play at keeping house,' says this cosy little place. 'Let's do,' answer we who would stay always in Never-Never Land." But the writer finally allowed, "Diminutive and playlike as this little house may be, its realization of many substantial conveniences [including a compact "dining alcove" opening off the living room] and luxuries lift it from Make-Believe Land into that of grown-up actuality." Photos of the interior show not "Never-Never Land" but conventional furnishings—an upholstered sofa and Colonial Revival rocker along with a photo of Michelangelo's *David* in the living room, and wicker furniture in the sun room.[25]

Farm and Estate Buildings for Woolworth, Lewis, and the Inslees

Richard W. ("Duke") Woolworth (1899?–1959), son of C. S. and nephew of F. W. Woolworth, founders of the 5-and-10-cent stores, attended Princeton but did not graduate. He was known for raising Guernsey cows on his 280-acre "Northshire Farm" in Salem Center, Westchester County, and as an accomplished amateur golfer. Keefe's work for Woolworth included a dairy building (1926–29) where Keefe, the Colonial advocate, advised "windows with shutters," over barn-like windows to "add . . . a little touch to the very simple buildings." Woolworth also commissioned an addition to the main house after the birth of a son, which inspired Keefe to write his client: "Please give this little chap my good wishes for the holidays and tell him I consider him the friend of the architects for his arrival made necessary an addition to your house." Keefe's Woolworth file contains a 1925 blueprint of a stone Colonial house for Woolworth by Hopkins, but noted architect Mott Schmidt was responsible for the existing brick Georgian mansion of 1934.[26]

It was, however, Keefe's Colonial cottage (1926) on the Woolworth farm that received wide publicity. The cottage resembled the architect's other estate cottages—story-and-a-half, white siding, with shutters and dormers providing accents—although here the façade was partially recessed behind a shallow front porch. *House Beautiful* included the cottage in its November 1928 issue with floor plans and a photo by Louis H. Dreyer. Since the walls were split cypress shingles, Keefe received a request to use a photo of the cottage in advertising for the Southern Cypress Manufacturers Association. In March 1930 it was featured on the cover of *Your Home*, where prospective home builders (women were the magazine's target readership) were told that architect Keefe called it "an ideal home for a newly married couple!" Why ideal? Because with two bedrooms on the first floor, the second floor could be left unfinished or, as the write-up was headed, here was "A House that Has Room to Grow." As in his earlier bungalows, the bedrooms were separated from the living room by a hallway. Readers, who were assumed to be "folks of moderate means," were not told that "this dream house" was a small part of a wealthy family's estate. The Woolworth cottage next appeared, taking the hint from *Your Home*, as "A Honeymoon Home" on the May 1930 cover of *The Franklin News*, published by The Franklin Society for Home-Building and Savings of 217 Broadway, New York.[27]

Clarence McKenzie Lewis (1876/1877–1959), one of Keefe's most faithful clients, was a Columbia-trained civil engineer for the Baltimore & Ohio Railroad and later a Blair & Co. investment banker in Manhattan with an apartment at 1000 Park Avenue. In 1912 Lewis purchased Sheffield (or Sheffield-Hope) Farm, in Mahwah, New Jersey, and had Alfred Hopkins, together with Keefe, design farm buildings there. Blueprints dated 1914 for Lewis's "Farm Buildings" in Mahwah are Colonial in style and signed "Alfred Hopkins, Architect, Charles S. Keefe."[28] At Sheffield Farm, Lewis developed a keen interest in horticulture and eventually became a trustee of the New York Botanical Garden, which now houses his papers. He also became familiar with Skylands Farm, a grander estate owned by another horticulture enthusiast nearby in the Ramapo Mountains.

In 1912 Hopkins had designed a gate lodge for Skylands Farm, **Francis L. Stetson's** vast estate on the New York-New Jersey border, which is today the New Jersey State Botanical Gardens at Skylands. (Skylands Farm's mailing address in Keefe's time was Sterlington, Rockland County, New York.) Stetson (1846–1920) was an attorney who numbered among his clients J. P. Morgan and Andrew Carnegie, while demonstrating a serious interest in plants and serving as a

The Franklin News

Published Bi-Monthly by
The Franklin Society
for Home-Building and Savings

217 Broadway　　　　　　　**New York**

VOL. 7—No. 4　　　　　　　　　　　　MAY, 1930

A HONEYMOON HOME

Built for Young Married Couple, It is Practical for Others as Well

"A HONEYMOON home," the architect, Charles S. Keefe, called this house. "An ideal home for a newly married couple!"

As you will see from the plans, it is a complete home on the first floor, with provision to add more rooms on the second floor later. The entire second floor may be left unfinished or a single bedroom

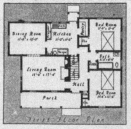 installed as shown on the plan. On the first floor are living room, dining room, two bedrooms, kitchen and a bathroom. The second floor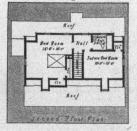

(Cont. on page 2)

Workroom for greenhouse at Skylands Farm.

member of the board of managers of the New York Botanical Garden (1908–20). Stetson developed Skylands both as a garden showplace and gentleman's farm with a full range of farm animals handsomely housed.[29] Hopkins's *Modern Farm Buildings* (1913), which illustrated Hopkins's own work, had as its frontispiece a photo captioned, "Buildings of reinforced concrete. A beautiful environment and a restful composition. Farm buildings for Francis Lynde Stetson, Esq., Sterlington, N.Y." Also pictured were several other Hopkins buildings at Skylands Farm ranging from the Coach Stable and Coachman's Cottage to Milking Cows Barn and Piggery. None of these structures was Colonial, but they followed the picturesque quality of Stetson's Tudor mansion completed in 1897 by Algernon E. Bell. It is likely that Keefe had a role in the design of Stetson's farm buildings while in Hopkins's office.

In 1922, after Stetson's death, Lewis acquired Skylands Farm, and Keefe soon was employed in further developing it. The Stetson mansion was torn down in order to satisfy Lewis's mother, Helen Salomon, who wanted something bigger and more accurately old English for insertion of her collection of antique English woodwork. Keefe in 1923 did his best to obtain the commission for this grand house, which would have been the largest in his career. He assured Lewis that "this would be the big job of the office" and that, while he would have overall responsibility, "Mr. Salomonsky here in the office . . . [would] devote his entire time to this work," and Mrs. Salomonsky would be involved "whenever needed." Keefe knew that Lewis had been discussing the job with the renowned architect John Russell Pope, but Keefe argued that "we can give the work more individual attention and . . . we can follow it more closely than a larger office can. . . ." Still, the combined talent of Edgar and Verna Cook Salomonsky and Charles Keefe could not compete with the prestige of Pope, whom in fact Keefe had earlier recommended to Lewis. Pope went on to complete the Lewises' splendid Tudor manor house in 1928. Despite this failure, Keefe did secure lesser but cumulatively important jobs at Skylands; overall 1923 was Keefe's best year to date, as he told the Skylands superintendent.[30]

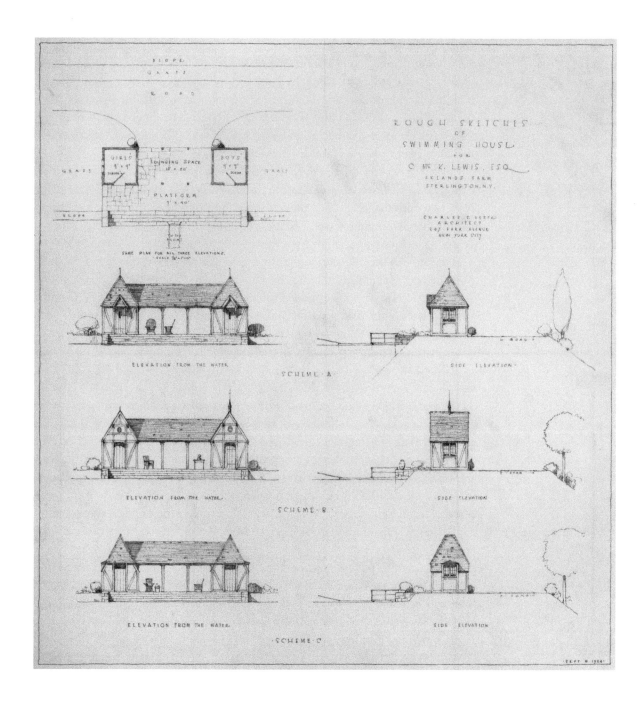

ROUGH SKETCHES
OF
SWIMMING HOUSE
FOR
C. McK. LEWIS, ESQ.
SKLANDS FARM
STERLINGTON, N.Y.

CHARLES S. KEEFE
ARCHITECT
247 PARK AVENUE
NEW YORK CITY

SCHEME·A·

SCHEME·B·

SCHEME·C·

Lewis called upon Keefe to undertake extensive work on Skylands's farm and outbuildings. The architect made sketches and measurements of existing buildings, presumably lacking the original plans and having alterations and additions in mind. Understandably the swimming house, laundry building, cow barn, pigeon-poultry house, and other outbuildings which were to be built or altered were never thought worthy of enlisting the talents of the great John Russell Pope.

Swimming house at Skylands Farm.

Keefe, however, put his best efforts into these buildings. His 1923 drawings for alterations to the Sheep Fold Cottage provided two alternatives, one Colonial, the other half-timbered. In his "Rough Sketch of Workroom for Greenhouse" (January 7, 1926), Keefe produced a handsome drawing of a low Tudor structure (with matter-of-fact rain barrel and watering can) about to be entered by a man and dog—perhaps the dog-breeder Lewis. In October 1924 the journal *Architecture* had seen fit to publish Keefe's laundry building, tool house, and garage.

Lewis's request for Keefe to design a "Swimming House," as he titled his 1924 drawing, allowed the architect to exercise his talent as a draftsman, creating lively pen-and-ink sketches of the boys' and girls' changing rooms joined by an open-fronted "lounging space." Keefe's 1925 sketch for the Swimming House's weather vane portrayed a nude youth standing atop a sleek fish. The facility was located far from the mansion, up in the hills on Lewis's reservoir, called "Gatun" after the lake created in building the Panama Canal. Still, the Tudor mansion determined the style of the small structure: English half-timbered, the framing was joined with visible wood pins and a carved wood beam extended over each door. As in any project, however, Keefe was obliged to spend time designing and obtaining mundane components, here the spring board and ladder.[31]

Keefe the artist—or at least the draftsman who appreciated the role of art and illustration— suggested that Lewis "try something new in signs for country estates by having a good sign made with a painted design. Then you could get as much sky as you want. I think it would look well and give a touch of color to the entrance. We could make a good looking post with iron brackets to hold the painted panel." Keefe's idea for emphasizing the sky involved "outlining the trees and buildings and placing the sign so it will be against the sky as one approaches it." What Lewis thought of the proposal is unknown, but Keefe successfully collaborated with Lewis in designing a sundial that was placed on the stuccoed chimney of the Elizabethan-style Lodge erected by Stetson and designed by Hopkins.[32]

The architect-client relationship was enhanced by their shared interest in dogs and books. Lewis raised Black Chow dogs and gave the Keefes their beloved Bingee. Keefe and Lewis were both book collectors, although Lewis's Skylands library, "enviably rich in horticultural works of every land and age," far surpassed Keefe's architectural library. They discussed books, and once, when Lewis was disappointed with a new architectural book, he passed it along to Keefe: "it seems to me to have been written more with the point of view of guiding the young architectural practitioner through some of the intricacies of his relationship with clients rather than with the idea of making the most of the humorous possibilities which are also inherent in this relationship." Keefe, in acknowledging the gift, suggested, "Why don't you try [writing] a book . . . from the client's point of view? You have had experiences with several architects so you are properly equipped. To other folks most architects appear peculiar to say the least, for their ways are not those of other folks as you well know."[33]

The two men also communicated on European travel plans, and Grace, who rarely accompanied Keefe on business trips, did so April 11, 1925, according to Keefe's note about travel expense by auto from Kingston to the Lewis cow-barn job. Still, the Lewis-Keefe relationship was not entirely harmonious; Lewis found his architect's billing peculiar and not infrequently questioned Keefe's charges, never fully understanding how Keefe arrived at his fees. He called upon Keefe to offer advice and plans on countless items, tiny and large, that Lewis was vaguely considering, and so the architect pointed out to his patron, "I do enough drawings at cost to entitle me to a profit on the occasional job that goes ahead."[34]

Like Lewis, **Charles L. Inslee** (1873–1934) was an Ivy-League-educated civil engineer with country property in New Jersey. But his Windy Brow Farm, located outside Newton, was of a much smaller scale and its architecture less grand than Lewis's. Still, as the family homestead where Charles had been born, the farm must have had sentimental appeal. After graduating from Cornell in 1895, he took a post-graduate course in engineering and eventually became president of Guarantee Construction Company in New York. In 1925, in his late 40s, he married a Smith College graduate and widow, Marguerite Tuthill Leonard, an event that may have inspired Charles to contemplate a new house.[35]

The large Colonial with white-shingled walls, planned by Keefe in 1927-28 and represented in J. Floyd Yewell's rendering, included a charming, informal service wing on the north side and a sleeping porch on the south. The expansive surface of the gable roof was interrupted by dormers and a massive stone chimney. What was first called a "book room" later became an "office" at one end of the long, low, west-facing porch. Its dark shadows and falling vines imply cool shelter on a warm day for the man standing nonchalantly on the porch in Yewell's drawing, suggestive of the pleasures of life in a Keefe country house. Among the drawings is one from September 30, 1927, for the Colonial three-car garage, with,

Charles Inslee house.

unusually, notes about the lengths of five cars—Cadillac touring, Packard, Nash, Studebaker, and Ford.

The design of Charles Inslee's house resembled that of his younger brother, **Ralph Hamilton Inslee** (1881–1951), also a Cornell graduate (1904). Inslee married Sarah Van Blarcom of Newark in May 1928, and that month Keefe drew a "proposed residence" for Inslee, a two-story symmetrical Colonial. That proposal was replaced by another in June that advanced to working drawings in July for a white-shingled Colonial home. Like his brother's, it was neither a grand Tudor manor house nor a modest Cape Cod. Its long, story-and-a-half west façade with asymmetrical projecting gable, a variety of dormers, and lower service wing made for an interesting picturesque composition in a professional rendering, unsigned but attributable to J. Floyd Yewell. (The rendering names Keefe as architect and "Edward Crook Associate.") The main entrance was distinguished with Federal-style leaded fanlight and sidelights, while a second-story screened sleeping porch opened at the rear or east.[36]

E. Hope Norton and Better Homes in America

E. Hope Norton (1873–1961) was among Keefe's most important clients, as he commissioned a number of buildings from Connecticut and New Hampshire to Ecuador between 1925 and the architect's death. Typically Norton took an active interest in all aspects of the design and construction of the buildings he ordered. A graduate of the University of Virginia, Norton was an industrialist known for developing the Guayaquil & Quito Railway linking the Pacific Coast of Ecuador with its capital over the Andes Mountains in Quito. He went to South America in 1911 as president of the railway and in 1914 founded the Ecuadorian Corporation, which developed and operated a brewery, cement plant, electric light company, street railways, and banana-rice-cocoa plantations.[37] Norton spent a great deal of time in Ecuador, but he maintained an office at 43 Cedar Street, Manhattan, and had an active social life in America. He was listed with his wife Lily in the 1930 New York Social Register as having his residence at Homewood Farm, Darien, Connecticut, and club memberships in New York at the Racquet & Tennis, Riding, and India House.

Soon after 1900 Norton was among the founders of Tokeneke, an exclusive residential park of some 560 acres in Darien, named for a local Native American sachem and located on the shore of Long Island Sound. Norton occupied Shorewood, his Tudor-style summer home from about 1907 to 1917. Later he resided at Homewood Farm, and he remained actively involved with development of the park in 1930 through Norton Inc., which required approval for new construction.[38] A 1928 list of property owners and residents had 120 names, including a dozen represented in Keefe's drawing files. Always private, Tokeneke appealed to Charles Lindbergh, who purchased a property in the 1960s, and gate posts have long warned away curiosity seekers.[39]

Norton cottage and garage.

Norton guest house.

The Keefe-Norton connection began in May 1925 when **Harry Parker** of Tokeneke furnished Keefe a "tip" that Norton, his neighbor, might be interested in Keefe's services. Parker himself in 1926 had Keefe prepare working drawings of very minor structures—a wood shed and poultry building. Keefe's 1927 pencil sketches for a large gable-roofed Georgian house and appealing pen-vand-ink sketches for a stone, hipped-roof house failed to attract Parker, whose residence was finally designed by the better-known Julius Gregory.[40]

Following up on Parker's tip, Keefe wrote Norton and offered to discuss the buildings Norton had in mind for his "country place." By July, Keefe had prepared a Colonial design for "Proposed Stable Buildings" for Norton at Homewood Farm, including a cottage, garage, kennels, and stable. In January 1926 Keefe submitted his final bill for the new cottage and garage, which had required the architect to make sixteen trips to the site.[41] The September 1926 issue of *The Architect* published a plan and photos of the cottage, garage, and kennels built on two sides of a court. Unpainted shingle walls were interrupted with Keefe's characteristically modest and tasteful white-painted Colonial doorways, porch, and trim. Other buildings featured in that issue were far grander: Grosvenor Atterbury's richly furnished living room in New York, or William Lawrence Bottomley's nine-story Stuart Court Apartments in Richmond, Virginia.

While the group designed for Norton was not the sort of commission architects like Atterbury or Bottomley would rush to publish, Keefe designed an even smaller building, a guest house on Norton's estate, that Keefe in 1937 called "the smallest house I've done." The guest house was also described as a "Two-Room Cottage," or "compact, comfortable little bungalow," although an early note by Keefe simply referred to it as "Norton Butlers."[42] This modest commission brought Keefe a measure of renown in the form of a bronze medal—Honorable Mention—in the One-Story Class from the 1931 Better Homes in America competition. The medal was designed by Gutzon Borglum, famous for his monumental presidential heads at Mount Rushmore.

Better Homes in America had been organized in 1922 with private funds, but also with the help of Secretary of Commerce Herbert Hoover, to "interest leading architects in small house design . . . and to acquaint the American public with good small house architecture." In thanking Ray Lyman Wilbur, President Hoover's Secretary of the Interior, for the bronze medal, Keefe entered into the spirit of the movement and specifically endorsed the idea that good (Colonial) buildings influence good citizenship: "Better Homes in America is to be commended for its labors in awakening public interest in good design for the modest home. Beauty in such homes has its effect in making good citizens and creating higher ideals for those that are fortunate enough to live in them."[43]

Designed and built in late 1925 and 1926, the cottage had received Norton's usual attention; the contractor's bid was cabled to him when he was abroad. Keefe gave it a dignified front, despite its rough, hand-made, weathered shingle walls, thanks to its white, highly refined four-column porch with lightly molded swags in the pediment and thin leading in the pediment's shield-shaped window. *Your Home*, a magazine for potential home builders, pointed out that the porch "faithfully copied" the "white-pillared porch" of "'Homewood,' a beautiful old Maryland home erected by a signer of the Declaration." Homewood had also served as inspiration for the Harkness garden house, and Norton had presumably named his Connecticut estate after the Maryland landmark. The original Homewood was again of a larger scale than Keefe's cottage and with none of the rustic note evident in the cottage's shingled walls.[44]

When asked by people at Better Homes in America how the cost of the building (about $3,000 without the land) could be reduced to appeal to prospective homebuilders during the Depression, Keefe pointed out that prices were currently low and that the rived cypress wall shingles would last over a hundred years, in contrast to cheaper shingles. A stock mantel and brick instead of stone chimney would lower the cost, but substituting a stock entrance porch was impossible "as this is the only decorative thing on the building and the effect depends upon it."[45]

In plan, the house consisted of a bedroom and living room separated by a bath and tiny kitchenette with sink but no stove or refrigerator. *Your Home* proposed that "this ducky little house . . . originally designed for . . . week-ending guests," could meet "the earliest and growing needs of the young home-making couple, thanks to the "electrically equipped kitchenette." However, this Better Home was clearly not intended for regular occupancy by even one person and was solely intended as an adjunct of a rich man's estate. The gold medal winner in the One-Story Class, a California house by Winchton L. Risley, and the other honorable mention, a California house by H. Roy Kelley, were also traditional designs, but fully equipped for family living.[46]

Norton seems to have enjoyed tinkering with Keefe-designed Colonial Revival improvements to his Homewood property. The existing main residence was a rambling story-and-a-half frame house, and between 1927 and 1930 Keefe planned alterations and additions including a "Pine Room" and "Book Room." Norton's enthusiasm for new and old pine paneling and flooring for Colonial effect, common at the time, was tied to his admiration for furniture of the type, and so Keefe purchased for Norton a book about New England's old pine furniture, probably Russell H. Kettell's *The Pine Furniture of Early New England*, 1929.[47]

Keefe made drawings in 1938 for altering the existing roof lines from something like a bungalow to something more Colonial with shingled walls and multiple gables.[48] For the garden, between 1929 and 1931 Keefe designed a Summer House and Garden House, as well as a heated Tool House with adjoining hot beds. The Garden House was to be an octagon, fourteen feet in diameter with a bell-shaped roof, reminiscent of one designed by Peter Harrison about 1766 for Abraham Redwood's Rhode Island estate but long preserved at the Redwood Library in Newport.

Norton's daughter **Hope Norton** (1903–99) married **George Edward Stevens**, a Yale alumnus, and Keefe designed and supervised construction of

Hope and George Stevens house.

their new Colonial house on Locust Hill Road in Darien. It was completed to the "entire satisfaction" of E. Hope Norton, the client, in October 1929. Norton wrote Keefe that the result of his efforts was "most gratifying to both my daughter's family and my own, and I have only heard favorable comment from outside parties as to the beauty of its design and perfection of arrangement." Keefe in turn praised client Norton: "It gives me a great deal of pleasure to know that you and your folks are pleased with it all. I have had a lot of fun doing it and appreciate your help and cooperation in getting the results we did. You must remember a client has his share in building a house and if it turns out happily the client's contribution . . . is just as definite as that of the architect."[49]

Keefe expected to obtain photos of the Stevens house in June 1930 with plantings in place, and the *Architectural Record* thought the house worthy of a seven-page photo spread. Its white-painted stone façade was not quite symmetrical, and the side and rear elevations of clapboard painted white had the appearance of additions made over time. Father Norton had had Keefe plan a "book room" for his house, and the Stevens house was given one at the outset with a fireplace that abutted the living room fireplace. The Stevens's status was clear in the plan, for while the kitchen was small (9 feet by 13 feet), other spaces were set aside for pantry, stores, maids hall, bath, and beds for three maids (in two maids rooms). Upstairs the family had four bedrooms, each with twin beds, as well as a sleeping porch. Interior photos show standard Colonial Revival furniture in the light-toned dining room, and Mr. Stevens's slip-covered armchair ready for a relaxing smoke by the dark-wood-paneled fireplace wall. However, the marriage was not long lasting, and in 1938, after a Reno divorce, Hope married Paul Thayer Iaccaci, who had attended Harvard before becoming an ace in World War I. Perhaps spurred by Norton, in 1932 an Argentine architectural review, *Nuestra Arquitectura*, requested and received from Keefe photos of the Stevens house for publication, but the review seems not to have sent the issue including the photos as Keefe requested.[50]

Norton also commissioned Keefe to plan buildings in Ecuador, surely intriguing for an architect whose practice was closely centered on New York and the Northeast. Keefe had become a friend of Norton's assistant, John Oldrin, who, on New Year's Day 1928, sent Keefe a photo of a church doorway in Quito, an example of the city's historic church architecture that Oldrin considered "perfectly astounding . . . superb." Oldrin wished Keefe could see the Quito landmarks himself, but he never did. In 1934 Keefe designed for Norton a milking cow shed and calf barn with stucco walls in Guayaquil, and in 1934-35 Norton's combined house and office in San Miguel. [51]

The house-and-office's front elevation—composed of a classical door frame around a windowless wood door ornamented with twenty-five metal bosses, a shallow balcony with iron railing above the doorway, an iron grille over the kitchen window, and a low-pitched tile roof—is not at all American Colonial, but intended to fit in with Spanish tradition in South America. Exterior walls were stucco over concrete blocks. One side of the first or ground floor was given over to the kitchen and servants' rooms, while the other was devoted to two offices

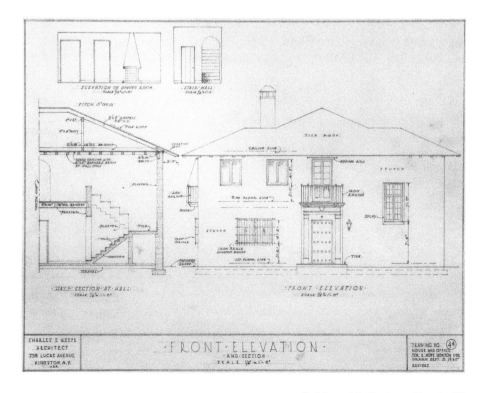

Norton house and office.

TWIN OAKS
HOUSE OF HERBERT WHEELER,
TOKENEKE, DARIEN, CONN.

CHARLES S. KEEFE, ARCHITECT

Photographs by Louis H. Dreyer

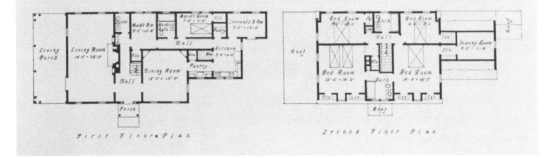

(one with a cashier's window opening onto a back porch), a store room, and stairs. Norton's living quarters occupied the second floor; the dining room, with fireplace, was at the front, while a long living room opened out to a gallery in the rear, with three bedrooms placed in the middle of the second floor.

Norton maintained a vacation home in Hebron, New Hampshire. In the thirties Keefe was assigned the task of "restoring an old New England Colonial house for Norton," noted the *Daily Freeman*, which also reported that its hometown architect "has been enjoying a pleasure as well as business trip with E. Hope Norton to Hebron, on New Found Lake, N.H." Norton's house stands near the village common in Hebron, which remains a pristine example of the quaint New England hamlet. The house, a two-story frame house from c. 1820, had its long front porch removed, and in May 1935 Keefe designed a new, reduced, entrance porch, as well as a side porch. A year later he drew a squirrel profile pattern as a wooden ornament for the front porch gable, no doubt a gesture of friendship that remained in place in 2016. When the *Freeman* note appeared in 1938, Keefe was planning "Changes in Service Wing," a long, narrow wing connecting the main house to its barn. [52]

Other Tokeneke Commissions

Herbert Wheeler (c.1880–1942) had excellent social credentials—educated at St. Paul's School in Concord, New Hampshire, and Princeton University (class of 1900) where his role as halfback in defeating Yale was featured in the headline for his 1942 obituary in *The New York Times*. After a career as an insurance broker, Wheeler and his wife, **Katharine Smith Wheeler**, had a real estate business in Darien from 1927 until his death. (Sketches by Keefe in the Wheeler folder for Colonial storefronts—"Smith Candles and Candies/Groceries/Beauty Shop/W. T. Grant"—may have been related to their real estate interests.) In 1927–28 Keefe designed the Wheeler home, Twin Oaks, in Tokeneke. It was larger than his standard story-and-a-half Colonials, with a high first story and room for four bedrooms and two baths on the second, thanks to generous dormers. Much of the first floor was given over to a maid's room, maid's bath, maid's bedroom, and servant's dining room, although the kitchen was only 8½ by 11½ feet. Photos published in *Architecture* show the centerpiece of the living room was the fireplace flanked by bookshelves filled with uniformly bound volumes and with an upholstered wing chair and smoking stand drawn up by the hearth. Alongside the fireplace, a small iron door appeared to

Herbert and Katharine Wheeler house.

Wheeler house, living room.

Farrell gardener's cottage.

open into an oven, but Keefe's drawing shows it lined with wooden boards, so perhaps it functioned as a small Prohibition liquor cabinet.[53]

John J. Farrell (1890–1966), son of U.S. Steel chairman James A. Farrell, was himself educated at Yale and head of a steamship company offering freight and passenger service to Africa. His wife, the former **Maud Hadden**, was the sister of Briton Hadden, co-founder of *Time*. Farrell commissioned Keefe to design a number of improvements in the Colonial mode to his property at Tokeneke. Between 1928 and 1930 Keefe planned alterations and additions to Farrell's Colonial Revival residence, notably a Print Room, with wood paneling suited for framed prints, and a fireplace with marble hearth and facing. Other improvements included a substantial kennel building and a four-car garage with a laundry and quarters for two men. [54]

As so often in Keefe's career, it was not the main house, but an outbuilding, in this case a small gardener's cottage, that was widely published. Fortunately, the cottage survives. Designed and erected in 1928, it was a very basic version of a Cape Cod cottage—shingled walls with batten shutters, no front porch but a simple stoop defined by side seats, and cramped spaces within. Keefe gave the doorway some distinction—the carefully proportioned six panels of the door, a Colonial knocker, five-pane transom, and finely detailed cornice. *Your Home* (October 1930) called the cottage "A True Connecticut Yankee" and interpreted its simplicity as a virtue: "refusing to accept ornamentation that goes beyond a fundamental simplicity of line" being "the strength that marks the architectural design of New England." The magazine also described it as a "clever cottage home," and the "clever" or charming aspect was certainly heightened in the published photos by the endearing presence of a child's doll on the front stoop. Keefe included a silhouetted witch-on-a-broomstick in his drawing of the north porch's gable, but this clever and slightly eccentric detail did not appear in published photos of the house.

Mrs. Albert Young house.

Like other Colonial Revivalists, Keefe's Colonial houses clad in wood siding or shingles were usually painted white with green trim. Such was the case with the shingled Farrell cottage and his remodeled Nelson house. However, his Cape Cod designed for *The American Home* magazine (Sept. 1930) might have white or cream walls, green or blue shutters, with a brown-stained roof; his Norton guest house had walls of weathered shingles with "a bit of color . . . added in blue panel blinds" (shutters). While Cape Cods were often painted white, Keefe advised that the shingled walls of Cape Cods be "left to the weather," especially when "situated by the sea, the shingles would turn a lovely silver gray because of the salt mists and the flying sand." [55]

The Farrell cottage garnered additional publicity for Keefe over the next several years. It brought him his second honorable mention and Borglum-designed bronze medal in the 1932 Better Homes in America Competition's one-and-a-half story class when Herbert Hoover was honorary chairman of the organization. (The gold medal went to Royal Barry Wills.) Noted architect and Keefe acquaintance Dwight James Baum chaired the jury and was pleased to observe that only one "radical modern" design had been submitted. Instead "the traditions of our country's domestic architecture are being continued and improved yearly by the contributions of architects in all parts of the country." [56]

Keefe reported to E. Hope Norton in December 1927 (when Norton was in Quito) about very extensive alterations and additions beginning at the mansion **Mrs. Albert (Minnie) Young** (1855–1931) had acquired in September 1927 on Tokeneke's Osceola Drive. An heiress of an American Tobacco Company fortune and widow of a stockbroker, she also had a Park Avenue residence in Manhattan. The radical alterations, completed in 1928, resulted in a house Spanish or Italian in style; stucco surfaced the walls, the roof was laid with "dull green Spanish tiles," and the façade was fitted with ironwork on the balcony over the

entrance, an iron canopy over the entrance door, and iron grilles at the two small windows flanking the entrance. [57] The Young files include a page torn from a magazine picturing the stucco-walled, Spanish-style residence of Col. David May by Curlett & Berlman in Beverly Hills, California, apparently admired by the client.

Ownership of the property, known as Round Meadows, was transferred from Mrs. Young to her daughter **Edna Young Brenchley** (1881–1952) in December 1928, and Edna's close involvement with Keefe's work there is indicated by his correspondence with her in 1927 and plans of that year including a bedroom identified as hers. Edna, while married to Alfred Dieterich, eloped in 1907 with Harry Brenchley, Alfred G. Vanderbilt's coachman and horse trainer; they were married in 1908 and divorced in 1926. In 1931 **John Oldrin** (1901– 85) was Edna Brenchley's private secretary (a role he seems to have played for Norton), and in 1932 they married, although Edna was twenty years his senior. It seems plausible that the choice of the Spanish (or Italian) style was influenced by Norton's and Oldrin's enthusiasm for South America.

While working on the mansion in 1927, Keefe also planned a Colonial "garage group" for Mrs. Young, a four-bay garage connecting a cottage and laundry building. The cottage garnered a good deal of publicity. *Your Home*, catering to a readership of modest means, pictured only the cottage and concluded that "almost unlimited are the laudatory adjectives that can be applied to this house." The *American Architect* later devoted four pages to photos, plans, and elevations of the group and indicated that the exterior shingle walls and woodwork were painted gray, the doors and shutters bottle green, and the chimneys whitewashed.[58]

A second cottage (1928–29), distinguished by a gabled entrance bay surfaced in stone and with a sundial in the gable, was published in *House & Garden* as "A Stone and Shingle Cottage in Connecticut for Mrs. E. Y. Brenchley." The

*Edna Young Brenchley
cottage.*

magazine found the house "typical of the rather rambling, comfortable looking little dwellings found throughout the more rural districts of New England" and, appealing to readers who might afford the cost of a three-bedroom home, admired "the easy manner in which the attached garage has been carried into the general architectural scheme." [59]

Mrs. Young was the client for both cottages, but Keefe consulted with both women. Mother and daughter's approval of a door knocker design was noted on its blueprint. The unusual stone entrance bay and sundial may have been Mrs. Brenchley's idea to add a bit of old England, where she had lived for a time with Harry Brenchley, as she told Keefe, " I do like the Tudor houses the best, the windows & gables are so lovely." [60]

Keefe's familiarity with his clients is captured in the light tone of his July 1, 1931, letter to Mrs. Brenchley a few months before her mother's death; he had heard that Mrs. Young was "quite ill. Please tell her I hope she will soon be out in her little auto, that is, if her friends haven't used up all the 'juice'"—the auto was battery-powered. As with other major clients, Keefe took up small as well as large assignments for Mrs. Brenchley. In 1930 he sent her "a sketch for the proposed tool shed," a stone building with incinerator at one end. "The men can eat their lunches in the little room where I have arranged for a stove to keep it warm in cold weather. I have also shown a toilet as the men have no place to go when the garage group is closed." When she complained that her refrigerators were not producing enough ice cubes, Keefe reminded her that "You use more than the usual family which is one of the penalties of being hospitable." He suggested she acquire a small unit devoted exclusively to ice-making.[61]

John Oldrin was involved with Keefe's jobs for Norton, Young, and Brenchley, and Keefe's letters to the younger man reveal some of the banter that must also have marked their conversations when, for example, Oldrin picked up Keefe at the Stamford station and drove him to Norton's place. During Prohibition, Keefe, no teetotaler, teased Oldrin about water vs. "demon RUM," and in closing another letter advised, "In the meantime be good, but if you cannot, then be careful."[62]

While Edna Brenchley became Edna Oldrin in 1932, she retained ownership of the Tokeneke property until her death, when it transferred to John by her will. To the world, however, the property was the couple's. In 1935 the *Freeman* reported a visit by "Architect Charles S. Keefe and Mrs. Keefe . . . [who] motored from Kingston . . . [and] were entertained in the beautiful gardens of 'Round Meadows,' the country place of Mr. and Mrs. John Oldrin, clients of Mr. Keefe, who designed the spacious Italian residence, cottage, green houses and other buildings." And it must have been Edna's mansion that Keefe in 1937 told the *Freeman* was "the largest single family dwelling I've built from the ground upwards." It was "for John Oldrin in Darien" and was "of Italian style and has 14 bedrooms . . . and nine baths." Keefe seems to have glossed over the fact that the house was the result of alterations and additions, and he misidentified the number of bedrooms; his plans show ten in the main house.[63]

Wyntje S. Pentecost was the garden designer for Mrs. Young, and as such consulted with Keefe about the site. Keefe designed a Cape Cod cottage for Pentecost to be built at Tokeneke. Working drawings for the cottage are dated Feb. 1928. In October he thanked her for "the photograph of the charming little garden you made at Mrs. Young's place," and asked her to return the "plans, etc. for your cottage," probably indicating it was not carried out.[64]

Keefe's designs for Tokeneke included proposals for the beach-front **Tokeneke Club** between 1930 and 1938. They range from a "Seat in Mr. Norton's Cabana" (1931), to a "Children's Pavilion" (1930) with fish silhouette in the gable, and finally to the long, Colonial façade of a new clubhouse (1932). This probably was not built, as the Keefe archive does not have working drawings, and in 1938 he prepared a sketch for the club entrance, with one rendering sent to John Oldrin and a copy to William Young, the contractor closely allied with Keefe. Young then wrote Keefe: "I received the sketch for Club, & I gave J. Oldrin app. price. I would advise you not to spend too much time on them as they are a cheap bunch, & they had another sketch of a porch that some Landscape Gardener drew up. He is figuring on doing some planting there." The club was incorporated in 1907, and its clubhouse, subject to fire and storm, has been rebuilt several times, most recently in 2008.[65]

Houses in New Canaan, Connecticut, and North Salem, New York

Client John Farrell was a yachtsman as well as chairman of the annual horse show of the Ox Ridge Hunt Club in Darien. Serving on his committee was **Charles C. Bellows** whose wife, **Doris Rude Bellows**, entered her horse in the 1930 show. Charles Bellows was with the Wall Street firm of Brown Brothers; his

Charles and Doris Bellows house and the old Cape Cod house that was sacrificed. (House Beautiful)

father and grandfather had for a century owned a wine and liquor importing firm; his grandmother was of the distinguished Delano family.[66]

In 1929 the Bellows had Keefe design their home on Ferris Hill Road in New Canaan, Connecticut, not far from Tokeneke and Darien. The house was built using parts from an old Cape Cod house the couple had purchased, measured, and demolished, along with old materials from other sources. In Keefe's papers is a June 21, 1932, list of old materials collected by Mrs. Bellows for her house, including paneling, stairs, doors, mantels, beams, rugs, and furniture. The W. P. A. Federal Writers Project created a photographic and written record of the Bellows house that describes the interior woodwork and lists some of the sources of old material. One paneled wall and fireplace of the Bellows's downstairs bedroom was originally in a c. 1690 Providence meetinghouse and then painted lemon yellow for the bedroom.[67] The central section of the new house resembled the original Cape Cod and included parts from it—doors, windows, and paneling—as well as an old staircase found by Mrs. Bellows and new elements drafted by Keefe. He also added, in harmony with the center section, one wing with a first-floor living room and second-floor master bedroom, as well as another wing with kitchen and rooms for two maids. This utility wing was connected by a long arbor to a combined garage, stable, and kennels.

Bellows house, bow window and hollyhocks. (American Architect)

The architect worked closely with Doris Bellows in designing the house, while her husband was responsible for the bills. Acknowledging a payment when the project was nearing completion, Keefe wrote him: "I hope you are getting as much of a kick out of the house as Mrs. Bellows does. She certainly can find interesting things to build into it." Keefe seemed to enjoy collaborating with Mrs. Bellows to make the house as a whole seem old. He advised "hand rived cypress shingles on walls and cedar shingles of roofs, all left to the weather." (When completed, the exterior wall shingles were stained dark brown.) The outside entrance to the cellar was to be "the same as some I have seen on the Cape," while "stone work to look like old foundations, using stones with fairly flat faces and pointed flush with the face of the stone with grey mortar." Unless she wished otherwise, he proposed, probably for the front door, "fourth quality double thick glass as this is the nearest to the old glass." He added wryly that "when you look at your friends thru this glass they make them look rather queer, but you will understand it's the glass and not your friends that are off in form."[68]

Still, occasionally the architect felt obliged to rein in Mrs. Bellows; she intended to use a cornice whose "crude finish" Keefe objected to, especially given the quality of the interior details. Never a purist, Keefe reasoned that, "Just because some old fellow did a poor job there is no reason for our perpetuating it." Instead, Keefe wanted to use "a typical Cape Cod cornice" design he had used elsewhere, here adding dentils on the front of the old or central part of the house.[69] Keefe won this point, as the Federal Writers Project's description of the house notes that "a dentil course" was added at the cornice. Whether the Colonial Revival George Washington profile Keefe designed as a cutout for the shutters was carried out remains uncertain.

The result of the architect-client collaboration was one of Keefe's most appealing and well-published houses, one in which he took special pride. Sadly, the Bellows house has been demolished, but through publication it can be said to live on. *House and Garden*, directed toward women, credited Mrs. Bellows with ownership of the house, gathering vintage materials, and working with the architect to achieve "a group which reproduces the intimate vernacular of Cape Cod." Like the originals, the house "appears to have grown . . . with a bit added here and there as a family grew, or finances permitted." So the composition seemed "unstudied," but inspection of the plans demonstrated that in fact "all divisions of the house are well segregated and are positioned for maximum convenience." Thus the Bellows's bedroom was well away from the servants' wing

and even farther from kennels and stable. The photos in *House and Garden* charmed Elizabeth Morrison of the *Catskill Daily Mail* who wrote Keefe: "Mrs. Bellows home in February *House and Garden* made me long to enter, remain and have a cup O' tea, and poke around among the Hollyhocks in the lovely garden. Houses are like people."[70]

The Bellows house was featured in the *American Architect* with six pages of photos by George H. Van Anda along with Keefe's drawings. By 1933 Van Anda could record, in the photo introducing the house, hollyhocks flourishing by the bow window and shingled walls of the back of the house. While charming, bow windows were not features of early Colonial houses. The dining room, the main room in the central section of the house, was featured in two photos showing off simple paneling around the fireplace and unpainted old oak beams alternating with rough plaster surfaces in the ceiling. *House Beautiful* (August 1933) again pictured the dining room. Its furniture was appropriately not Chippendale but "Early American," plain and unpretentious—trestle table and benches, bow-back Windsor chairs, hutch and settle. Not pictured but opening into the dining room was a bar, included in the plans before the repeal of Prohibition in 1933, the year Charles Bellows entered the wine and liquor business identified with his family since 1847.[71]

Hooked rugs, chintz curtains, and HL hinges were found throughout the Bellows house. The dining room floor was dark oak, while other floors were

Bellows house, dining room. (American Architect)

Bellows house, staircase. (American Architect)

painted dark green with white spatter finish, a finish associated with Cape Cod. The August 1934 issue of *Painters Magazine* featured the Bellows hollyhocks and bow window on its cover, and page 14 focused on paint colors used in the living room, boy's room, stairs, and hall.[72]

In contrast to the Bellows house, essentially a new house incorporating many old parts, Keefe's 1927 plans for **David Patterson** consisted of alterations and additions to a standing eighteenth-century house at One Norton Lane in North Salem, Westchester County. Keefe's improvements to Roof Trees, as the house came to be known, are recorded in a fine rendering by J. Floyd Yewell and received a good deal of admiring publicity. Patterson and his wife maintained a "country place in Virginia, noted for its string of thoroughbred hunters," and in acquiring the North Salem house they intended to remodel it as a hunting lodge. Although the old house was said to date from the 1730s, it was not of elegant Georgian form but, as Harold Donaldson Eberlein put it, "dejected-looking," something "that might have started as more or less Colonial and afterwards drifted into quasi-early Victorian." Early on, Keefe drew an attractive "rough sketch," eliminating all signs of dejected Victorian and proposing an expanded Cape Cod, but finally he determined to make more modest changes to the existing house. He removed what Eberlein called "the ugly Victorian verandah" and designed a new porch so that its side profile presented "bell-flared eaves," thereby creating "a pleasant little house of distinctly Dutch Colonial affinities." Eberlein also admired Keefe's internal revisions: "by a small addition it became possible to readjust the whole downstairs arrangement and create a generous living-room and dining-room in one, but with the character of each distinctly preserved despite the fusion."[73]

The editors of *The American Home* found the remodeled house "so appealing . . . in its restful simplicity" that they featured Glenn W. Thomas's watercolor of the Patterson house on their September 1929 cover. Harriet Sisson Gillespie went on to describe Keefe as "an architect whose happy restorations of the Colonial constitute a real contribution to American architecture. . . Mr. Keefe's peculiar success in this field lies in a certain quality of reserve or restraint." Keefe's inspection of the house found it structurally sound, and the only significant change to the front was the Dutch Colonial porch. The rear was the focus of additions

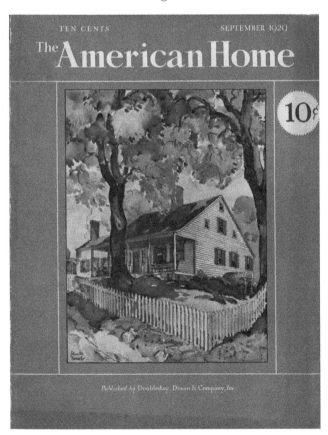

David Patterson house.

Constantine and Gertrude Hutchins house.

Hutchins house, rear, overlooking the Charles River.

for bedrooms and kitchen. New siding and shutters were required, and the chimneys had to be rebuilt above the roofline. A golden oak doorway gave way to a six-panel door of Colonial inspiration. Gillespie's conclusion: "White painted with blue-green shutters, its quaint beauty is further enhanced by the homely picket fence, which gives the final touch of old-time charm for which Charles S. Keefe's restorations are famous."[74]

Houses in Massachusetts and Vermont

Thanks to landscape architect Hallam Movius, Keefe received an important commission to design a superior Cape Cod for **Constantine Hutchins** (1884–1966) at a site determined by Movius—a knoll overlooking the Charles River in the Boston suburb of Needham. Hutchins, Harvard Class of 1905, was at various times a Boston banker and member of the New York Stock Exchange. He, his wife **Gertrude Amory Hutchins** (1892–1975), and their children summered near

Buzzard's Bay and Cape Cod. Consequently they "had a great liking for the low, rambling Cape Cod type of house." The Hutchins house, designed in late 1927 and early 1928, was beautifully illustrated in photos by Louis H. Dreyer in seven pages of the April 1929 *Architectural Record*, perhaps the finest publication of Keefe's work in a professional journal, with Movius credited as landscape architect.[75]

To a basic story-and-a-half, central-chimney, shingle-walled Cape Cod Keefe added a screened porch and stone terrace overlooking the Charles, as well as a service wing for kitchen, two maid's bedrooms, and a maid's sitting room—creating a long, low house angling along the hillside. Keefe took pains with details; the refined, white-painted pilasters at the front door were marked with subtle entasis (the Dec. 2, 1927, drawing, "Detail of Entrance Door," includes the notation, "Entasis on Pilaster"), while the step below the door was an irregular stone

Hutchins house, living room.

slab, and the exterior walls were rough, unpainted shingles with purposefully irregular lower edges. The living room's fireplace was topped with a delicate cornice serving as mantle shelf, while the dining room fireplace was utterly plain—almost modern. Cupboard doors above a bedroom fireplace had rat-tail hinges, possibly by Teller. In 1929 Keefe planned an addition to the garage including a man's room, two box stalls, and feed room, as well as designing a lesser Cape Cod to serve as a guest cottage. The ensemble, with the main house, formed a semicircle around a circular driveway and reminded one observer of "a tiny village on the Cape."[76]

The Hutchins's living and dining rooms were fitted with old pine paneling, some from a New Hampshire house, although the Colonial furnishings, chosen by Gertrude Hutchins, appear to have been mostly new, with "hooked rugs and bright-colored chintz [to] enliven the room." Photos in the *Architectural Record* of the paneling must have encouraged William Sumner Appleton, head of the Society for the Preservation of New England Antiquities, to write Keefe congratulating him on the "charming" Hutchins house, which "shows such an appreciation of the attractive quality of old New England work that I confidently expected to find it had been done by one of our members." However, Appleton found that Keefe was not a member and so invited him to join, which he did by sending the $6 fee for active membership.[77]

Charles Harris Whitaker (1872–1938), longtime editor of the *Journal of the American Institute of Architects*, was described by Lewis Mumford as "one of the few men of his generation in the East who understood the importance of Louis Sullivan, though his own taste was toward the traditional and rural values of his boyhood." In April 1930 Whitaker wrote Keefe requesting photos of the Hutchins house for inclusion in a proposed book, "The Modern House," by Dr. Walter Curt Behrendt (1884–1945), a German friend of Whitaker. Keefe must have been impressed that, according to Whitaker, Behrendt was "a writer on architecture well known in Europe" and that "the number of American houses to be included is fixed at a relatively small number."[78] Behrendt, in fact, was a key figure in promoting modern European architecture that rejected the revival styles. Still, he did find merit in simple vernacular building, and it was this that no doubt led Whitaker to request Hutchins house photos from Keefe.

Hutchins house, dining room.

Keefe, who may have been aware of Behrendt's modernist leanings, wisely described the Hutchins house for Whitaker and Behrendt as following "the lines of the early American houses on Cape Cod. It is typically American and is a good example of the simple type of our modern houses where good, simple, wholesome living is indulged in."[79] Having a guest house and quarters for two or three servants on what *House Beautiful* identified as an estate and only part-time residence of the Hutchins family did not, in Keefe's mind, remove the Hutchins family from "good, simple, wholesome living." In contrast to the mansions of European aristocrats and American robber barons, the Hutchins's place would have stood for the simple and wholesome.

We can only imagine Keefe's disappointment when, a year after sending six photos and plans for the first and second stories of the Hutchins house, Behrendt's book had not appeared. Keefe wrote Whitaker inquiring about the publication and, since Whitaker's address was Butterworth Farm, Foster, Ohio, Keefe observed that "Life on a farm is much better than that of an architect these days for you know you are going to eat and that is more than many of our fellows are sure of." Whitaker replied, not from an Ohio farm, but from Nauplia, Greece, that he was traveling to Berlin where he would ask Behrendt about the book. And there the book trail ended for Keefe. In 1934 Behrendt, who was Jewish, left Germany for the United States and, with the support of Whitaker and Mumford, secured a teaching post at Dartmouth College. Behrendt's book, *Modern Building*, published in 1937 and covering European and American developments, included nothing related to Keefe or the Colonial Revival other than a condemnation of the "eclecticist" architect who, "for the house of the bourgeois . . . uses the Georgian or Colonial pattern." On the other hand, Behrendt judged

William and Agnes Rice house.

that in America the "radiant triple star [was] represented by Henry Hobson Richardson, Louis Sullivan, and Frank Lloyd Wright," three architects whose work Keefe ignored or disliked.[80]

William Thompson Rice (1891–19??) headed A. H. Rice Co., makers of silk sewing thread in Pittsfield, Massachusetts. His father and grandfather had established the firm and, like them, William Rice was a graduate of Williams College and active in Pittsfield civic affairs. Like several of Keefe's Connecticut clients, William Rice was an upper-class sportsman and Keefe, on learning that Rice had broken his leg, could only "hope it was polo and not the stairs [Keefe designed] that caused it. If its the last, Mr. Pike [stair builder] and I will not call again." Rice was listed in the New York Social Register and was treasurer of the Pittsfield Riding & Polo Club in 1930. **Frederick Goodrich Crane, Jr.**, of Dalton, was vice-president of that club. Keefe, with landscape architect Hallam Movius, was responsible for a garage and stable group for Crane that was designed and built in 1925, and in 1930 Keefe designed a second stable and a riding rink for Crane.[81]

Keefe began the long process of planning a residence for Rice and his wife, **Agnes Van Santvoord Rice**, in 1925, at first collaborating with Movius. Keefe sent the Rices sketch plans and a perspective drawing of the proposed house via Movius to help convince the clients to build. Movius then reported to Keefe that the Rices "are now showing it to their friends and consequently it may do a little missionary work for us." Mrs. Rice, like other clients, clipped magazines for pictures of house details as suggestions for their architect (e.g., an "Early American" living room from *Country Life*, Apr. 1927). Her husband fussed at length over details and costs, requiring Keefe to make major revisions to his plans, so that in

Rice garden and summer house.

December 1927 and January 1928 Keefe despaired of designing a house of the size and character the Rices wanted within their $20,000 (or sometimes $25,000) budget. Keefe wrote Rice: "Very likely you can get a house as large as you desire by erecting a full two story building, rectangular in form and without any particular architectural pretensions. This type of building does give the most for one's money in actual cubic feet. . . . but it is that small additional cost that makes for a distinctive house."[82]

Rice finally endorsed Keefe's more complex and more expensive plans. In the spring of 1928, contracts were signed and construction mostly completed that year by contractor D. Herbert Pike, whose workmanship and patience Keefe praised. Pike's contract called for $30,098 for the house, while other contracts brought the total to $40,740.10 for the house and garage.[83]

As Keefe always hoped, the Rice house was no rectangular box but a long, informally composed, one-and-a-half and two-story, shingle-walled, white-painted Colonial. Keefe was successful in urging Rice to build the house and attached garage at the same time, making the ensemble "look longer and lower." The place was enhanced by a flower garden with formal, geometric beds designed, not by Movius, but by another Boston landscape architect, Mary C. Cunningham.[84] The flower garden extended from the living room to an elegant, open-sided summer or garden house designed by Keefe in 1929. Beautifully printed plates of the Rice house and garden appeared in the November 1930 issue of *The Architect* (pls. 63–71).

The Rice house is unusual among Keefe's buildings in having an important Arts and Crafts embellishment—tiles in the playroom fireplace by Henry Chapman Mercer picturing historic American subjects including Puritans, eighteenth-century Harvard, Boston harbor with a box of tea, and Bulfinch's Massachusetts State House. The clients, not the architect, chose the tiles, which would help teach New England history to their children. Special attention was paid to designing portions of the house for the Rice offspring; a photo of the "Children's Entrance," with extremely slender columns and thin, curving, shell-like roof was featured in *The Architect*.[85]

Also noteworthy is the house's white pine trim based on a Hampton, New Hampshire, bedroom in the American Wing of the Metropolitan Museum. The Rices visited the American Wing and were attracted by the strap hinges they saw there. Keefe, however, wanted to limit strap hinges to the outside of a Dutch door, arguing that the Rice house generally followed a later style (the front entrance was Federal style when "better hardware" was available).[86]

Despite the long gestation, Rice was pleased with the house and its architect: "I feel that we made a very happy choice of an architect and I am taking pains to tell people about it." In subsequent years Keefe was called upon by the Rices to design small and large enhancements. Early on they had trouble "getting a radio and cabinet that will go with the furniture in our living room," but then they "hit on the idea of making a pine case for it that would be in keeping with the rest of the furniture . . . a 'reproduction of an old New England radio cabinet.'" Rice asked Keefe to make a rough sketch for a local cabinet maker. Keefe complied and sent two prints for a pine radio cabinet: "I have tried to keep as far away from the usual type of radio cabinet as possible and used forms generally made by the early folks for cabinets or little shelves." Small HL hinges of wrought iron were the cabinet's most distinctive Colonial feature. The clients were pleased

Rice common room.

with their radio cabinet, giving the architect an opening to make light of their attraction to Puritans: "Glad to know you like the radio cabinet. I hope it goes alright and doesn't stop work on Sunday the way the Puritan fathers did."[87]

A basement space was to be transformed to look like what Rice called a "common room in an old inn." Rice named as inspiration both the Hotel Northampton, with its Colonial Revival Wiggins Old Tavern in Northampton, Massachusetts, and the Wayside Inn, made famous by Longfellow's poem and attracting travelers with its Colonial Bar Room, in Sudbury, Massachusetts. Keefe's 1932 drawings of the wood-paneled Common Room represents a bar with wooden grill projecting into the room, resembling the bar at the Wayside Inn. The sketch picturing an ingle nook, seats, and horizontal paneling also drew upon an illustration of a "basement space" treated as an "early American ingle, lounge and tap-room inspired by the 'Hall of Capen House' in the American Wing of the Metropolitan Museum." The illustration, part of an ad for Bryant Gas Heating, was torn from an unidentified magazine, possibly *House & Garden*, and given to Keefe by Mrs. Rice.[88]

In a letter to Rice, Keefe provided a thorough description of the Common Room (see Appendix IX) and acknowledged the influence of the ad illustration while noting that horizontal boarding "was done in some early houses. All the folks that use boards today put them on vertically so we will be different but still correct." A tankard and narrow-necked bottle appear in the sketch. Keefe explained that "in making such drawings bottles seem to fit in nicely but please understand that is as far as the suggestion goes." (Keefe liked to include such bottles in his drawings intended for clients, no doubt to suggest the pleasures of life in his houses. In a 1934 sketch for G. L. Ohrstrom, he drew a chair and table with bottle and glass—the bottle having the only touch of color in the drawing.) He tried to emphasize that "the room should be a pleasant place for everybody young and old. Turn the boys loose in there, all they can do is to antique the place." Earlier Keefe had suggested that the small storage space in the radio cabinet could house "radio logs" or function "to hide your dice and cards when the dominie [pastor] comes. That is if you own such 'tools of the devil' as I believe they are called."[89] Clearly the intention was to provide the Rices and their guests a tasteful, historically rooted setting to enjoy games and Prohibition-era alcohol sheltered from public scrutiny.

Keefe, in writing the contractor D. Herbert Pike early on about the room, predicted, unusually, "We should have some fun with this." However, like other projects for Rice, what he called "the room in the cellar" was put on hold in May 1932 pending better economic times.[90]

The Rices did, as Keefe hoped, recommend him to their friends, and Mrs. Rice's recommendation to **Ruth Moore Taylor** of Troy, New York, bore fruit in 1939. Miss Taylor, a 1916 Vassar graduate who then studied "household economics" at Russell Sage College, was the daughter of Robert M. Taylor, a prominent Troy businessman. She was a leader of the YWCA in Troy and of Vassar

Ruth Taylor house.

Alumnae. After her father's death in 1938, Ruth Taylor began planning with Keefe a "simple, comfortable, all-the-year-round house" on fourteen acres in picturesque Dorset, Vermont, some sixty miles from Troy. A Dorset history included Miss Taylor among the "'summer people' . . . who chose to live in Dorset for its scenic values and its culturally vigorous ambience." However, when the Dorset house was being completed in May 1941, Miss Taylor reported to Keefe that she had sold the Troy home she had occupied with her father—Dorset was to be her full-time home.[91]

Working drawings for her low, horizontally extended Colonial home on Hollow Road are dated May 1940. Eugene A. Quick of Kingston had the general contract for the new house and spent extended periods there, on at least one occasion driving Keefe from Kingston to visit the site. Keefe had invited D. Herbert Pike, Pittsfield contractor of the Rice house, to take the Taylor job, but Pike declined because of the distance to Dorset and work he already had in hand.[92]

The east front of the house was planned as a long file of (from north to south) two-car garage, maid's room, kitchen, dining room, hall, living room, and porch. All were nestled into the slope leading gently down to the Mettawee River, better described as a stream at this point. The client's bedroom and dressing room were located at the rear, behind the living room. Keefe's first-floor plan indicates an "ironing board" in the dressing room, well away from the kitchen and maid's quarters. (The second story, finished only over the dining and living rooms, had two bedrooms and a bath.)

The relative informality of his correspondence with the Rices was surpassed by that with Miss Taylor who spiced her letters with playful banter. She who had studied household economics at Russell Sage insisted, "I wouldn't trust any man alive to pick out and place my ironing board!" And the ironing board "must be heavy enough—I'm a strong armed amazon!" Then when Keefe tried to recommend light fixtures, she responded, "you'll have me a fancy woman yet. . . . I'm sorry to have been so unladylike over the fixtures." Treating windows as faces and gable roofs as hats, she wrote, "I hear the dormer windows have their faces in and their hats on. What ornaments are you going to use on their hats? You said you would decide when you knew me better. Don't put anything over on me!" He responded: "The ornament on the dormers are rather delicate Colonial urns. I tried out other things & the urns seemed to fit in the best. I hope you like them."[93] Despite being strong as an amazon, Miss Taylor raised no objection to the delicate urn ornaments, which in fact Keefe routinely chose.

Miss Taylor, like the Rices, had Keefe design a garden house (in her case functioning as a tool house). Its walls were of stone partly from the previous house on the site; its roof was topped with a birdhouse in place of a belfry. The garden house, along with a ten-foot-high, gable-roofed "well cover" and daffodil-lined cellar hole from the previous house, added to the charm of the landscape. Keefe, however, was not responsible for the terrace and other landscape features designed by landscape architect and 1931 Vassar graduate Molly S. Drysdale. Responding to her inquiry about the location of a Colonial lamp post he had designed, Keefe professed to "like your layout very much," but when Miss Taylor tried to get Keefe to meet with her and Miss Drysdale to advise on the road and grading, "you always evaded us—too many women!" When Miss Drysdale objected to a picket fence wanted by Miss Taylor, Keefe sided with his client and assured her, "After everyone [i.e., Miss Drysdale] leaves the place maybe we can work in some picket fence. Mum's the word."[94]

Miss Taylor objected to some local marble being used in a wall in front of the white-painted house: "I don't want a dirty-white stone. . . . I'm not ready for a mausoleum yet! There must be some old ruin somewhere of stone." Keefe in reply argued that "marble is the local stone and to me it fits in with the type of house we are building." No marble was available from old walls, and Keefe preferred marble to the other local choice, cobblestones, which were "full of bumps and lumps." He considered the colors in the marble appealing and cited (McKim, Mead & White's) Tiffany façade on Fifth Avenue where the white marble had "turned a wonderful soft color." If these points did not convince her, surely she recalled that "according to the hymns all good people will dwell in marble halls & in this case you are getting it ahead of time." The architect also responded to Miss Taylor's objection to sagging stone work. "It looks just like the old wall in Manchester [at a bandstand] that I pointed out to Quick. Wait till its weathered & you'll not notice it. As it stands its just the type of stone work I wanted that is not perfectly true & even as to lines, and do I have a time getting such old appearing work for most masons want every line true & level and not at all like the old time work. I'd say it's just right. One old architect put it this way. For god's sake make a mistake once in a while & let's get some charm in the work."[95]

The banter never stopped. In 1941 when a contractor threatened to sue Miss Taylor over a disputed bill, she warned her architect who, as was his habit, seemed to be avoiding her, "Don't you get me in disgrace—we've never had anything like this in the family, before. You needn't think that new car of yours [a 1941 Chevrolet] is any camouflage—I know you by your hat."[96]

Keefe would have had little choice but to drive by Miss Taylor's home when he consulted with her neighbor, **Olivia Antoinette Helme Herbert**, the elderly widow of John W. Herbert, a lawyer and business executive. Mrs. Herbert, a summer resident, owned property across the stream from Miss Taylor. Between 1940 and her death in August 1945, Keefe drew a number of plans for her property, including a garage group with Cape Cod cottage in 1944. No correspondence with her survives, so the gossip Miss Taylor provided Keefe in 1940 may well be untrue: "I discovered from several sources that Mrs. Herbert . . . wants my land for a house for her colored servants, which is a charming idea."[97]

In October 1940 Grace Keefe came with Charles to enjoy the fall foliage and see the Taylor building site, although the owner was not present: Mrs. Keefe "was delighted with the location for your house." In July 1941 both Keefes called upon her, and as the architect subsequently wrote, "Mrs. Keefe likes your house a lot and is delighted with your color schemes." Charles had apparently been unenthusiastic about her preference for yellow rooms and yellow bathroom fixtures. "She enjoyed her little visit with you."[98]

The Keefe-Taylor friendship, odd as it may have been, was facilitated by his sense of closeness to Vermont, home of his father's family. Filed with the many Keefe letters relating to Miss Taylor's house is one he wrote her in 1941 with no architectural content: "Enclosed is a clipping of two new books about Vermont. I have noticed that folks who settle in Vermont seem to burst into print about what they find there. I am beginning to worry about you for I know you have discovered quite a few things already. The native Vermonters are not mute by any means. . . . but you don't find them putting any thing down on paper that can be cast at them later."[99]

As her house was nearing completion, Keefe wrote Miss Taylor that he had met the Dorset architect Henry Bowditch Van Loon, son of the popular writer and historian Hendrik Van Loon, and that Van Loon's wife "liked your stone work a lot." Miss Taylor had heard that Van Loon approved of their work—he and his wife had been "pretty concerned about some of the atrocities going up in Dorset," and he had asked to design her home. Keefe was unaware of Van Loon's offer, and now imagined that "Mrs. Rice had been quite definite in her remarks to induce you to take a strange architect. I have been very fortunate in the clients I have been able to get and I try hard to give them homes they will be happy in."[100]

In November 1940 Miss Taylor paid tribute to her architect by planting what she called "the Keefe elm" near the corner of her bedroom. He acknowledged that, "I feel greatly honored to have a tree named after me particularly . . . an elm." Soon after being planted, the tree, she noted, "had become large and Siamese." He replied that "the Keefe elm evidently has a split personality or something like that." Keefe reciprocated by following his usual practice and offering a gift to his client, a small wooden roadside sign lettered TAYLOR.[101]

Finally, in 1942, when the architect dealt with an "explosion" of her American Standard boiler and also took photos of the completed house without announcing his arrival, Miss Taylor wondered, "Did you sneak in behind me . . . ?"[102]

Crane Museum

Just before the Depression, Keefe was involved in the establishment of two museums by businesses hoping to use history to enhance their reputations and ultimately sales. The first, and more successful, was the **Crane Museum** in Dalton, near Pittsfield, set in landscaped grounds on the bank of the Housatonic River in the Berkshires. Crane & Co., papermakers with a long-time monopoly on producing paper for U.S. currency, traced its origins to Zenas Crane and 1801. The Crane family, which retained an ownership role, stood out as one of Dalton's "two ruling clans" or "paternal dynasts" and were known for their civic benefactions. Cranes had given Dalton's people both the combined Public Library and Town Hall (1892) and the Colonial Revival Community House (1923).[103]

In 1928 Keefe corresponded with the Yale-educated president of Crane & Co., Winthrop M. Crane, Jr., and his associates about reworking into a museum one of the company's oldest structures, a stone building from 1844 currently used for storage. Keefe credited Earnest Elmo Calkins (1868–1964), "dean of advertising men in this country," with conceiving "the idea for this building and exhibit." Calkins was an early advocate of a "soft sell" approach to advertising where establishing goodwill and creating a brand over time replaced seeking immediate results. *The Berkshire Evening Eagle* opined that while the museum would be "good advertising," it would also "aid in preserving the story of Dalton's past. . . . The townspeople will be proud of the museum and its exhibits, and will proudly point it out as 'Dalton's' museum."[104]

Keefe presumably was hired thanks to his success in working for the Crane-Rice circle in Pittsfield and Dalton and to his reputation as an expert on Colonial architecture. While Movius may have been responsible for introducing Keefe to this circle, Keefe now recommended Movius to Winthrop Crane as the museum's landscape architect, but in the end the distinguished landscape architects, Olmsted Brothers, were chosen to collaborate with Keefe.[105]

On November 14, 1928, after meeting with Winthrop Crane and Calkins, Keefe prepared a typed, three-page justification for and description of the "Proposed Museum for the Crane Company" and suggested the old stone, 30-by-55-foot storage building, from an early incarnation of the paper mill, would offer "a proper background" for the museum's exhibits. He believed it was "reasonable for a company closely identified with the growth of the paper business in America and with the historical events of over a century to form a museum of

Crane Museum.

papers." Establishing the museum would also "reflect the greater interest now taken in good paper."[106]

A preliminary rendering by J. Floyd Yewell for Keefe showed an industrial-looking, two-story façade, but as completed the exterior took on a more Colonial appearance with new front and rear doorways (the front or north with new wooden columns), new circular window over the front entrance, and new sash and shutters for five windows on the west side (one old west window was closed up to achieve symmetry). The storage building had been of two stories and a loft, but the museum would occupy only one story. Keefe offered alternative treatments of its ceiling: remove the second-story beams to expose roof beams and trusses; remove the second-story beams and put in a nearly flat arched plaster ceiling like some early American meeting houses; or retain the second-story beams and add a flat plaster ceiling that would make for a "home like look." Keefe favored the last alternative, but Winthrop Crane and his associates were of divided opinions.[107]

Soon, however, a new option emerged, probably from Keefe's experience of the new American Wing at the Metropolitan Museum. This option, which was adopted, called for a new roof frame constructed of heavy arches in hand-hewn oak inspired by the restored Old Ship Meeting House in Hingham, Massachusetts, as it had been adapted for a gallery in the American Wing.[108] While the museum walls would be plastered, Keefe designed the interior as a great assemblage of unpainted wood from wide oak floor boards to roof trusses.

The sturdy simplicity of the tradition-bound architectural woodwork hid some modern materials—steel girders were cased in wood to create the effect of ceiling beams, and the oak plank floor rested on a four-inch concrete floor reinforced with triangular mesh woven wire. The woody interior surfaces would be in harmony with Wallace Nutting's finely finished furniture in early Colonial style. Nutting had gained fame as an advocate of the Colonial Revival through his reproduction Colonial furniture, tinted photos of staged Colonial interiors, and books on antiques and the picturesque beauties of northeastern states. Keefe wrote Nutting, "I am erecting a room for exhibition purposes designed along the lines of the Old Ship Meeting-house in the Metropolitan Museum of Art," and he sought quotes for eight oak trestle tables (to be fitted with bronze and glass display cases), four oak benches, and six maple chairs.[109] Nutting, through his associate Ernest John Donnelly, fulfilled the order, which was expanded to include four stools and an additional table. While Nutting's Colonial pieces seemed best suited to Colonial houses, he did seek corporate customers, and chairs similar to Crane's were installed in "The Pine Room" at Aetna Inc. in Hartford about 1935.[110]

The 1844 mill building was to be made into an exhibition space redolent of early America, but not a reproduction of any one historic space. Many felt that every good Colonial interior needed a fireplace, even one with a roof structure harking back to a cold, fireless, Puritan meetinghouse. At first Winthrop Crane was content with a fake fireplace, but he changed his mind. Keefe wrote that he "had a sneaking idea your folks would finally decide upon a real fireplace," and he had prepared drawings for one. Zenas Crane's portrait hung above the

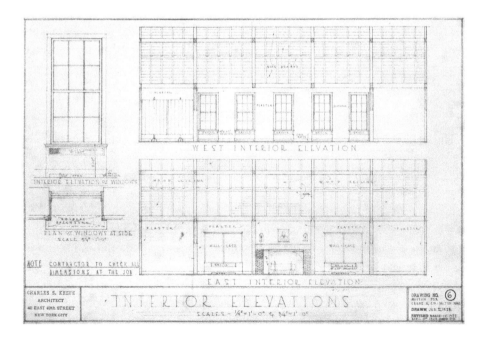

Crane Museum, interior elevations.

fireplace and confirmed the historical antecedents of the company and its museum. Further, since Crane's advertising featured a loosely Colonial fireplace with crane, the museum's fireplace must have a crane.[111]

The early industrial origins of the building and unpainted surfaces of the sturdy woodwork and furniture meant that hand-forged iron was in order, and Myron Teller was just the man to provide the crane along with andirons, trammel iron, pot hooks and chain for the fireplace. Keefe also ordered hardware for five pairs of shutters required for the new windows, as well as four pairs of false strap hinges for front and rear entrance doors. Stock hinges would perform the actual hinge function. Teller was not pleased and chided: "My dear Charles: . . . Sorry you had to resort to this make-shift as it certainly is only an imitation, though I assume something has forced you to meet this condition."[112] Teller was a friend but also a rival. While Teller was the expert on Colonial hardware, as an architect who also made and sold hardware Teller went against the Canon of Ethics of the American Institute of Architects, which ruled that "to engage directly or indirectly in any of the building or decorative trades" was "unprofessional."[113] This probably explains why Teller was not a member of the A.I.A. Keefe must have taken silent satisfaction that he, not Teller, could append "A.I.A." after his name.

Keefe could also take pleasure in Winthrop Crane's letter expressing satisfaction with the completed museum: "We are all very pleased with what you have done in planning and executing the changes in our museum."[114] The architect was also able to design two texts drawing attention to his museum: first, in 1929, an oval memorial tablet of marble countersunk in ledge stone, "To Commemorate the founding of the First Paper Mill in Dalton Mass. by Zenas Crane 1801. Crane & Co. 1929"; and then in 1931 a sign to attract visitors, tastefully, from automobiles on the road, basing the design on a 1775 sign from Lexington and an old Cape Cod lamp post.[115] Today the Crane Museum of Papermaking remains open to the public in the 1844 mill building thoughtfully transformed by Keefe.

Wheatsworth

F. H. Bennett was founder and owner of **Wheatsworth, Inc.**, "Millers and Bakers of Whole Wheat Specialties," with mills in Hamburg, New Jersey, fifty miles west of New York City. In 1928 he commissioned Joseph Urban, celebrated architect and stage set designer, to create a Ginger Bread Castle, a "unique outdoor stage setting . . . quaint, beautiful and fantastic" for a small amusement park close to the Wheatsworth Mills, which themselves were open for public tours.[116] Bennett preserved within the modern concrete mill complex an 1808 grain mill built of stone. Pictorial tiles at the mill site by Flint Faience & Tile Co. show the "Old Stone Mill Built 1808" next to the modern concrete mill.

Bennett was an admirer of Henry Ford's restoration of Longfellow's Wayside Inn at South Sudbury, Massachusetts, and in 1929 obtained Keefe's advice

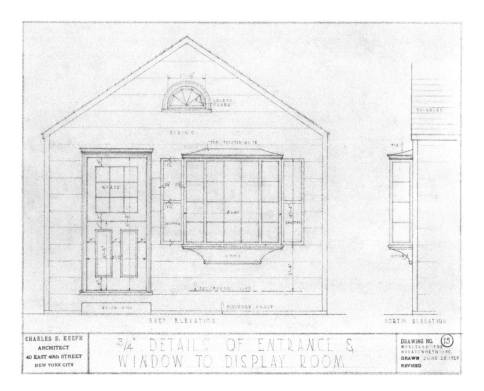

3/4" DETAILS OF ENTRANCE &
WINDOW TO DISPLAY ROOM

DRAWING NO. (15)
WORKSHOP FOR
WHEATSWORTH INC.
DRAWN JUNE 28, 1929
REVISED

*Wheatsworth workshop,
display room.*

in repairing the gambrel-roofed mansion put up by the builder of the 1808 mill. Keefe explained to a Crane official that he was working on a museum similar to theirs in New Jersey: "While Wheatsworth is not an old concern, they make whole wheat products in the old way and are restoring this old house to get some of the right atmosphere about their mill. We are also going to erect a shop of old timbers where workmen will make reproductions of old pieces just to add another touch."[117]

The mansion Bennett planned on opening as "an antiquarian house and colonial type inn" had been the residence of Governor Daniel Haines in the 1840s, and Bennett called it the "Haines Mansion." The D.A.R. expressed interest in Bennett's preservation effort, and it was his intention to exhibit at the inn "treasured mementoes of the state's earliest days" as well as "revive . . . some of the handicrafts of colonial days, such as weaving, spinning, and hook rug-making." Keefe wrote his California client, Elizabeth Tyng, that "a room to be attached" to the Haines mansion would "form a back ground for part of what I consider the best privately owned collection of early American antiques in America.[118] The shop Keefe described as built with old timbers appears in his June 1929 drawings as an L-shaped "Workshop" building with "Display Room," smaller "Workshop" and still smaller "Finishing Room." The entrance to the Display Room was to be appealingly Colonial with Dutch door and small-paned bay window.

The craft project seems not to have come to fruition, and Keefe's involvement with the mansion itself was minor.[119] Bennett wrote Keefe on January 6, 1931, that he was consolidating Wheatsworth with the National Biscuit Company and asked Keefe to provide architectural arguments for preserving the Haines Mansion that Bennett could pass along to Nabisco. Bennett himself believed that "it should be maintained . . . for the sake of the good will and publicity that will ensue. . . . I believe the property has possibilities of creating as much interest as Henry Ford's Wayside Inn. . . . That is why I admire Henry Ford—for carrying on as he does, with relics of bygone days."

Keefe, hoping to keep the project alive, replied to Bennett the next day:

Laying aside all sentimental reasons for owning the Haines Mansion its value as an advertisement should justify its retention. It is situated on a main highway. . . . If it is properly restored and furnished and used as a tea room or lunching place, as you intended, it would offer a good illustration of the uses of your products. People are interested in such houses as the number of visitors to the American wing of the Metropolitan Museum prove. We might also point to the increasing number of antique dealers along all the main highways and the number of visitors to all the early American houses that are open for inspection.

The Haines house is a very fine example of the type of house erected in New Jersey at the beginning of the nineteenth century. Restore the house as nearly as possible to its original condition, put in the garden as planned [Keefe had prepared drawings for a new open-sided summerhouse and a 98-foot-long pergola in the fall of 1929.] and you have a place that would soon become as famous as Mr. Ford's Wayside Inn. It is certainly near the largest centers of population. . . .

I might say that my idea of the advertising value of such places is not based on my own opinion alone. I refer to the building I just remodeled for the use of Crane & Company, paper makers, at Dalton, Mass. There we took the oldest building that remained and made it into a place to exhibit interesting things connected with paper making. . . . The idea for this building and exhibit was conceived by Mr. Earnest Elmo Calkins the dean of advertising men in this country. . . . This building and exhibit have created a great deal of interest and Crane & Company feel its value has been proved already, tho it has been open but a short time.

Although the Wheatsworth Inn (later known as The Governor Haines) did serve tea and meals to travelers on Route 23, it never achieved the renown of the Wayside Inn and eventually was razed after a fire. The mills and Gingerbread Castle have long been abandoned and the mills are ruinous.[120]

Kingston and the Mid-Hudson Region

While practicing in New York and designing for clients as far away as California and Ecuador, Keefe continued to design houses in his hometown. His drawing, **"Houses at Kingston, New York,"** called for three houses and four apartments joined behind a symmetrical façade with Colonial details. The drawing was published as "Housing at Kingston, New York," in the *American Architect* (September 20, 1920), but this rare venture into multifamily housing was probably never built.

Between 1916 and 1922 **Alexander B. Shufeldt** (1884–1968) rose from bookkeeper to general manager of the Universal Road Machinery Company in Kingston.   For Shufeldt and his wife, **Louise Wilkinson Shufeldt** (1884–1941), who was active in the Kingston Hospital Auxiliary,[121] Keefe drew a number of house designs in 1920, some for a modest-sized, symmetrical Georgian house with walls of white clapboards (in one proposal the symmetry was broken by a short arcade linking house to garage), and others for a more Mediterranean-looking house with stucco walls and arches over French windows.

For reasons unknown, the earlier designs were set aside and Keefe in 1921 designed what he called a "Dutch Colonial" house for the Shufeldts, built at 71 Johnston Avenue. The Dutch Colonial label was justified by the entrance stoop with benches and by the long dormer emerging from the lower slope of the gambrel roof, but the flat stucco walls and casement windows relate to the Arts and Crafts movement. The delicate pilasters framing the doorway provide a Colonial or Federal-style touch; in the panel above the door Keefe placed the numerals 1921.[122] The front door and vestibule, located to one side of the Johnston Street façade, allowed for a long living room facing the street. Pennington photos from 1922 of the living room show a Colonial mantelpiece, prominent upright piano, and an eclectic mix of wicker and old rush-seat chairs. Keefe drew a "planting

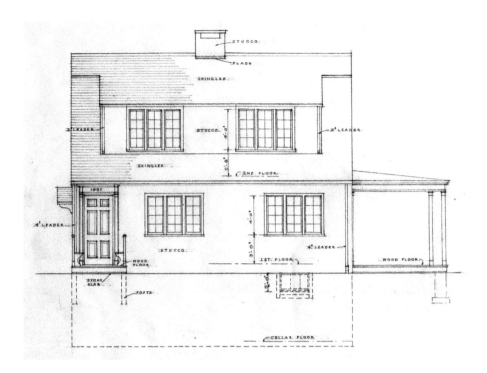

Alexander and Louise
Shufeldt house.

Shufeldt planting plan.

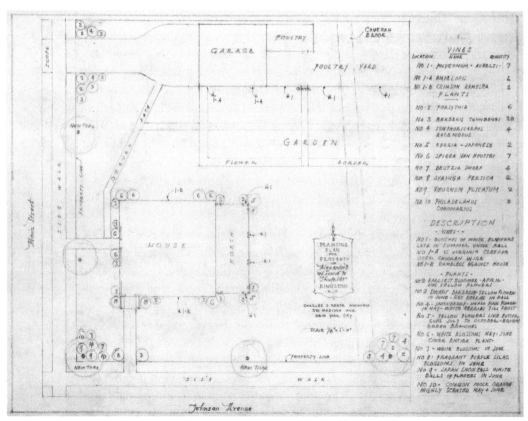

EAST ELEVATION   NORTH ELEVATION

Gertrude Doyle house.

plan" for the small yard including a section for poultry and shrubs such as forsythia and (the invasive) Japanese barberry. He signed the planting plan by placing his name and 331 Madison Avenue address on a Colonial signboard, as he did in the planting plan for the Cates in Long Branch.

The Shufeldt house resembles the house Keefe designed in 1924 for **Gertrude M. Doyle** on Waring Avenue near Yates Avenue in the Bronx. However, Keefe heightened the Colonial aspect for Doyle, substituting wood siding for stucco and double-hung sash with shutters for casements, as well as giving the front porch a Colonial elliptical arch and pediment with cut-out urn ornament. The thirty-nine-foot-wide house and the driveway to the garage were squeezed into a fifty-foot lot, yet in 1925 Keefe again drew a "planting plan," here for the small front and larger back yards. The plan, with Keefe's name and address again on a Colonial signboard and Doyle's on a flowing ribbon, listed plants from "Forsythia . . . Earliest Bloomer—April has yellow flowers" to "Syringa Persica . . . Fragrant Purple Lilac—Blossom in June." Keefe took special care in creating the planting plan, and a draftsman sketched several choices for lettering "Doyle" or "D" on the door knocker, but unfortunately nothing is known about the client, one of his few residential clients to build in New York City.

For **Walter E. Price** (born in Scranton, died in Kingston in 1932), a "commercial traveler," and his wife **Mabel M. Price** (?–1959), Keefe designed a "brick Colonial" or symmetrical Georgian house in 1922 that was built at 219 Albany Avenue.[123] An early perspective drawing called for a three-bay façade with doorway and windows surrounded with generous wall area, while in the final, five-bay design the façade appears crowded with more windows and shutters, as well

Proposed Walter and Mabel Price house.

Louis and Mary Basten house.

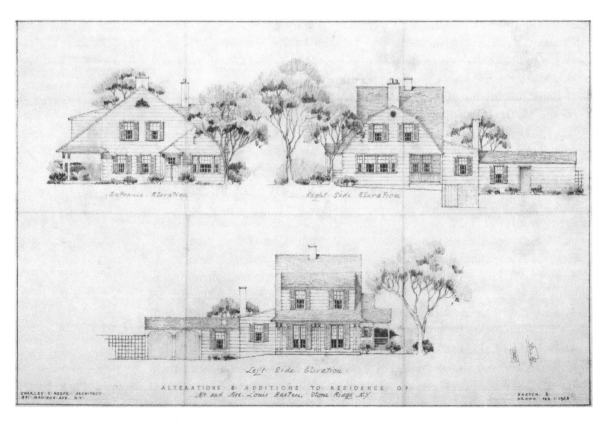

Proposed American Legion Memorial Building.

as an elliptical-arched porch at the central doorway. A sun room was appended on the south side in both designs.

Louis Bevier Basten (1856–1951), a direct descendant of Louis Bevier, a seventeenth-century New Paltz patentee, was born in Cottekill and became a vice- president of Everett & Treadwell, wholesale grocers in Kingston. In 1922 his wife, **Mary Scott de la Montanye Basten** (1857–1949), was on the Wiltwyck D.A.R.'s committee on the preservation of "Historic Spots."[124] Both were active in St. James Methodist Church, the Keefes' church, and the wives may have been related. The Bastens maintained a summer home in Marbletown, and in 1923 Keefe designed alterations and additions for a Stone Ridge house, at first planned as a frame Colonial distinctive in its broad triangular entrance elevation fronting a library and living room. However, working drawings eliminated the library and diminished the breadth of the façade.

Keefe, the Spanish-American War veteran and patriotic American, took particular pride in successfully completing the **American Legion Memorial Building** in 1926 for the city that would always represent home for him. Veterans of World War I founded the American Legion in Paris early in 1919, and in July Kingston's veterans held their first American Legion meeting. Three years later, in 1922, Keefe wrote a letter supporting creation of quarters for the Legion and provided sketches of a Colonial Revival building. He observed that, "as a member of the Spanish War Veterans, I have seen that organization in Kingston fade away to nothing, simply because of the lack of a home. Neither families or organizations can long survive without a place that they can call HOME." The Legion reminded its members that Keefe had designed a comparable building for the Knights of Columbus, "which is indeed a credit to the city." Keefe was motivated to push the Legion project because his half-brother Robert Keefe, a flyer in the Aviation Corps in France in 1918, suffered head injuries in a plane crash and was described as "a total disability of the World War." Charles's commitment was such that he donated his architectural services.[125]

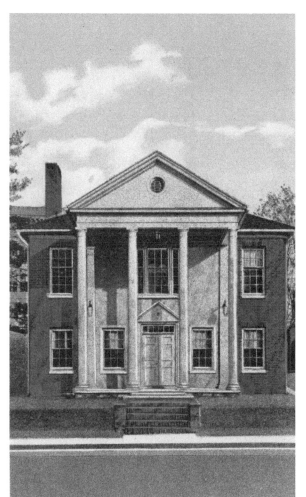

American Legion Memorial Building. (Curt Teich postcard)

The site chosen for the Legion quarters on West O'Reilly Street, just off Broadway, was not far from the Knights of Columbus and around the corner from City Hall and Kingston High School—that is, in the civic center of Kingston. The Legion quarters would resemble the Knights of Columbus as a two-story, brick Colonial Revival building, but it would have greater dignity thanks to its two-story, four-column portico. The memorial function of the building was explicit in a bronze memorial tablet, designed by the architect and cast by Gorham Company, set in a marble panel in the entrance hall. It quoted from Lincoln's Gettysburg Address and stated: "Erected by Kingston Post 150, American Legion and Patriotic Friends in Memory of Those Who Gave Their All for Freedom and Democracy. November 11, 1925." Above the bronze tablet was an American eagle, while below was the emblem of the American Legion with crossed swords—all in bronze. A stand or console furnished a surface for placement of "floral offerings" of anniversaries of major events during the war, but "relatives of the boys who lost their lives also place flowers there on certain individual anniversary days."[126]

The building also served as a home from which to carry out welfare work for veterans. Welfare could be broadly interpreted, and the building was designed primarily as a Prohibition-era clubhouse: "a place we can go on the cold winter evenings, a place we can meet our old pals, where we can talk over the old times, a place with an auditorium, where we can hold our own dances, movies or stage our own minstrels." The two main rooms on the first floor were called the "lounging room" (with "comfortable chairs . . . and large open fireplace") and the "reading or card room" (later functioning as the barroom). An early photo of the lounging room shows General Pershing's autographed photograph over the Colonial mantle. (A magnificent framed drawing, "Columbia Gives to Her Son the Accolade of the New Chivalry of Humanity," signed and dated 1919 by Edwin Howland Blashfield and donated to the post in 1927, has long replaced Pershing.) On the second floor were a kitchen and an assembly room with sliding doors available to separate meetings of the men of the post from gatherings of the Ladies Auxiliary.[127]

At the dedication in 1926, the building's "Colonial architecture" was said to be "in keeping with the history of the city of Kingston which has long been known as the Old Colonial Town." Colonial architecture was commonly understood to be distinctly American, not foreign, and so perfectly suited for use by patriotic Americans. The American Legion, through its Americanism Committee, saw itself as a source of patriotic education for schoolchildren and new adult citizens. Conrad J. Heiselman, chairman of the Americanism Committee and later a Republican mayor of Kingston, further emphasized the Legion's role in "fighting radicalism" in the person of "reds" or Bolsheviks. Heiselman assured potential donors to the construction fund that "This Memorial Building will not be a lounging room. It will be Kingston's Service Station, from whence will come words, thoughts, influences and actions that will be 100 per cent American, for God and country."[128] These last four words are incised on the cornerstone, along with the date, 1925.

Stanley and Mae Matthews house. (James Bleecker photo)

Post 150 was happy with the completed building, constructed inexpensively for about $32,000, and put on a dinner as a "testimonial to Charles S. Keefe, the architect who gratuitously planned the Memorial Building and superintended its construction." Pleasing as that dinner must have been, Keefe was probably even more gratified that **Stanley J. Matthews**, elected commander of the post in 1923 and having an important role in the completion of the Memorial Building, hired Keefe to design his Tudor residence in 1926. The next year Keefe succeeded in having the Memorial Building published in the *American Architect*.[129]

Stanley Matthews (1895–1996) was an officer in his family's wholesale grocery and grain business; his wife, **Mae Everett Matthews** (1896–1979), was active in the American Legion Auxiliary.[130] The residence Keefe completed between 1926 and 1929 for the couple at 61 Lounsbury (or Lounsbery) Place is one of Keefe's most appealing. Turning aside from his usual preference for some variety of Colonial, Keefe employed instead the English Tudor, known from publications and his 1910 English visit, and evident in the stucco walls, casement windows (their metal frames marking them as twentieth-century), batten doors, and asymmetrical composition of the low façade with its cross gable. The Matthews house

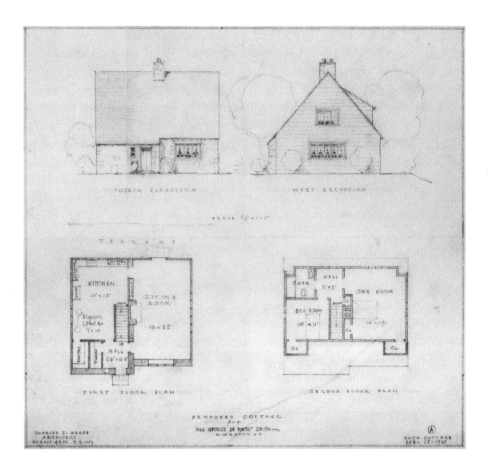

Frances Smith cottage.

seems to fit comfortably into its site on a quiet city street in one of the city's pleasantest neighborhoods. While the design is not Colonial in detail, the simplicity and restraint of the exterior—there is little ornament and no half-timbering of the kind often found in Tudor houses—is comparable to Keefe's work in the Colonial idiom.

A cozy cottage Keefe planned in 1929 for a doctor's elderly widow, **Frances S. Smith** (1858–1945), was probably intended for a lot she owned near the Matthews house on Lounsbury Place. The lot (which she sold in 1944) was also not far from 251 Pearl Street where she had lived with her husband, George DeForest Smith (1852–1921), an "eminent specialist in nervous diseases." The cottage Keefe proposed, using a delightful little elevation drawing, called for a low, one-story, stone-veneer façade with doorway flanked on one side by a narrow window and on the other by a broad, three-part window comparable to the Matthews's casements. The gable roof rose high, without dormers, calling to mind the great roof of the early eighteenth-century Jean Hasbrouck house in New Paltz. The interior was laid out for a single person—living room and combined kitchen and "dining space" on the first floor, two bedrooms and a bath on the second. Frances Smith, a member of the Ulster Garden Club, in 1925 had a prize-winning rock garden, and her cottage would have been well suited to accompany a lovely garden, but the cottage, perhaps a victim of the Depression, was never built.[131]

Also not built was the substantial country house planned between 1925 and 1934 for **Lester and Barbara Moehring** near the Ashokan Reservoir at Winchell's Falls on the Esopus Creek in the Town of Olive, Ulster County. Lester A. Moehring (1892–1947) was a Brooklyn native who in 1925 was on the treasurer's staff of the Maxwell Motor Corporation. He became assistant controller of the Chrysler Corporation in Detroit in 1926 and controller in 1927, a post he held until his death. While the Moehrings maintained a residence in Grosse Point Farms, wife Barbara Darling Mohring (1886–1953) often drew them back to Kingston and rural Ulster. She was the great-great-granddaughter of Lemuel Winchell who had established a store and mills at Winchell's Falls. Barbara's mother, Ella Winchell Darling, resided at 142 Washington Avenue in Kingston (various Keefes were at 291 Washington Avenue), and Charles's sister Celeste was part of a circle of friends that included Barbara.[132]

In April 1926 Keefe produced working drawings for a hip-roofed Georgian house sturdily built with eighteen-inch-thick stone walls and a wing for kitchen and garage with gun and sewing rooms above. The main block included a butler's pantry and a bedroom for Ella Darling. In 1934 Keefe created a much-revised set of plans with bird's-eye views. Still stone-walled, the house was to be gable-roofed and larger with a book room, pleasant first-floor breakfast porch, and porch above for lounging and looking out over the countryside. But this, Keefe's most ambitious

Lester and Barbara Moehring house.

Ulster County residence, remained strictly on paper, as the Moehrings simply restored the old Winchell homestead near the picturesque falls.[133]

In the old Hudson River towns of Hudson and Catskill, Keefe was part of the effort to bring up-to-date elegance to what appeared to be drab late-nineteenth-century commercial blocks, in his case by adding stylish Colonial fronts. First, in 1920, he designed a Colonial façade for **Granville M. Joslen** in Hudson that was to serve **Carlton & Co.** on the ground floor, while doctors' offices occupied the second story. His color rendering pictures a debonair couple strolling on the sidewalk while a little girl, all in white, with a big, broad-brimmed hat, stands in front of the expansive window, transfixed by whatever is inside.[134]

While the Joslen project was probably never carried out,[135] Keefe retained his interest in Colonial street fronts. In 1925 he executed one of his most accomplished pen-and-ink drawings with applied color—a view of the Betsy Ross House on Arch Street in Philadelphia. Although the flag flying above the sidewalk and the signboards "BETSY ROSS" and "BIRTHPLACE OF OLD GLORY" clearly announce the patriotic shrine and tourist attraction, the drawing also reflects Keefe's fascination with picturesque urban clutter, evident in his earlier New York drawings—taller commercial buildings with prominent signs and iron-and-glass store fronts press in upon the little Colonial landmark, which itself has been disfigured by signage and the addition of a shopfront of iron and large panes of glass. Only the dormer window and second-story windows

Store building for Granville Joslen.

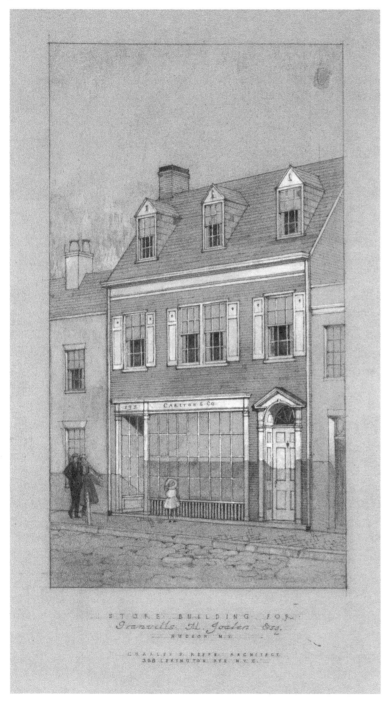

with shutters look to remain from Betsy's time. (However, the curtains, shades, and small cutouts in the top panel of the shutters could be found in Keefe's new Colonial homes.) Keefe no doubt was amused when he sketched pictures of tiny, odd figures in the Betsy Ross and right-hand store windows. And how satisfying it must have been for Keefe, the New Yorker, to crop "COMPANY" in the left-hand store sign to just "NY." A postcard from the period indicates that Keefe generally recorded the actual streetscape, although he multiplied the number of window panes in the upper stories of the commercial buildings, perhaps to be in harmony with the Ross windows. Keefe had probably traveled to Philadelphia by 1914 when he cited Congress Hall as a source of his Knights of Columbus building. The Betsy Ross House drawing, initialed and dated

View of the Betsy Ross House.

1925, implies a visit to Philadelphia that year, when he may also have toured Valley Forge; in the Keefe Archive is a guide to Valley Forge Park published in 1922. In 1937 the Betsy Ross House was thoroughly restored by R. Brognard Okie, thereby losing the bits of disorder that appealed to Keefe the artist, if not Keefe the architect.

In 1927–28 Keefe did succeed in applying a street-level Colonial front, similar to his Joslen-Carlton design, to a nondescript commercial building for the insurance, real estate, and law offices of **Harring & Betts** at 385 Main Street in Catskill. The *Catskill Daily Mail* welcomed the "new glass front that is quite a novelty and different from anything . . . in Catskill." Its large window, unlike Betsy Ross's, was composed of "many smaller panes, enclosed in copper frames," which helped give the new front "a fine colonial style, adapted to modern convenience."

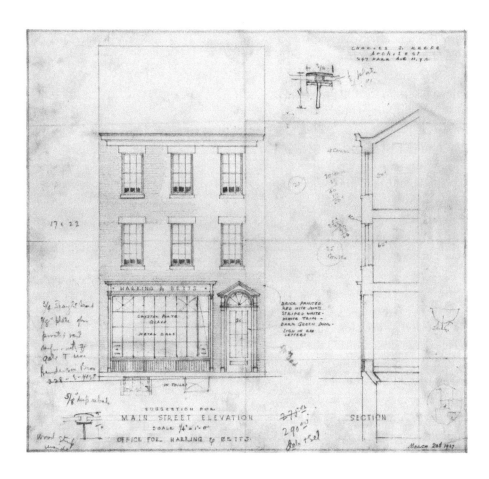

Office for Harring & Betts.

In the main office, the Colonial note was found modestly in Windsor chairs and settees on an inlaid linoleum floor. Keefe received national recognition for the façade remodeling through its publication in the *American Architect*, November 20, 1927, while the local newspaper featured a photo of the renovated façade in October 1928, calling it "a masterpiece of architecture."[136] Masterpiece or not, by 1984 Keefe's contribution to Main Street had mostly vanished; the handsome window was removed, replaced by a characterless office front. But Keefe had also designed a side doorway with Colonial fanlight and broken pediment, and that survived; even the lead eagle and rosettes in the fanlight remained.

Also in Catskill, but of an entirely different character, was Keefe's **Catskill Country Club** (1926–27). In the summer of 1926, Keefe designed alterations and additions to a nineteenth-century Italianate building that included removing the bracketed cornice and adding a tall Colonial portico. In October, while the remodeling was underway, the building burned to the ground. At once Keefe set to work designing its replacement, using the old foundations, and by December he arrived at the final design for a one-story clubhouse, bungalow-like with its low hipped roof encompassing the club rooms and porches around three sides. The prohibition-era interior was given over primarily to a forty-three-foot-long "lounge" opening out to the front porch. There was little insurance to cover the cost of the new clubhouse, and the club functioned modestly with a nine-hole golf course and two tennis courts. Keefe's building was erected without frills; the lounge's walls and ceiling were not plaster but Celotex. The only markedly Colonial architectural feature was the fireplace centered on the lounge's long back wall. Still, the *Catskill Daily Mail* judged the new clubhouse "of a beautiful architectural design" and "the interior decorations . . . most artistic . . . a harmonious blending of colors." The predominant color was "a tint of lemon," while some of the furniture was in "jade green" or "upholstered in oranges, blues and violets." Seaman Brothers, a long-established furniture store in Saugerties, provided "two large wrought iron electric chandeliers, each with eight lamps," as well as wrought-iron wall lamps. The wrought iron created a Colonial or at least handmade look, also found in "several old-fashioned Hutch tables and Console tables" and in "quaint electric lamps, made from demijohns" and placed on living-room tables.[137]

In 1928, not long after the completion of the Catskill building, Keefe, probably aware of his limitations as a designer of country clubs, recommended John A. Thompson of Thompson, Holmes & Converse and formerly of McKim, Mead & White when William Rice of Pittsfield sought a country club architect.[138]

Catskill Country Club.

CHAPTER FIVE

Persevering during
the Depression

Van Deusen house.

Architects were hit hard by the building slump during the Depression—in 1933 it was estimated that architects east of the Rockies had less than a seventh of the work they had in 1928, and that six out of seven draftsmen and other skilled workers in architectural offices had lost their jobs. Keefe did not escape the hard times, although he, like others with small offices, could adapt to the reduction in work more easily than those who ran large "plan factories."[1]

In spring 1930 Grace Keefe was able to travel to Europe for the first time, but Charles it seems felt he could not afford to accompany her. He told client C. McK. Lewis that, "she is not taking an extended trip but is reserving the places I want to visit until we can go together." That time never came. Grace's trip focused on Holland, not on Charles's earlier itinerary but land of her Hoetaling and Schepmoes ancestors. It took two months and occurred around the time Lewis set out for the Balkans and Austria. Lewis wondered whether Mrs. Keefe might be in London or Paris when he was there, but Keefe replied that she would not. Still, Keefe alerted Lewis that he might "run across Mr. E. Hope Norton . . . another one of my clients. The world being so small after all, your paths may cross."[2]

The couple was able to celebrate their silver wedding anniversary, October 12, 1930, with a catered event for some forty guests at what the *Freeman* described as their "artistic home." "Place cards were cleverly decorated with pictures showing the styles of 1905. Favors for the ladies were hand-painted flower baskets and amethyst cut crystal ash trays were the favors for the gentlemen." But the caterer was a diner-delicatessen owner apparently in debt to Keefe, who, when asked for another loan, responded that his practice was in trouble—that he had had to let go one of his two draftsmen.[3]

By 1931 Keefe's situation was dire. Charles Bellows, Keefe's Wall Street client, was unable to pay his bill, forcing the architect to write dunning letters

136

making clear his own and his profession's fallen state: "I will be pleased when you can pay even small amounts on account. Most Architects are about out of business these degenerate days." In July 1932 Keefe told his long-time client William Rice that, while most architects were "out of business . . . I'll go down fighting."[4]

Keefe still took time to maintain good relations with suppliers of building materials, writing the American Radiator Co. that their salesman, unlike others, continued to call at his office "to present the value of new products" and "comes in with a smile and has no tales of woe to tell." He also wrote Armstrong Cork Co., describing the useful service the permanent exhibit of The Architects Samples Corp. provided New York architects and their clients in selecting materials.[5]

But it was impossible to ignore the bad times, which impacted his health. Keefe was ill and unable to work most of January 1933, explaining to Robert Mac-Murphey, a client whose inquiries went unanswered, "I spent more time in bed with these colds than I have in all of the last fifteen years. Seldom ill, I guess business conditions made me worry enough to fall below par." By March he had recovered his health and sense of humor, but he was caught up in the bank holiday, as he wrote Ann MacMurphey: "Everyone seems cheerful here [in New York] even if they have to count their pennies. I neglected to go to the bank in time and had to borrow money to come to New York." It must have been a rare pleasure to accept the invitation of John Oldrin to an expensive lunch in the Chrysler Building's fashionable Art Deco setting: "John Oldrin and I had lunch in the Cloud Club atop the Chrysler Building. The way he talks about four foot fish is scandalous. The height may have affected him as he has always been truthful before."[6]

The summer did not improve business for Keefe, who wrote his old associate in Burnett's office, Stanley Cunningham, in July informing him that he had been forced to destroy Burnett drawings when he moved to a smaller office. "Business has been flat for two years but up to date I have been able to survive. Have some work in hand now but nothing of any size. . . . I go after country work of all kinds and up till now have been able to get it. . . . Get quite a lot of publicity even if I do not get much work. That will come along however."[7]

Publications

Keefe did succeed in keeping his work in the public eye during the Depression. He welcomed the publication of his designs and his thoughts in *Your Home*, a magazine catering to the general public. In March and April 1929 it had published his Young gardener's cottage and Wheeler house, then in March 1930 it praised Keefe as "an architect whose reputation as a designer and creator of beautiful and livable homes is national." In the same issue Wainwright Evans interviewed Keefe about the advantages and disadvantages of "Cost Plus versus . . . Fixed Price" contracts.[8]

In the August 1930 issue, Evans reported on one of his "many talks" with Keefe "whose skill in adapting authentic and established styles of home architecture to modern needs is well known to the readers of this magazine." Evans asked Keefe to comment about errors in design using pictures of houses not designed by Keefe; he found fault in houses whose lines were too vertical, chimneys were too prominent, or where the house failed to "'cling to the ground.'" He also condemned "'the fake Dutch colonial in many new communities, where it is really a two-story house, not a story and a half as its lines allege.'" It was the use of a long dormer that allowed the subterfuge. However, Keefe himself routinely used long dormers at the rear of his houses and occasionally in the front (e.g., the Shufeldt house). Then, too, Keefe could not abide "a piece of structural nonsense which is often indulged in—the extending of the gable end of a house to sweep down and include a gate in a wall which is not needed." (An offender in New Paltz was the Dayton house of 1937, whose design was probably furnished by a lumber dealer. Rhoads, *Ulster County*, 150.) But Keefe twisted logic to justify his own use of faking: "'One client of mine . . . built himself a half timber house, which was a reproduction of an old mansion in England. In order to give to the exposed timbers the same effect of age . . . we used a sand blast . . . to wear it down and 'age' it at once to a point that would have taken a lifetime of weathering to achieve. Also, the timbers were surfaced with an adze, that being the way the timbers in those old houses were smoothed down. The combination worked perfectly.'"

Evans also captured some charming tidbits of Keefe's architectural musings: "'I think the psychology that leads people to take pleasure in the small paned window is the feeling of being shut in and protected by those bars. It emphasizes the sense of security, and seclusion which is part of the fun of having a home of their own.'" Continuing on the idea of seclusion, Keefe proposed that "'The Englishman likes privacy. For the same reason he puts a high wall around his garden, perhaps with broken glass on top of it; and he would as soon think of having a front porch on the street where his neighbors could see him taking his ease as he would of taking his morning bath out on the sidewalk where he could splash.'" On the other hand, an open-plan interior appealed to some clients, especially, Keefe found, to a husband and wife without children.

In October 1930 *Your Home* published Keefe's Farrell cottage as "A True Connecticut Yankee," exhibiting "the strength that marks the architectural design of New England, refusing to accept ornamentation that goes beyond a fundamental simplicity of line." The brief text did not identify the cottage with Cape Cod, which was odd since the December 1930 issue presented "Just What Is a Cape Cod House? by Charles S. Keefe, A.I.A., As told to Wainwright Evans." While Keefe simply penned on the magazine's cover, "JUST WHAT IS A CAPE CODDER (INTERVIEW)," the interview allowed Keefe to argue for the importance of tradition and good breeding in house design just when he was feeling threatened by the rise of modernism (see below, "Against Modern Design").

The American Home, like *Your Home*, was a fan of Keefe's houses. In September 1930 it published "An Interesting and Unusual Colonial Plan," a two-bedroom

AN INTERESTING AND UNUSUAL COLONIAL PLAN

Designed for THE AMERICAN HOME *by Charles S. Keefe*

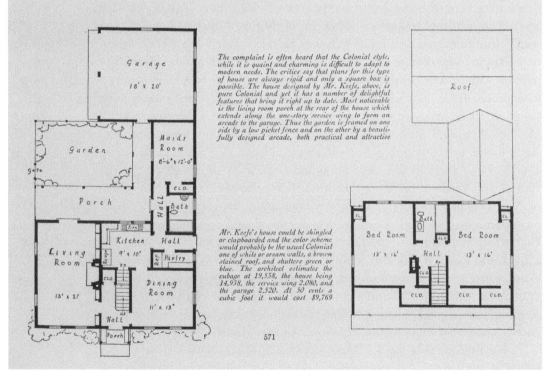

The complaint is often heard that the Colonial style, while it is quaint and charming is difficult to adapt to modern needs. The critics say that plans for this type of house are always rigid and only a square box is possible. The house designed by Mr. Keefe, above, is pure Colonial and yet it has a number of delightful features that bring it right up to date. Most noticeable is the living room porch at the rear of the house which extends along the one-story service wing to form an arcade to the garage. Thus the garden is framed on one side by a low picket fence and on the other by a beautifully designed arcade, both practical and attractive

Mr. Keefe's house could be shingled or clapboarded and the color scheme would probably be the usual Colonial one of white or cream walls, a brown stained roof, and shutters green or blue. The architect estimates the cubage at 19,538, the house being 14,938, the service wing 2,080, and the garage 2,520. At 50 cents a cubic foot it would cost $9,769

571

Cape Cod or "pure Colonial" designed by Keefe for the magazine. Critics of "the Colonial style" complained that it allowed only a rigid square box, "difficult to adapt to modern needs," but the magazine emphasized that Keefe's plan was hardly a simple box. He expanded the Cape at the rear with maid's quarters and living room porch, both connected by an arcade to a two-car garage. An intimate garden then was framed by the porch, arcade, and garage. The house therefore had "delightful features that bring it right up to date."

Keefe kept a careful list of the many magazine publications of his work. He relied less on newspapers. One example, which appears in his list of publications, was the March 8, 1931, *Herald Tribune*; his Woolworth Cottage was included in the Sunday series, "The American House and Its Setting," directed by William Harmon Beers of the A.I.A. The caption writer proposed that "future generations will find [the house] as charming as we of today find the older Colonial work. Without striving to observe to the letter all the archeology of the Colonial style, the architect has contrived to convey fully its real spirit and to design a house convenient to live in"—a statement Keefe would have heartily endorsed.

Keefe no doubt was especially pleased to be recognized by *House & Garden*, which was more stylish than *Your Home* or *American Home*. In 1932 *House & Garden* requested biographical information and a snapshot of Keefe, both of which he happily provided. (The snapshot was taken by sister Celeste.) He considered this preface to the self-promoting paragraph: "I once knew a draftsman who would finish a drawing, stand off and look at it and say, 'gosh! that's good! I don't know how I do it.' This would make the other fellows wild. I'll be like that fellow. I'll now talk about myself." But he crossed out the passage from a draft, and gave a brief synopsis of his career:

An Interesting and Unusual Colonial Plan" for The American Home.

> Have specialized in country and suburban work mostly residences and the other buildings that go on a country place. My work is pretty well scattered from California to Massachusetts, most of it being near New York. Author of "The American House" a book on residential work ["mostly plates" crossed out by Keefe] and editor of the revised edition of "The Georgian Period," the standard work on our Colonial architecture. Member of the A.I.A. and Architectural League. Design anything that people ask me to do for a house down to a door stopper and like it all. Take my vacations looking for old houses and have trained my wife to keep her eyes open for good ones. Give her hell if she lets any get by. So in self defense she spots them altho sometimes she gets dizzy trying.[9]

Keefe's Bellows house appeared in the February 1933 *House & Garden*, but without his biography.

In October 1932 Rexford Newcomb, Dean of the College of Fine and Applied Arts at the University of Illinois, solicited Keefe for photographs of his two houses for Elizabeth Tyng in Palo Alto for publication by J. B. Lippincott in *The Colonial and Federal House: How to Build an Authentic Colonial House*.[10] Newcomb selected the houses from clippings he had gathered from *House Beautiful*.

Persevering during the Depression 141

In the end, after referring to illustrations in *Architecture* (November 1930), Newcomb included both Tyng houses, the porch of the Norton Guest House in Darien ("an exquisite modern rendition" [p. 93] of the Federal period porch at Homewood in Baltimore), and the Farrell Cottage in Darien. The latter also became the prime illustration in publicity for the book—Lippincott's four-page brochure printed in red. Newcomb seems to have sought geographic balance between well-known Eastern designers (e.g., Electus Litchfield, Dwight James Baum, and Keefe) and lesser-known practitioners from the South, Mid- and Far West.

Travels

It is clear that despite the frustrations and anxieties brought on by the Depression, Keefe took pleasure in what work he had. As he wrote Ruth Meginnis of Reinhold Publishing, "It's fun to work at something one knows and likes." And by vacationing on Cape Cod, he was able to offer Grace and himself time away from routine but also a chance to surround himself with his favorite residential type. In 1931 he wrote a client (Charles J. Kittredge of Crane & Co.) about an upcoming vacation trip "to Cape Cod where there are some fine old houses. My wife claims that I only go places where there are such houses and I guess there is something in it." On returning to the office after ten days on Cape Cod, he wrote another client (William Rice): "I like those little houses and photographed a lot of them. Mrs. Keefe was along and after we looked at about two hundred houses or so she spied a man all bent over. There! she said, is a man that lived in a Cape Cod house all his life. The ceilings are low but I hope they do not effect people that way."[11]

A number of negatives remain in the Keefe Archive, probably from this 1931 vacation/study trip. Many are of turned fence posts, others are of doorways, and a few are general views of Cape Cod houses. The only clearly identifiable Cape Cod cottage has a sign, "The Wee Hoose Antiques"—it stood in West Falmouth according to a postcard of this shop. Negatives of the G.A.R. Hall in Falmouth, originally a Baptist meeting house and currently the Scituate Historical Society, were identified by Keefe as stemming from this trip and show that he was recording, as sources for his designs, classical porticos and cupolas as well as Cape Cod houses. Keefe's drawings of lattice in Provincetown, a 1750 house cornice in Yarmouth, and details of the 1690 Yarmouth Inn on Cape Cod—hinges, a cupboard door "turn," and the fireplace side—while undated may also stem from the 1931 trip.

Keefe traveled to study old houses on Cape Cod and in New Castle, Delaware, but there is no record of Charles and Grace making the journey to Colonial Williamsburg, the popular and influential Rockefeller-sponsored restoration of Virginia's colonial capital that opened in 1932. However, in 1936 Keefe offered to write a foreword for a booklet he proposed about the Colonial colors used in the Williamsburg restoration.[12] Keefe also had in his files an undated catalog, "Williamsburg Tapered Asbestos Shingles by Mohawk," with photos of roofs with these shingles at Colonial Williamsburg Restoration.

Retreat to Kingston

Keefe advertised their home for sale in the October 8, 1933, *New York Times*. It did not sell. Sometime that year Keefe closed his New York office and retreated to Kingston, where he set up a makeshift office in what had been his and Grace's bedroom. In 1937, when ordering back issues of the White Pine Series (useful for designers seeking Colonial motifs), he told Ruth Meginnis, his friend at Reinhold Publishing, that "since the depression caused me to close my office in New York I have been working from home but when things really get under way I expect to open up again." Unfortunately, his practice never recovered enough to justify opening an office outside his home, whether in Kingston or New York. When Grace's estate was appraised in 1973, the former bedroom-office retained two draftsman's tables and drawing cabinet units. Keefe probably met clients downstairs; Letha Gedney recalled the dining room used as an office. Keefe's situation was better than some; Joseph B. Wertz, a draftsman who worked in his small apartment during the Depression, published drawings of a drafting table he devised that could also serve as dining and living room table.[13]

While the forced retreat to Kingston was a severe blow to the middle-aged architect, Meginnis tried to reassure him that he remained among her "old friends" and that "whenever I am asked for a list of some of the best architects in this vicinity, I always make sure to include your name. Hope some good has come of it." Keefe admitted, "since leaving New York I have lost touch with many of the folks I knew and it's good to hear from them." He was grateful for being included on her list, and while he could not cite any work resulting directly from it, "jobs sometime come out of the air as it were and one can never trace them back." Like Keefe, Meginnis was proud of her Irish heritage; she described herself as a descendant of Lord Henry J. Monks of Dublin.[14]

Keefe's financial problems during the Depression are highlighted in the file he made while working to settle the estate of his brother, Dr. Augustus Keefe, a Kingston physician, who died suddenly on May 12, 1934, a year before their father Andrew's death. Correspondence in the file reveals conflict between, on the one hand, Charles and his siblings Andrew and Celeste, and on the other, their stepmother Mattie, over distribution of income from a house at 292 Washington Avenue formerly owned by Charles's mother, Celestina, and finally sold by the three siblings in 1941. The conflict, exacerbated by Charles being in debt, approached Byzantine complexity because of Charles and Grace's friendly relations with half-brother Robert, World War aviator and (despite his war injuries) successfully employed by Aetna Life Insurance Company in Hartford, while Charles and Grace disliked sister Celeste yet tried to be supportive of Celeste's husband, Adam Porter. Suffice it to say, Charles's family life was far from peaceful.[15]

The family's troubles culminated in 1959, after Charles's death, when his half-sister Eileen, a retired Glens Falls science teacher, committed suicide in the family home at 291 Washington Avenue. She appeared "despondent" before hanging herself. In 1952 she had written a poem, "Progress," lamenting the passing of Kingston landmarks, the Kingston Academy and Eagle Hotel, as well as open trolleys and the Skillypot ferry. After her death, a booklet was printed, *Poems of D. Eileen Keefe*, which included "For My Great Grandfather," with the lines: "But if on some magical carpet/I could fly back to old Lisneskea/To see the green hills of Fermanagh/I think I would ever say nay."[16]

Invitation from the Royal Institute of British Architects

Keefe, reduced to working out of his home in small-city Kingston, found some satisfaction in being invited by the Royal Institute of British Architects to have his work represented in the International Exhibition of Contemporary Architecture, which was opened in London by the Princess Royal on November 30, 1934. The RIBA was marking its centennial and the opening of its new headquarters. New York architect Julian Clarence Levi, writing for the American Institute of Architects on behalf of the British institution, requested from Keefe a photo and plan of his **Reginald Burbank** cottage and garage group. This consisted of a low cluster of white Colonial cottage, three-car garage, and two-box-stall stable around three sides of a courtyard in Dalton, Massachusetts. A pre-Depression work of 1927 and illustrated in *Architecture*, January 1929, the Burbank job was not an especially interesting or important work of Keefe's. He was certainly honored to be included in the exhibition, but there was a $10 fee as well as the expense of preparing and sending the mounted photos. Sending his $10 check, Keefe told Levi, "Times are bad with me but I'll try and spare that for it's worth it."[17]

Dr. Burbank, an arthritis specialist, was listed in the 1930 New York Social Register as residing at 6 East 78th Street in Manhattan—a five-story house he purchased in 1926—but he and his wife Marion also maintained the Dalton residence and supported the Pittsfield Riding and Polo Club. When informed by Keefe of the honor paid his work for them, **Marion Burbank** replied that "the garage group is spoken of by all who come here and the little cottage is far more livable than our old house." Brief notices of this recognition of a local man appeared in the January 4, 1935, *Freeman* and *Catskill Daily Mail* that were clipped for his file. Keefe understood that the exhibits would remain in London as "part of the institute's permanent collection," but form letters sent to him after the exhibition made ambiguous requests and went unanswered.[18]

While pleased to be recognized by the RIBA, Keefe must have been disappointed by the exhibition catalogue. His entry ("87. Cottage and Garage, Dalton,

Mass."), like most, was not illustrated. Worse, the text and illustrations celebrated modernism, designs by Gropius, Mies, Le Corbusier and others of the avant-garde so beyond Keefe's comprehension.[19]

In February 1935 Keefe told his English correspondent, James Taylor, that he felt "greatly honored" to be included in the RIBA exhibit, but that hardly outweighed the trial of closing his New York office and "trying to carry on business from my home." Keefe reported that in spring 1934, "93 per cent of the architects & draftsmen of the country were out of work," and now there were only "some signs of building starting again in a small way."[20]

Keefe was celebrated in the *Freeman*, his hometown newspaper, in August 1936 in its series "Our Neighbors Whose Fame Is International." Clara Norton Reed was the writer of the article surveying Keefe's career, and the abundance of detail suggests that Keefe cooperated fully with her. A long-time writer for the *Freeman* and active in Kingston's civic affairs and social life, Reed took pride in her home, the c. 1790 Dr. Matthew Jansen stone house. Despite a lengthy list of accomplishments—designing buildings as far away as California and Ecuador, exhibiting his work in London at the invitation of the RIBA, receiving two Better Homes in America medals from the Secretary of the Interior, numbering Lowell Thomas among his noted clients, belonging to the American Institute of Architects and Architectural League of New York, publishing well-regarded books, and having his houses featured in many magazines—Keefe still appeared to

Reed as "the quiet, courteous gentleman, better known abroad than at home, who goes about our streets, the Charles S. Keefe whose life has been a part of our city and county."[22]

A Maine Client

In May 1932 Keefe told a potential client in Maine, **George Russell Branson**, that he had so little work that he was contemplating closing his office, if he could cancel his lease. Drawn to Keefe by his design for a Dutch Colonial house in the *Herald-Tribune*,[22] Branson was a hunter and fisherman at Grand Lake Stream, a place renowned among sportsmen in remote eastern Maine near the Canadian border. Rather than employ a surveyor to determine site levels for his own Dutch Colonial, Branson saved money by firing his rifle at corner posts. The client, full of design ideas, clearly enjoyed the give and take of dealing with his architect, but Keefe worried that Mrs. Branson was not sufficiently consulted by her husband: "Remember she is going to use this house and if we can make her work easier, all the better." It was not simply a matter of saving housekeeping work, as Keefe urged Branson to consult his wife about how their furnishings would fit into a living room with larger doors; "Ask Mrs. Branson about this because she can see the furnishings better than a man."[23]

Branson flooded Keefe with handwritten letters going over countless details, paid for preliminary and working drawings and specifications, but apparently never built the story-and-a-half, shingle-walled Colonial house designed by Keefe. Branson enjoyed the process of designing the house with input from himself and his well-respected architect. For Branson it seems that having plans by Keefe was almost as good as having the completed house: "Whether I am ever able to build . . . or not I will I am sure have a set of plans to be proud of." Never confident that he had sufficient funds to build, Branson did understand that Keefe was spending considerable time on the project, so, without being billed, he sent Keefe $100, knowing he was being "very unbusinesslike." In his last known letter to Keefe, Branson reported that a Portland contractor estimated the house would cost $14,600, much beyond Branson's expectation, but he would try other contractors and perhaps "personally drive a nail here & there."[24]

A Depression-Era Connecticut House

Despite the hard economic times, **Ann MacMurphey** (1899–1976) and her husband **Robert Hyde MacMurphey** (c. 1895–1976) were able to complete, over several years, their Keefe-designed house in New Canaan. Ann had admired Keefe's house for Edna Brenchley published in *House & Garden* (August 1931) and was acquainted with her. John Oldrin, after his marriage to Edna Brenchley, drove Keefe to the site of the MacMurpheys' unfinished home.[25]

The very extensive correspondence between the MacMurpheys and Keefe began September 10, 1932, when Robert wrote Keefe expressing enthusiasm for

WEST ELEVATION

EAST ELEVATION

his Hutchins house in the September 1931 *House Beautiful*. Robert was a graduate of the University of Minnesota and was employed as a salesman to the college market by Henry Holt & Co., Publishers, often writing from New England and New York State hotels. Ann's stationery read, "Students Club House, Ten Prospect Street, Northampton, Massachusetts." This was a Smith College student clubhouse in 1932, but Ann's connection to the college is unknown, and Robert also used the same address. Not surprisingly, the clients wanted "plenty of bookcases, as we have a pretty good stock of books and will have many more."[26]

The MacMurphey house was designed in 1932-33, although only the two-car garage (with pump room and wood shed) and passage (including what would become the maid's room and bathroom) were built in 1933 as a makeshift home. Makeshift and at first without heat, still Ann thought it delightful, "like a play-

Ann and Robert MacMurphey house.

house." Keefe and his clients took pleasure in coming up with names for the house, to be applied when it was completed. Robert told Keefe that his and Ann's names "are plain foolery, and I have made the very worst name of all, Topsy Ridge, for when it is done, our house like Topsy, will have 'just growed.'" In the abbreviated home, Keefe managed, despite the client's limited budget, to use Myron Teller's H L hinges on batten doors. Teller, ever ready to correct Keefe on his choice of hardware, wrote him, "Sorry to see you using H L hinges on batten doors—straps, of course, are the proper thing."[27]

Bids for completing the house were received in 1935. William Young, the low bidder, received the general contract. Some details were designed in 1936, and small photos of the completed house were published in the April 1938 *House & Garden*. It stands, much altered, at 177 Chichester Road in New Canaan. Although a neighbor objected vehemently to the siting of the house near the property line, the delay in completion was mainly caused by the client's financial struggles during the Depression. Keefe, with such troubles of his own, tried to assure MacMurphey that there was "some hope ahead"; he had "thought all the draftsmen are dead," but one "startled" Keefe by coming into the office and asking for a job.[28]

The main house, added to the service wing, was a Cape Cod with central chimney and two small dormer windows on the façade. The first-floor plan called for a large living room, which incorporated a dining area since there was no dining room, following Keefe's theory that childless couples favored open plans. A guest bedroom was also on the first story. Preliminary plans dated September 21, 1932, included two bedrooms on the second story. The couple soon asked for an "upstairs library" that could become a bedroom were they to sell the house. Working drawings from April 1933 retained just one bedroom—the other becoming the "study" with a fireplace (faced with black brick) and a built-in "bunk." Keefe, not a structural or historical purist, suggested adding "a couple of old beams partly embedded in the ceiling [of the study] . . . to give it an old appearance."[29]

The clients were conscious of compositional matters, for while the Cape Cod front was ordered by tradition, the rear elevation might be, and was, tinkered with. Ann told Keefe, "I am *terribly* keen about the sketch. The uneven, jagged roof line is far more interesting than the straight one, and gives the garden side of the house exactly the informal look we want. . . ."[30] Windows, including a bow window lighting the living/dining room, were asymmetrically arranged on the rear elevation.

Keefe and the MacMurpheys developed a friendship at least initially based on their admiration of his work. Ann visited the Crane Museum in October 1932 and found it "so attractive, and the setting so nice now. The leaves are colored which makes a beautiful background for the gray stone. I particularly like the doorway. It is so snug." Also fostering their friendship was the Irish ancestry Keefe had in common with both MacMurpheys. During the dispute with their neighbor, Robert wrote Keefe, in green ink, "we're not looking for trouble, tho there is Irish in both the MacMurpheys." Keefe maintained the theme in draft-ing for the MacMurpheys' enjoyment a humorous mockery of the French including their tendency to end words with an "e." In this Keefe announced "I ame IRISHE."[31]

Client and architect met over meals to discuss plans, and Keefe teased Mac-Murphey about his tiny handwriting: "I always wondered who the man was that wrote the ten commandments on a ten cent piece. Now, I know, he must have been one of your ancestors." Robert explained, "My writing got this way print-ing!" Both MacMurpheys found Keefe's comments amusing, and Ann replied in her usual large cursive script that her writing "makes up for lack of size in his, the difference being the legibility of his and the illegibility of mine." Keefe's own handwriting was sensible, neither large nor small, and legible without being pre-cise. Sometimes he allowed himself flourishes in his signature—notably bold cir-cles around the C of Charles, as in his July 22, 1926, letter to R. W. Woolworth or March 10, 1933, to Ann MacMurphey. The light cheerfulness passed into Keefe's drawings; he carefully titled one of his pencil drawings of the MacMur-phey house, "ROUGH BIRD'S EYE VIEW/NOT A CUCKOO EITHER." Ann com-plimented him on another sketch, "I love the little bird-house and the weather-vane on the last sketch!"[32]

When sending a check in partial payment of Keefe's fee (5 percent of the estimated $8,000 cost of the house), MacMurphey expressed complete satisfac-tion with Keefe's professional services and also admitted, "Perhaps the nicest thing of all is that we both like and enjoy you so much personally. You have made a terrific hit with Mrs. MacMurphey." (First names were almost never used by any party in Keefe's professional correspondence.) As work on the first stage of the house concluded, Keefe wrote the clients: "I have enjoyed working with you and Mrs. MacMurphey a lot. You are both most reasonable about things and have done your share in making what I hope is a comfortable home. If all clients were like you folks architects would have more hair and teeth and fewer lines in their faces. If you don't believe this ask 'Dad' Hawkins."[33]

Grace Keefe was to be part of the friendly relations. Ann provided nastur-tiums for Grace's dress, and Charles noted that "the nasturtiums passed the censor with a big O.K." The MacMurpheys, unusual for out-of-town clients, spent a weekend in January 1936 with the Keefes at their home in Kingston. Keefe took the opportunity of announcing (with pardonable exaggeration) in the *Freeman* that "work [is] now under construction to complete a group of New England Colonial buildings at the MacMurphey estate."[34]

Major Alterations to Houses

During the Depression, Keefe's house designs continued to be published in jour-nals for the architectural profession and magazines catering to readers interested in building new homes for themselves. Professional journals were open to including work from the twenties predating the stock-market crash and to alterations whose lower budgets made them appealing in the Depression. Among the latter was Keefe's complete alteration in 1930 of a nondescript house into something Colonial for J. Albert Nelson in South Norwalk, Connecticut. This was published in both the *American Architect* and *Better Homes and Gardens*, although the latter chose

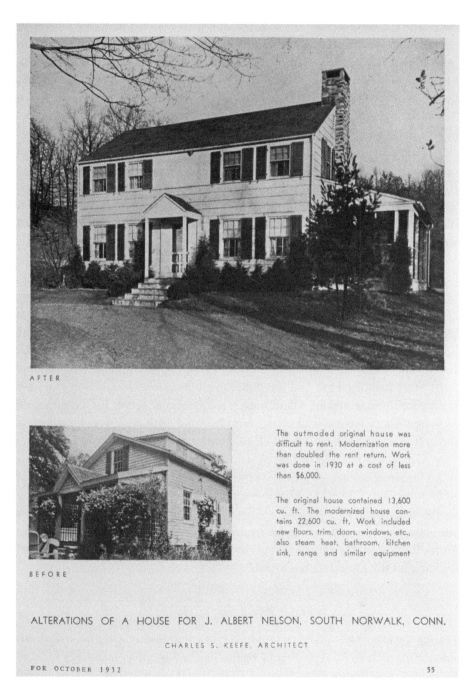

AFTER

The outmoded original house was difficult to rent. Modernization more than doubled the rent return. Work was done in 1930 at a cost of less than $6,000.

The original house contained 13,600 cu. ft. The modernized house contains 22,600 cu. ft. Work included new floors, trim, doors, windows, etc., also steam heat, bathroom, kitchen sink, range and similar equipment

BEFORE

ALTERATIONS OF A HOUSE FOR J. ALBERT NELSON, SOUTH NORWALK, CONN.

CHARLES S. KEEFE, ARCHITECT

FOR OCTOBER 1932   55

J. Albert Nelson house before and after alteration.

Walter and Millicent Hafner house before and after alteration.

not to identify Keefe as architect. Keefe explained that altering and enlarging the house significantly improved its rental income. Subsequently the National Emergency Council and Federal Housing Administration sought Keefe's cooperation in publicizing the Nelson alteration.[35]

In 1930–31 Keefe carried out another thorough and well-publicized makeover for **Walter Alfred Hafner** (c. 1897–1984) and his wife **Millicent Thornton Hafner** (c. 1894–1973), this one on Brookside Road in Darien and very near Tokeneke. Walter Hafner was a member of the Williams College class of 1919, but did not graduate with his class as he served in World War I as an ambulance driver and received the Croix de Guerre. When Keefe's client, he was in his family's book business, G. E. Stechert & Co., importers and dealers in new and second-hand books, located on East 10th Street near Broadway and with branches in Leipsig, Paris, and London. The commission came to Keefe thanks to the recommendation of noted country-house architect Frank J. Forster, who apparently was not in need of relatively mundane though not inexpensive alteration work early in the Depression. Walter Hafner's father, Alfred Hafner, was involved in the project, reviewing the plans and requesting estimates for a wing of stone vs. one of wood.[36]

The building subjected to Keefe's improvement was a large, c. 1900 frame house of no particular style. While Keefe was in the process of making plans, Millicent Hafner sent him snapshots taken by Walter of "the strange building we possess," as the clients thought "they might interest you for a 'before' and 'after' comparison." In fact the federal government later expressed interest in borrowing before and after photos for its modernizing exhibition. The "strange" elements (comparable to the "excrescences" of the Van Deusen House in Saratoga Springs) included the front porch, porte-cochère, and a bay window—all of which Keefe would remove.[37]

Keefe made the Hafners' home adequately Colonial, and so it was written up by Ernest Eberhard in a well-illustrated three-page spread in *The American Home*. Eberhard described Keefe as getting "a thrill out of transforming ugly ducklings," and the Hafners' new façade (its Georgian doorway crowned with broken pediment and urn) was said to possess "a really well-bred, elderly charm." The writer went further and called the arched window lighting the new staircase, "a dainty, almost a saucy touch," likening it to "the flirtatious gleam in the eye of a silver-haired belle who still retains her old charm."[38]

While not mentioned by Eberhard, the fact that the plumbing fixtures were in distinctive colors—white for one bathroom, green for another, black for the "toilet room," and yellow for the kitchen sink—must also have enhanced the house's up-to-date appeal. A "recreation room" with old-fashioned bar and fireplace was originally planned for the basement, but later omitted as the room was to have been below the stone-fronted living-room wing, whose construction was postponed. Concerned about the health of their baby, Robert, Millicent cut out an ad for Lustrglass in the June 1930 *House Beautiful* that promised to transmit healthy ultraviolet rays. She sought and received Keefe's approval to use this glass and to maximize the area of window glass on the east wall of the baby's room. Also departing from a standard Colonial Revival interior was a mural in oil on canvas depicting deer in a wintry landscape placed in the entrance hall at the foot of the curving staircase, apparently without Keefe's involvement.[39]

Keefe developed a warm, friendly relationship with the Hafners, no doubt enhanced by their mutual interest in old books. Keefe's plans called for a library, and he shared his copy of *The Month at Goodspeed's*, the well-known Boston book shop, with Walter. Keefe recommended landscape architect Wyntje S. Weidner to the Hafners, and in turn recommended the Hafners as "charming folks" to Weidner. The architect made lists of possible names for the Hafners' place, including "Hard Pan," "Ho Ha Farm," "Hafhaus," and "Mein Haus—probably wrong." He told the clients he doubted the choice of "Meadowlands"; while it "had a good sound and brings to mind the odor of new mown hay," it might suggest "hay fever" to others. A visit after the alterations were complete was delayed until September 1931 by the grave illness of Keefe's father-in-law. Then he sketched a loaf of bread and butter, and confessed to being tardy "to ante my bread & butter." After Keefe and contractor Young did additional work for the Hafners in 1938, Young wrote Keefe that, "Mrs. Hafner is tickled to death with the room," and Keefe replied that "she is so nice about everything."[40]

Pawling: Lowell Thomas and Thomas E. Dewey

During the Depression years, Keefe attracted two clients who were the most famous of his career: Lowell Thomas (1892–1981), the radio news commentator, traveler, and author, and Thomas E. Dewey, Manhattan district attorney and future governor of New York and presidential candidate. Between 1934 and 1937 Keefe designed alterations and additions to **Lowell and Frances Thomas**'s big "Colonial" house (built in 1827), as well as other improvements to their Cloverleaf Farm (or Clover Brook) at Quaker Hill, Pawling, Dutchess County. *House & Garden* noted that "when Mr. Thomas acquired the house he engaged Charles S. Keefe, an authority on early American architecture, to make this severe old house into the country home of a modern American gentleman." Rather than "tear out a lot of walls, muss up things generally and give the house a changed appearance . . . Mr. Keefe's main purpose was to improve and develop the form and lines of the old house. . . . The lines were generally good, though rather severe and plain, perhaps like the old Quaker who had originally built years before."

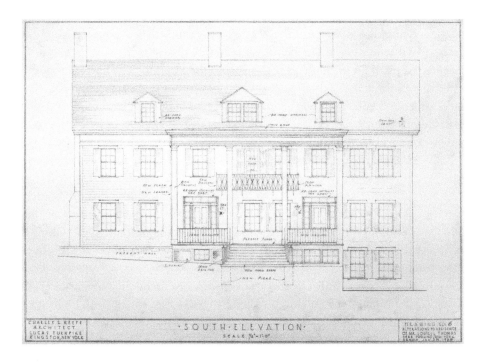

Lowell and Frances Thomas house.

Keefe regraded the ground adjacent to one side of the house to conceal the lowest of four stories and so better its proportions. He also created a dining terrace and added a bay window, as well as half-columns to severe doorways. Most striking was his replacement of a small porch with a two-story portico on the south or garden façade, with Keefe's usual slender and simple shafts—here, square piers. (The portico resembled that of the Charles Van Deusen house [1919] in Saratoga Springs.) From the porch and from the new wrought-iron balcony above the doorway, the view was "across the broad, tree-fringed meadows of the farm." In 1944 *Life* magazine devoted a full page to a photo of the Thomases on this elegant porch.[41]

According to *House & Garden*, the interior of the house as found satisfied the Thomases' family and entertaining needs, and so Mrs. Thomas served as her own decorator with only limited architectural interventions by Keefe. However, Clara Norton Reed reported in the *Freeman*, probably on the basis of a conversation with Keefe, that the upper floor of the main house "has been converted into a work room with a great fire-place at either end, for Mr. Thomas. Here he has gathered together his most interesting and priceless trophies of his world wanderings. . . . the basement has been fitted up as a ship and here the host entertains his celebrated friends."[42] Further, Elsie Sloan Farley, Interior Decorator, at 435 Park Avenue, wrote Keefe, April 13, 1937, that Mrs. Lowell Thomas had been in to see her about the Pawling house.

Keefe told the *Freeman* that he had designed for Thomas "on his farm . . . a large out-door grill, beer well, large service tables and a semi-circular arrangement for guests or an entertainment band. . . . Mr. Keefe also designed the Saints and Sinners softball diamond adjoining the Thomas fur farm. There one finds a novel pop stand and above it a platform for Fox Movietone News cameramen . . . a group of bleachers and a large clubhouse and locker room for visiting teams."[43] Keefe drew plans for an addition to the estate's stable, alterations and additions to its farmhouse, and at the main house, a library with (projection?) booth as well as servants' and "Duffle" or sports equipment rooms. An early (December 9, 1934) plan identified a "Tap Room" in the basement. He even provided designs for road signs and a key board with many hooks, lettered "Lowell Thomas His Keys."

Working closely with a celebrity of Thomas's sort on large and small projects clearly gave Keefe a sense of pride. When writing an encouraging letter to a Vermont lumber supplier who had been ill, Keefe closed with some homely (and not altogether cheering) wisdom from Thomas: "Take life a bit easier and don't worry about tomorrow. My friend Lowell Thomas knows an old Chinese saying that I think we all might take to heart . . . enjoy yourselves for it is later than you think."[44]

In 1936 Thomas undertook, with Keefe's involvement, the moving and subsequent alteration of **Aiken Hall**, erected in 1880 for religious and literary use; since 1895 the hall has been the location of Christ Church's interdenominational services. The short move was to a more elevated site that offered an extended vista of the rolling hills to the southwest. (The enormous boulder marking Thomas's grave is located just below the church and in the foreground of this vista.) The alteration and enlargement, which concluded in 1948, transformed what Thomas and his generation considered ugly "Victorian" into beautiful "Christopher Wren" or Colonial. In moving the building, timbers were placed under the church, and these timbers were then used in moving the house of Thomas's sister, Pherbia Thornburg, another Keefe client.[45] In 1937 Keefe designed a Georgian cupola with wood urns, cast-iron urns, and a copper finial for the hall, but the cupola in 1985 lacked these embellishments, and how much Keefe contributed to the remodeling remains a question.[46]

Thomas had acquired a vast estate at Quaker Hill with the idea of selling off large parcels to be built upon by congenial people. In a promotional booklet, prospective buyers were advised that a "master architectural plan protects the region against the unhappy eccentricities of residential construction which so often mar lovely countryside. . . . the heavily forested hillsides permit variety from attractive chalet-type homes of native stone or logs to comfortable Colonial frame." Keefe designed Colonial houses free of eccentricities at the Quaker Lake development, but he had no monopoly; the fall of 1941 also found Royal Barry Wills, the prominent Boston Colonial Revivalist, designing a Colonial house at Quaker Lake for G. Lynn Sumner, president of the Advertising Club of New York.[47]

In 1940 Keefe planned a one-story house with wood siding and stone veneer for one of the congenial people, **Glen L. Whiteman**, an AT&T executive, and his wife. The picture window is unexpected in a Keefe design. The *Freeman* reported in December 1940 that "Mr. Keefe is building a federal colonial home designed by him for Mr. and Mrs. Whiteman" at Quaker Hill, and the Keefes had the Whitemans as weekend guests and entertained them "at a small dinner."

Mr. and Mrs. Glen Whiteman house.

Thomas recommended Keefe to **Edwin M. Whitney**, NBC program director, and weeks before Pearl Harbor he designed a one-story Colonial for the Whitneys at the Quaker Lake development. This house would have a large, north-facing studio window lighting the living room.[48]

Frank E. and Ellen Mason were also among Thomas's chosen people—he was an NBC vice-president. Keefe sent them sketches for a new house in August 1941, but the couple soon abandoned the project. Frank Mason was spending time in Washington (during the war he was an assistant to Navy Secretary Frank Knox), and they could not justify the expense of a home far from there. Disappointed to learn of the abandonment, Keefe still encouraged the Masons to visit the Whiteman home. The Whitemans "were obliged to move about the country but at last they have a real home. . . . it will show you how an owner and an architect can work together to get the house the owner wants." Keefe also urged Thomas to visit the Whiteman home and the MacMurpheys' in New Canaan as part of his unsuccessful effort to convince Thomas to build additional small houses.[49]

Keefe did succeed in completing major alterations and additions to a house at Quaker Hill for Thomas's sister, **Pherbia Thomas Thornburg** (1904–80), and her husband, **S. Raymond Thornburg** (1892–1981), who were, however, less than ideal clients. Both were graduates of Ohio Wesleyan University. She had been a teacher and an assistant to her brother; he had traveled the world and would hold a variety of jobs in the oil, film, and rubber industries, as well as a stint in the early 1940s as resident manager of a camp in Pawling for New York City sanitation workers. Thornburg, known as "Pinky" to his friends, was credited with being instrumental in bringing to Pawling pastor and author Norman Vincent Peale and served as publisher of Peale's *Guideposts*. Pherbia Thomas, who had been married previously, was married to Thornburg in Akin Hall or Christ Church in 1936.[50]

Soon after the Thornburg wedding, Keefe began sketches to create what the Thornburgs called "Glenness" on property above Quaker Hill Falls. The existing large, vaguely Gothic house would be stripped of its Gothic elements and made over into something generically Colonial. The transformation involved moving the house 150 feet to a new foundation and adding living-room and library wings. Working drawings were completed in 1937 to create what Keefe called "a large federal-colonial residence" with shingled walls, six-over-six window sash, and two principal doorways, one with an elliptical arched fanlight, the other with elliptical arched pediment.[51]

The Thornburgs, especially Pherbia, were enthusiastic about planning their Colonial home that would connect to the natural setting. Pherbia at the outset asked for a house that would "'snuggle' into the hillside—and ramble—Not stand up too high." Her architect often had expressed just such an ambition to keep his houses low. But Pherbia noted in the same letter that, "In the last House & Garden there is a Mount Vernon porch with slender pillars that appeals to us.

Pherbia and Raymond Thornburg house.

Do you think this kind of a porch would be in keeping?" and she sent Keefe her crude pencil sketch of a two-story Georgian façade with six pillars, not conducive to snuggling into the hillside. Keefe wanted to please his clients, including Lowell Thomas who had a key role in the Thornburg project and had added such a porch to his own house, and so the architect designed a six-column porch for the west façade of the living-room addition. "To avoid getting the west front too high in the air," Keefe advised "cutting back into the bank at the front to secure a level space for the drive."[52]

Pherbia clipped and mounted for Keefe pictures of new Colonial houses and their exterior and interior details. The house must be Colonial, but she also wanted to take advantage of views of "our valley," urging "'picture' windows" for the library and dining room; "I have a feeling that a great plate glass window would be like framing an ever changing painting." Still, she was concerned that Keefe might feel picture windows would not "be in keeping with the design of the house." She acknowledged that building the house was one of the major "adventures" of their lives, and so they were including it in a "log" of such adventures. She asked Keefe to return for the log "the first crude sketch that we made and sent you." Later Keefe sent the Thornburgs drawings of their house, which Raymond acknowledged "are beautiful—absolutely perfect for the log."[53]

Pherbia's desire for outsized or bay windows eventually met resistance from Keefe after she urged him to allow a small bay window in an alcove off the living room, "something similar to the little room off of the dining room at Clover Brook," her brother's home. "Or make one like the picture you showed me of your [Bellows?] house in Conn.—where the window was also small panes—and only slightly bowed." Keefe replied: "Now about the window in the alcove. This is to be a single large window. . . . I believe we have enough bays and large windows now. Let's have one room that wont be very open." However, as late as April 1946, a few months before his death, Keefe designed two "picture windows" as alterations to the living room.[54]

In April 1937 Keefe wrote Raymond Thornburg, who was chronically late paying his architect and contractors, asking to be paid his fee but also sending a circular for New Castle Day in Delaware. "You are interested in fine old houses so if you can find the time I suggest your going." Keefe wrote later that he himself would be spending the May weekend in New Castle seeing the old houses. The next month Pherbia was touring the South and wrote Keefe that she was eager to visit Colonial Williamsburg "where I want to make a close inspection of colors and ideas for our house. . . . We can hardly wait to see our house—nothing along the way can compare to our view and house." From Williamsburg Pherbia sent Keefe a postcard of the Raleigh Tavern: "This is one of the charming towns— of any country. The more we explore Williamsburg the more we love the plans of our house—they even use the same door knobs you selected. We do wish you were here with us."[55]

Pherbia paid close attention to details from door knobs to linoleum, and also tiles for the dining-room fireplace, after Keefe persuaded her to have tile rather than brick facing. She selected twenty tiles of Dutch polychromed flower baskets at C. H. Vanderlaan, Inc., in New York soon after her Williamsburg visit. However, the interior would not be wholly Colonial. Reflecting their experience as world travelers, a small Buddha statue was placed in an Oriental-style niche designed by Keefe for the living-room alcove.[56]

In 1938 Glenness was completed, and that year the Thornburgs' daughter Pherbia was born. Keefe was charmed by little Pherbia: "The baby is a grand young lady. These 1939 models are certainly the best yet."[57]

As the project came to its conclusion, Raymond Thornburg wrote Keefe in May 1938 that they liked its "simplicity" and would change nothing. "Many people comment on the beauty and thoughtfulness in the details. In the course of a year or so the planting will have grown into its place and the house will look as if it had been on its hillside perch for a long period of time." But working for the Thornburgs had been difficult for Keefe. Raymond had caused a good deal of trouble with late payments, and he and Pherbia with complaints over minor flaws in construction. Keefe admired the workmanship of William Young of Darien, contractor for the Thornburg house and other Keefe projects, who confided in Keefe about the difficulty of pleasing the Thornburgs, in contrast to

Oldrin and Hafner; "What a difference there is in people." Keefe was sympathetic, writing Young, "It's alright to do all you can for folks that appreciate your work and pay you when the bills are due but why put yourself out for someone that does neither."[58]

Whatever their feelings about Keefe's and Young's work, the Thornburgs were not averse to publicity for their house, and therefore for themselves. Thornburg told Keefe: "We hope we can be of some value to you—that from our house others will be inspired to do likewise. If we can be of service, let us know what we can do." Keefe delayed his reply, citing time spent on a competition and work in Connecticut, Massachusetts, and New Hampshire. He acknowledged that he was "proud of your house and tried not to neglect any little detail needed to make it right, "while politely assuring the clients that their "good taste" had been essential to his success.[59] For reasons unknown, Keefe never published the Thornburg house.

The Thornburg property included what the *Freeman*, from an interview with Keefe, described as "one of the most wildly beautiful glens in Dutchess County. At the head of the gorge is a stream which tumbles almost shearly for about 40 or 50 feet." The Thornburgs and Thomas were interested in erecting a water-powered gristmill at the head of the falls, which local lore suggested had been the site of a mill in Revolutionary times. At first the idea was to grind grain and generate electricity, but the latter function was soon dropped. The mill, with its large overshot wheel, "will grind the grain for the present squires and farmers of Quaker Hill." The mill would be something of an adult plaything, in the spirit of Lowell Thomas's grounds, and might also have a "place for supper."[60]

In December 1936 Keefe sent an inquiry to the Fitz Water Wheel Company of Hanover, Pennsylvania, "builders of overshoot water wheels since 1840." Fitz had completed installations at Henry Ford's Wayside Inn in Massachusetts, Rock Creek Park in Washington for Harold Ickes, and the Wheatsworth Gingerbread House in New Jersey. Keefe told John S. Fitz that while there remained an old mill dam with a good fall of water, no trace remained of the Revolutionary-era mill: "I will arrange to design the exterior for we want it to appear like an old time wooden grist mill. In your country [Pennsylvania] the old mills were often of stone but in this section they were generally wooden structures." At the end of the year Keefe met Fitz in Poughkeepsie and drove him to inspect the site and determine the location of the wheel and mill. Keefe was no old mill expert, but he gamely offered to visit two he had heard were near Kingston.[61]

Fitz produced a blueprint for the Thornburg mill in March 1937, but the correspondence indicates that Lowell Thomas was the one who would decide whether or not to erect the mill—and would no doubt pay for it. The mill was still a topic for discussion in 1939. Lowell Thomas found an old mill that might be moved; Raymond Thornburg loved the idea and was looking into the market for flour and the possibility of making a profit. But mill correspondence ends in July 1939, and the next year Keefe was caught up in a dispute between Thorn-

burg and contractor Young over an unpaid bill for the house.[62] The Thornburgs'
interest in historic mills is confirmed by their monument, a millstone, in the
Quaker Cemetery on Quaker Hill Road (not to be confused with Quaker Hill
Cemetery where Lowell Thomas is buried).

Thomas E. Dewey (1902–71), Manhattan district attorney, governor of
New York (1943–54), and Republican candidate for president (1944 and 1948),
remains the most famous of Keefe's clients, although the work itself was of no
great importance. In 1938 Lowell Thomas, on the lookout for famous men to
add luster to his Quaker Hill community, was able to bring Dewey, "the rackets-
busting young district attorney," into the Quaker Hill fold. 1938 also saw Dewey
running, unsuccessfully, for Governor. At first Dewey rented Dapplemere Farm
and its "stately" white-frame house flanked by twin porches. The house, said to
be 140 years old, had taken on the appearance of a Georgian Revival mansion
in 1914. In 1939 Dewey purchased the property, a mile northeast of the village
of Pawling. Doubtless recommended by Lowell Thomas, Keefe visited Dewey's
purchase in mid-October to assess what needed to be done. Dewey and his wife
Frances soon concluded that "the changes are so limited, we can do them with
the help of a builder," but volunteered to pay Keefe for the time of his visit.[63]

Keefe took up the challenge and, asking to be excused for writing in longhand as his stenographer was ill, tried to convince Dewey to hire him: "Before I
met Mr. Thomas he was carrying on his work just as you contemplate doing and
my inspection showed me many things that were not as they should be. . . . An
architect's services are not a luxury but an insurance that you get the best solution
of the problem at hand and that you get what you pay for." Keefe went on to lay
out his credentials: designing houses from three rooms to fourteen bedrooms and
nine baths in eighteen states from California to Maine, and in San Miguel,
Ecuador. He also urged Dewey to seek opinions of Keefe's services from John
Oldrin and Mrs. Walter Hafner in Darien, W. T. Rice in Pittsfield, and E. Hope
Norton and John J. Farrell in New York City. Wisely, given Dewey's limited funds
and frugal outlook, Keefe stated there would be no charge for his previous visit.
Dewey for a time remained unconvinced, while observing, "you never need apol-
ogize for the illness of your stenographer. If I could write as clearly as you do, I
wouldn't even need a stenographer." By mid-November Dewey agreed to deliver
blueprints by his New Canaan builder for Keefe's evaluation.[64]

Relying on the builder's alteration plans, Keefe's drawings were apparently
limited to three plans dated November 30, 1939, for the cellar, first and second
floors, and drawings for a few details. Among the changes were a new bay window and terrace off the enlarged living room, as well as a "new service room"
at the rear connected to the kitchen. Dewey had purchased a working farm and,
dressed in overalls, he found enormous pleasure in farm work, apparently neces-
sitating the addition of the service room to tidy himself for life with Frances in
her "immaculate" stately home. A small porch at the front of the house needed
repair but, to save money, Dewey wanted it removed and the parts stored for

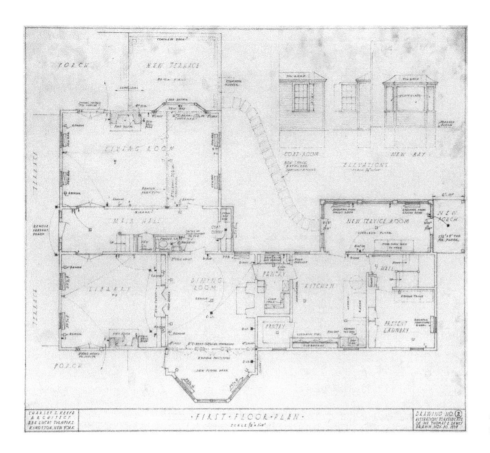

Thomas and Frances Dewey house, plan with new service room.

possible future reuse. To avoid antagonizing organized labor, Dewey obtained the approval of George Meany, president of the New York State Federation of Labor, for a provision in the contract specifying, "Union labor shall be employed in all of the work done to the extent that union workers are available in the Village of Pawling." Dewey instructed Keefe to insert this provision in the specifications, with the understanding that "unfortunately . . . there is little union membership in Pawling."[65]

Relations with the Deweys were good at first. He was prompt in paying Keefe's initial fee after the bill arrived with this unsubtle hint, "It's a long time between drinks for architects as you can see." However, like other clients, the Deweys were not hesitant to complain to Keefe about problems arising from work he supervised. William Young again had the main contract, and Keefe continued to hold his work in high regard. But Dewey wanted relief from "the pounding and creaking in the floors . . . all the money and effort that has been spent, is worthless . . . since it goes on in our bedroom in the middle of the night, it is not conducive to a quiet country rest." Similar complaints continued for months, until January 1941 when Dewey was sufficiently satisfied to pay Keefe's final bill. As a friendly gesture, Keefe then sent Dewey "a volume on the services of the

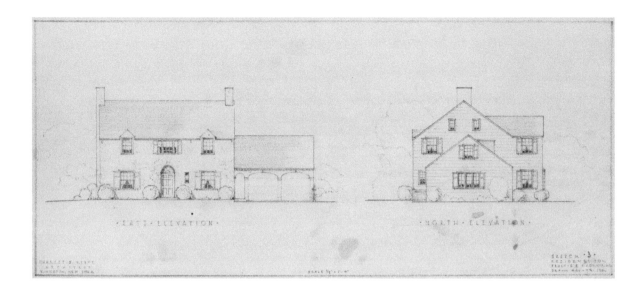

Metropolitan Police during the Draft Riots in New York, July 1863." The book was actually a gift to Dewey from "Egbert Beardsley, a friend of mine and, incidentally, a voter for you." During World War II, Dewey continued to receive Keefe's advice on heating and chimney problems, but the governor commissioned no new designs.[66]

Thomas's development of Quaker Lake, for prosperous and upstanding citizens epitomized by Dewey, represented the antithesis of Sanita, a camp located nearby on Whaley Lake where vacationing New York City sanitation workers were quartered in dozens of discarded but refurbished New York el cars. An effort had been made in 1941 to secure zoning for the Town of Pawling that would prevent the creation of Sanita and therefore "safeguard the Quaker Hill community." Thanks in part to the support of Franklin and Eleanor Roosevelt, the Sanitation Department overcame that campaign, and Sanita functioned successfully, with Raymond Thornburg ironically as resident manager for a time.[67]

Kingston

Keefe's clients included the rich and famous, but he clearly took a special kind of satisfaction in creating comfortable houses for men and women who lived respectable and useful lives in Kingston and vicinity but were neither rich nor famous. He designed two houses on North Manor Avenue, a neighborhood where noted New York architects Albro & Lindeberg were responsible for a relatively modest stucco and half-timbered Elizabethan mansion with casement windows for F. G. Schmidt in 1909. In the 1920s and '30s North Manor Avenue was a favored site for the homes of Kingston's rising middle class.[68]

Keefe designed 215 North Manor Avenue, a "federal-colonial style" house, in 1936 for **Francis E. O'Connor** (1899–1957), a physician, and his wife **Natalita** or **Natalie**. Born in Burlington, Vermont, O'Connor was a 1925 graduate of the University of Vermont College of Medicine. Dr. O'Connor was first president of the Kingston Athletic Association, forerunner of the Kingston Little League Association, and he piloted his own plane.[69] He was also a Catholic; were Keefe's Irish Catholic and Vermont roots a factor in O'Connor's choice of architect? The façade of the principal, two-story part of the house was given a stone (probably local bluestone) veneer, while other walls were of wood siding. The fanlight with lead eagle justified Keefe's labeling the house "federal-colonial style." The builder, Jay W. Rifenbary, kept snapshots of construction that clearly show the nonstructural nature of the stonework applied over boards nailed flush to the slender wood frame. Windows toward the street are limited, while the rear or western elevation, with a view over an undeveloped landscape, was fitted with a porch and wide bow window in the dining room. (Originally a two-car garage was connected to the north side of the house. Later this became living quarters and a new garage built, again connected to the north.)

Keefe designed the **Ella M. and Charles L. Arnold House** (1937–38) at 175 North Manor Avenue in the simplified "Tudor" style he had earlier adopted for the home of Ella's brother, Stanley Matthews, on Lounsbury Place. Ella Matthews (1897–1988) married Charles Arnold (1897–1981) in 1923; in 1936 she was president of the Junior League of Kingston. Charles in 1937 was treasurer of F. B. Matthews & Co., wholesale grocers, whose president was Stanley Matthews. Ella Arnold owned land on Manor Avenue transferred from her Matthews relations, signed the building contracts, and is named as the client on Keefe's plans, although

O'Connor house under construction.

Ella and Charles Arnold house.

Alfred MacDonald house. (J. Floyd Yewell rendering)

Arnold house, rear.

Keefe consulted her husband Charles when a question arose about the heating system, and Keefe sometimes referred to it as "residence of Mr. Charles L. Arnold." Both the O'Connor and Arnold houses were built by Jay W. Rifenbary (T. I. Rifenbary and Son), whose shop was nearby on Albany Avenue.[70]

The Arnold house resembles Keefe's Tudor design for the larger **Alfred J. MacDonald House** (1930–36, probably unexecuted) in Tenafly, New Jersey. Both had stone walls, casement windows, and picturesque silhouettes. For Keefe, the Arnold House's Tudor label must have been justified by the arched entry and walls of dark "blue stone" (a veneer, doubtless from an Ulster County quarry, of various colors including rusty browns) combined with metal casement windows and terracotta chimney pots. (Keefe marked an Atlantic Terra Cotta Co. catalogue as the source of the two red chimney pots.) The rear façade, with bluestone veneer below and wood siding above, was fitted with a flagstone terrace and screened dining porch oriented to what Keefe described as "a wide view of fields . . . and the Catskill Mountains in the distance"—an unexpected delight given the site's proximity to the city.[71]

In the living room, the molded stone mantel had a shallow Tudor arch, as did the built-in bookcases. The room's wide oak floorboards and wood beams might be called Colonial or Tudor, although the beams were so slender and sparse they appear as a decorative afterthought. Keefe had Paul J. Weber of Boston pho-

Arnold house, living room.

tograph the house; his photo of the living room shows comfortable upholstered seating, a radio cabinet in the corner, and only one framed picture—a print of the Doge's Palace and St. Mark's in Venice over the mantel, perhaps the gift of the architect. As in the living room, the dining room and halls had oak woodwork and plaster walls, "like old English plaster stained and glazed." However, the black fixtures in the powder room, the result of a change order from white fixtures, seem more Art Deco than Tudor.

Earl and Letha Gedney were young neighbors of the Keefes when their small (two-bedroom, living room, kitchen, no dining room) Cape Cod cottage at 60 Merritt Avenue was completed in 1935 to the architect's design. While an inexpensive cottage, it had features Keefe and his clients must have considered homey touches: a fireplace in the living room, visible ceiling joists there and in the front bedroom, and shutters with evergreen-tree cutouts. Earl R. Gedney (1907–81) was a linotype operator for the *Kingston Daily Leader*; his wife Letha A. Gedney (1909–2003) was an organist and pianist, a member of Kingston Musicians Local No. 215 for over fifty years.[72] In 1985 Letha Gedney still resided in the cottage (slightly expanded about 1960 with an addition to the living room) and recalled that Keefe had made a model to encourage the couple to build the Cape Cod design.

No Keefe models are known to survive, but while his office was on Lucas Turnpike he produced "Photographing Models," a two-page typescript, probably meant for publication. He described how to combine the model building with a realistic landscape by photographing the model outdoors with trees behind. He also recommended the use of toy automobiles from the 5 and 10-cent store and grass from cornmeal painted green. This lover of corn muffins ended on a sad note: "When one gets started on this work almost everything at hand can be made to serve. We used up all the cornmeal in the house so missed some good corn muffins as there wasn't enough time to procure more meal."

Letha also remembered that Keefe had helped the young couple get an FHA loan and expressed a kindly concern about the welfare of the household in general, steering them to Dr. Poley for treatment of their dog and taking an interest in improvements to their yard. On his visits Keefe enjoyed telling stories, including his favorite account of designing the Westchester prison with his personal escape route. "We all loved him," she concluded.[73]

In designing a "French Provincial" house and office for the veterinarian and city meat inspector, **Dr. Philip P. Poley**, in 1936–37 at 456 Albany Avenue, Keefe diverged from his customary Colonial or Tudor. The brick street façade became slightly French because of a front door frame with handmade pegs, casement

Earl and Letha Gedney cottage.

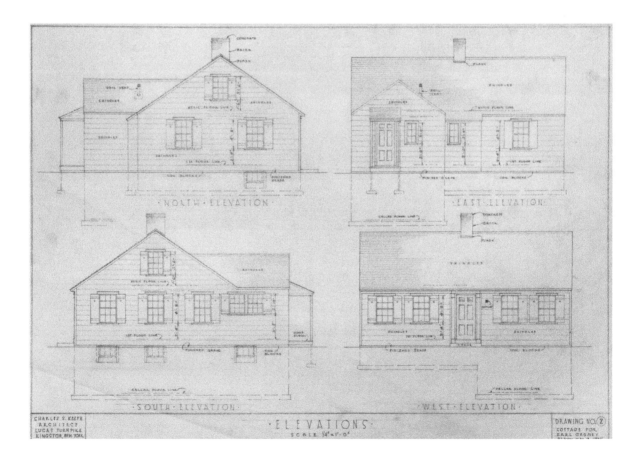

windows, and a panel of half-timbering (brick or plaster between wood posts) projecting on the second story. The other elevations were clad in wood siding in Keefe's usual Colonial manner. Dr. Poley was among Keefe's Jewish clients, but there is no evidence that this was a factor in the choice of style. A few year earlier, in 1934, a letter to Keefe from the *Pictorial Review*, apparently in response to a design Keefe submitted, commented: "The little French house is fine, but it does not seem to be anything you would do. I mean, we always associate you with Colonial stuff."[74]

Keefe's house with office for **Mortimer B. Downer, M.D.** (1896–1976) and his wife **Carol Hallstrom Downer** (c.1913–2014) is among his most prominent works in Kingston, visible from busy Wall and Fair Streets. Dr. Downer was the son of a well-known Woodstock physician who was close to the colony's artists and also named Mortimer Downer. The younger Downer attended the Ulster Academy, served in the Navy's hospital corps during World War I, graduated from Georgetown University, received his medical degree from Columbia in 1926,

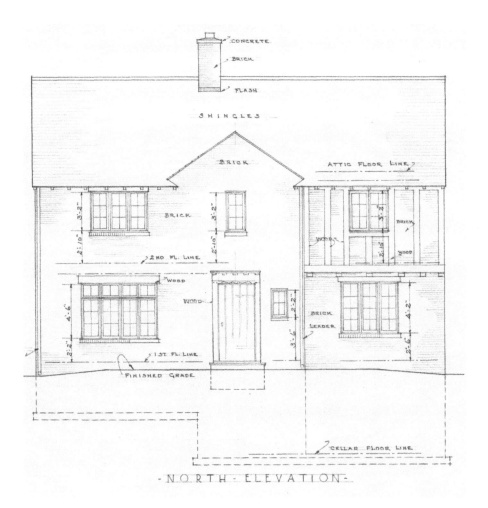

- N O R T H - E L E V A T I O N -

Dr. Philip Poley house and office.

Dr. Mortimer and Carol Downer house and office.

and became the first commander of the Woodstock American Legion post in 1930–31. As a Kingston physician in the 1930s, Dr. Downer was also active in the Lion's Club, but his widow stressed that he lived for his work as an allergist— he cared little about architecture or the arts. However, in 1929 the noted (and to some, notorious) artist Robert W. Chanler painted his portrait, a cool, Picasso-influenced portrayal of the young doctor wearing a blue necktie, with the artist's signature also in blue.[75]

The Downer house and office stands out as the only Keefe commission where the author was able to interview extensively one of his clients, Carol

Downer. In 1931 Mortimer Downer married Carol Hallstrom when she was about eighteen and he was planning to continue his medical studies in London and Vienna. Her bridal portrait, dated 1931 and painted by Carol Brooks Mac-Neil (1871–1944), wife of the better-known sculptor Hermon MacNeil, depicts in stiff profile a lovely, self-assured woman with white veil.[76]

When a young woman, Carol Downer appeared frequently in the *Freeman's* society or women's pages, joining the College Women's Club (having attended the New Jersey State College for Women) and active in the auxiliaries of Kingston Hospital and (with Grace Keefe) Ulster County Tuberculosis Hospital. In the late 1930s she was especially active as an amateur singer in the Musical Society of Kingston where her repertoire included "Home on the Range" as well as "Wien, du Stadt meiner Traume." Friends recall her adventuresome spirit and love of music and travel even as an old woman. In 1943 her thirty-mile trek when lost in the wilderness of northern Vermont attracted the attention of the national wire services: "Bloodhounds Are Used in Hunt for Mrs. Carol Downer, Doctor's Wife Is Missing in Vermont."[77]

When the author met Carol Downer at her home on June 25, 1982, she made it clear that she was informed on architectural matters as the daughter of an architect of Swedish background, Arvid Hallstrom (died 1936), who had worked in the offices of Howells & Stokes and Cross & Cross, prominent New York architects. She admired Keefe and the building he produced. He was "scrupulous about details," and while he tended toward being "an absolute purist," she recalled "his concept of the role of an architect, 'To consider, first and foremost, the wishes of the client and make them part of the workable whole.'" As a person, Keefe was "a gentleman of great sensitivity." The Depression had "knocked the stars out of his eyes," and he led a "hand to mouth existence in his last years." Grace Keefe, even in the 1930s, seemed "eccentric."[78]

Mrs. Downer dismissed Keefe's Kingston rivals as house designers. She disliked Gerard Betz's own house with its casement windows, dark wood interior, and living room with dropped floor—one step down and thus creating a serious threat of falling on her face. Keefe insisted, she said, that lowering the living room two steps would have raised a cautionary alert. Harry Halverson she associated with Cape Cods, "and we were not Cape Codders." But of course it was actually Keefe who was better known for designing in that idiom. She particularly disliked the small windows of Cape Cods with their "cottage curtains." Mrs. Downer considered her own home "Federal" in style, an apt term for this free interpretation of the Colonial, particularly given the overall sense of lightness of the two-story house and its low hipped roof.

Designed in 1938, photos of the completed house are dated 1939. The lot at 55 Fair Street (or 207 Henry Street) is unusually prominent, for while the main or south façade faces Henry Street, the sides of the house lie along Wall and Fair Streets, key thoroughfares. In exhibiting photos of the house, Keefe described this as a "problem," meaning it "had to appear well from all points." The architect also had to arrange the plan so that the doctor's office was integrated with the house while maintaining privacy for both functions. The Downers had no children, but Carol's mother, Francesca Neander Hallstrom, was assigned a bedroom in Keefe's plans.

Carol Downer took credit for the large window in the dining room and tall (French) window in the living room. The small porthole window in the second story in an alternate scheme (of Regency character) for the façade horrified her. She favored the curve of the staircase, though the soaked plywood for the wall below the staircase broke on the first try. Keefe commissioned a photo of the entrance hall and staircase, whose handrail and posts were very slender. Stars, interestingly, made up the pattern of the floor covering. Near the foot of the staircase and by the front door was a demilune table whose legs were also slender, indicating an attempt to coordinate architecture and furniture within the Federal style. Hanging above the table was an embroidered sampler of a garden with thin young couple in Colonial garb and the saying, "TURN ALWAYS TOWARDS THE SUNSHINE AND SHADOWS WILL ALWAYS FALL BEHIND YOU."[79]

The small kitchen with no eating area conformed to Mrs. Downer's idea that one should eat in the dining room. Keefe chose in New York the old Dutch painted tiles for the living-room fireplace. She found the attached garage convenient, but was annoyed by patients ringing the bell after hours—not Keefe's fault. Her only complaint attributable to her architect was his choice of roll screens inside the windows.

Downer house, entrance hall and staircase.

Olive M. Marsh (1903–95) was a Kingston elementary schoolteacher, trained at New Paltz Normal School. In 1985 when the author corresponded with her and spoke with her on the phone, she was pleased to help with information and wrote (with perfect penmanship), "I am glad to know that you are making a study of the career of Mr. Charles S. Keefe. I thought he was a very fine man." Miss Marsh was fully engaged with her community. The *Freeman* noted in 1921 that she appeared as a "maiden" at Kingston High School's May Day exercises and later mentioned her acting as a chaperone on a Girl Scout hike, serving on a PTA committee, and singing with YWCA and Clinton Ave. Methodist groups. She was also active in the New York State and Ulster County Teachers Associations and, according to her obituary, she was "an avid painter."[80]

In 1937 Marsh and two women friends from Kingston schools vacationed on Cape Cod, while the following Easter she and one of them spent the holiday at Williamsburg, Virginia.[81] No doubt these travels to Cape Cod and Williamsburg were signs of her interest in Colonial traditions. Marsh was introduced to Keefe by Kathleen Shurter, a school nurse who knew the Keefes and had read about him in the *Freeman*. Further, Olive's mother Ina, who lived with her, liked a California house by Keefe that she had seen in a magazine. Olive recalled that Keefe's inclusion of laundry tubs at the back door, rather than in the basement, appealed to her mother. It was his first Tyng house in Palo Alto, published in *House Beautiful*, that had this feature. In 1939 Keefe agreed to design a smaller, less expensive version of the Tyng house, facilitated by the fact that the two women were not tall and so ceilings could be lower. In a preliminary drawing Keefe proposed a façade with off-center cross gable (as in the Tyng house) and small front porch fitted with a trellis and three-part concave roof. As built at 134 Madison Avenue in the Roosevelt Park neighborhood of Kingston, the substantial cross gable was replaced

Olive Marsh house.

with two small dormer windows, and the somewhat elegant porch was simplified to two posts supporting a shed roof given a slight curvature. A trellis graced the front entrance until removed in the 1980s when new siding was applied.

The house was designed in March 1939 and built between Labor Day and Christmas. It resembled a Cape Cod cottage, although in 1985 Marsh did not identify it as such. She was pleased and proud of her home, not least because of her architect's careful attention to detail and ensuring that the house was built within her $6,000 budget, including Keefe's fee of $375. Keefe, as was his custom, commemorated the conclusion of the project by giving the client a print, in this case a nineteenth-century lithograph of Suez, and he came to visit the Marshes and see their Christmas tree in the new home.[82]

Another small house by Keefe in Kingston in this period is the Colonial cottage (1935) for Miss **Berthe Parrish** (or Parish) at 41 Park Street, which she shared with her unmarried sister Emma. Berthe organized the medical library at the Kingston City Laboratory in 1950 after working at the Brooklyn Library.[83] Apparently as an afterthought, Keefe designed bookcases for the living room in 1936. According to Grace Keefe's 1954 will, "Berthe Parish" was to receive an onyx lavaliere.

During the Depression, Keefe's designs for Kingston clients were limited to residences. In 1941 he was approached about submitting sketches to a competition for an **addition to Kingston High School** providing for vocational education and a gymnasium. Keefe wrote Arthur J. Laidlaw, the Superintendent of Schools, that he would not submit sketches. In 1913 Hopkins and Keefe had been unsuccessful entrants in the competition to design the high school, and Keefe's reputation was based on his houses, not schools. But Keefe's reasons for not submitting had to do with the organization of the competition, which did not follow the standards established by the American Institute of Architects. He suspected there was a "nigger in the wood pile," as he put it— that the board of education in fact had already settled, privately, on an architect. "My advice (unasked for, of course) is that if the Board prefers some certain architect to go ahead and hire him. This will cause less feeling than the above procedure."[84]

Hurley

Early twentieth-century Hurley was essentially a suburb of Kingston, a little over three miles from the county courthouse, but it had a proud history of its own. Established in 1663 by the Dutch as the village of Nieu Dorp, Hurley retained its Colonial aura through the nineteenth century and even into Keefe's time, or that was the impression romantically inclined visitors promoted. Harold Donaldson Eberlein observed in his *Manors and Historic Homes of the Hudson Valley* (1924): "With characteristically Dutch conservatism, Hurley has slumbered on through its more than two and a half centuries . . . little changed in outward appearance . . . and tucked away . . . in a backwater past which the swirling eddies of feverish

American progress have raced." At New Year's 1917, Charles and Grace brought his colleague John Scarff for a visit to Hurley, doubtless to show him its venerable stone houses.[85]

Prominent among the old stone houses lining Hurley's Main Street is the **Van Deusen House** (begun c. 1720) at 59 Main, where New York's Committee of Safety briefly found refuge and a meeting place after the British burned Kingston in October 1777. Keefe had included a photo in his 1918 article, "The Development of the American Doorway," and he made several undated pen and ink drawings of the quaintly picturesque Van Deusen House, some at least intended for Christmas cards. In one unfinished colored drawing Keefe restored the front of the house—with 12-over-12 window sash, shutters, a Dutch door without the historically inaccurate exterior strap hinges a recent owner had applied, and none of the dormers that were also a later addition. In the street a handsomely turned-out woman is seen in profile, suggestive of the gentility and fine manners the twenties associated with the Colonial era.

Van Deusen house, rear.

The **Spy** or **Guard House** (also known as the Du Mond House, at 37 Main Street) where, tradition says, the British spy, Lieutenant Daniel Taylor, was held before his hanging in October 1777, was the subject of several drawings by Keefe. In one case he pictured an attractive young couple strolling in Colonial garb, in another an older bonneted woman with market basket, and in a third a svelte young woman wearing a long skirt and bonnet and holding a Christmas wreath (clearly a design for the Keefes' Christmas card). None of these represented the stirring masculine drama of Hurley in the Revolution. In a fourth Spy House drawing, Keefe allowed just a bit of "feverish American progress" to intrude; signs for gas and oil, candies and other refreshments announced the building's current commercial use. But in all these drawings Keefe edited out the

Victorian bargeboards and, in general, Keefe was part of the effort to maintain the Colonial appearance of Hurley even as the twentieth century necessarily brought on changes. In 1942 he designed a stone-fronted store in harmony with the adjoining Spy House, both owned by the architect's friend, **George Kent**.[86]

Earlier, in October 1937, Keefe measured and made rough pencil sketches of an eighteenth-century stone house called **Nieu Dorp** (after the original name of Hurley), at 66 Main Street, in preparation for a restoration carried out in 1938. His client was another friend, **Eugene Morehouse**, a retired state Supreme Court stenographer and prominent Mason. Keefe applied a fieldstone veneer around a frame addition at the rear of the house, substituted shed-roofed dormers for a nineteenth-century front gable and Dutch stoop for a nineteenth-century porch, and modified the interior with new bathrooms, kitchen, and a front room now designated "library" with extensive shelving. Teller's Colonial Wrought Iron Hardware billed Keefe for gutter hooks on August 19, 1938. *House & Garden* published the result in May 1945 (after the Morehouses sold the house) as a successful effort "to unify the design in the spirit of the old Hudson Valley Dutch original." The magazine also called it a "scholarly restoration," which

*"A Merry Christmas."
(Spy House)*

*Spy House with "GAS &
OIL" sign.*

In the Dutch tradition

SCHOLARLY RESTORATION ON AN OLD

HOUSE NEAR KINGSTON, N. Y.

Mr. and Mrs. Eugene Morehouse house restoration.

■ No one has been able to determine exactly when the oldest part of this house was built. The earliest record so far discovered says it was vacant and in bad repair in 1793. Just before the war it was bought by Mr. and Mrs. Eugene Morehouse who asked architect Charles S. Keefe to restore it and make it suitable for year-round occupancy. The plan of the house was not altered insofar as the main structural elements were concerned and only a few minor partitions were removed or altered to create a re-apportionment of the space. The exterior has benefited very greatly by the architect's skill in replacing anachronistic details with those appropriate to the original building.

The walls of the old house are about two feet thick and made of stone laid in clay and straw. The ceilings of the ground floor were formed by the floor boards above, supported by beams running lengthwise of the rooms. In the early days the occupants lived exclusively on the ground floor, the upper one being simply an attic or storage place. About a hundred years ago the owners needed more room and a frame addition was built across the entire rear of the building. At the same time, a gable was added at the front of the house so that the attic could be converted to useful living space. In the present restoration, dormers have been substituted for this gable and other alterations were made, as shown in the photographs on these pages, to unify the design in the spirit of the old Hudson Valley Dutch original.

BEFORE AFTER ▶

Compare the picture above with the large photograph at right and note how the architect stripped away the frame and clapboard construction which post-dated the original house, replacing it with a continuation of the masonry wall. The new section is veneered.

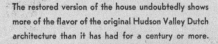

The restored version of the house undoubtedly shows more of the flavor of the original Hudson Valley Dutch architecture than it has had for a century or more.

▲ BEFORE   AFTER ▶

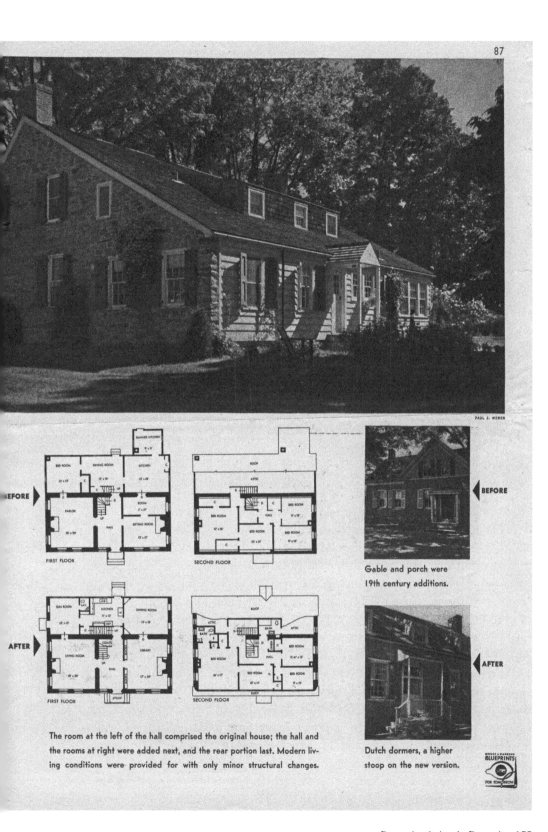

PAUL J. WEBER

BEFORE

AFTER

FIRST FLOOR   SECOND FLOOR

FIRST FLOOR   SECOND FLOOR

BEFORE

Gable and porch were
19th century additions.

AFTER

Dutch dormers, a higher
stoop on the new version.

The room at the left of the hall comprised the original house; the hall and
the rooms at right were added next, and the rear portion last. Modern living conditions were provided for with only minor structural changes.

HOUSE & GARDENS
BLUEPRINTS
FOR TOMORROW

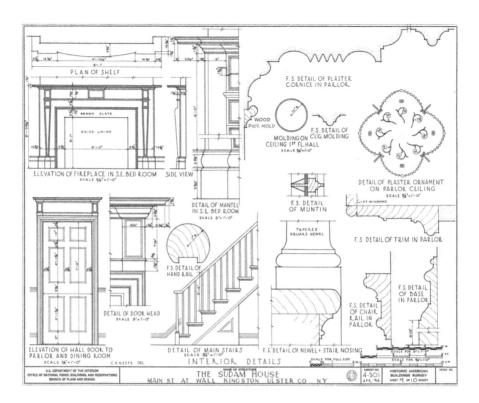

Sudam house, Historic American Buildings Survey.

was not a term Keefe would have used since his interest was in creating comfortable houses with traditional, but not necessarily strictly correct, forms.[87]

Still, Keefe retained the desire to record historic buildings, evident in his 1918 article on local doorways. In 1934 Keefe served as "Squad Leader" for the draftsmen making measured drawings for the Historic American Buildings Survey of the Federal-period **John Sudam House** in Kingston (currently the Fred J. Johnston Museum of the Friends of Historic Kingston). Keefe's "Field Party" consisted of Isaac Reuben and A. J. Kullman. While working on Nieu Dorp, Keefe used the *Freeman* to advocate preservation of the Sudam House: "The beautiful old residence . . . is one of the most outstanding examples of federal-colonial architecture in this section of the nation. . . . There are 10 rooms in perfect condition and they present an elegance difficult to match." Vacant and for sale, the house, Keefe recommended, should be purchased by the Ulster County Historical Society as its "permanent headquarters." Morehouse told Keefe he read his recommendation "with interest."[88] In fact the Sudam house was purchased and preserved by antiques dealer Fred Johnston in 1938, while the historical society was given the Bevier house in Marbletown as its headquarters in the same year.

A 1937 *New York Times* story, "Landmarks in Catskills," praised the Ulster County restorations by "the architects Charles Keefe and Myron S. Teller, both of Kingston, who, working separately, have done much for old dwellings." Keefe, it said, had discovered an example of "'leaded glass' . . . in restoring an old house," probably Nieu Dorp, but the "Dutch builder," lacking the resources available in the mother country, "had taken one-eighth-inch strips of hickory and had shaped them to simulate patterns common to Netherlands houses." Two months later the *Freeman* reported the same story and added that the architect found the Hurley restoration "absorbing, because of the unexpected problems and discoveries always bobbing up."[89]

The *Freeman* article, "Charles S. Keefe, A.I.A., Finds Small House Designing Thrilling Vocation," celebrated Keefe in what would be the most extended and laudatory account of his career to appear in his lifetime. (Sadly, it was accompanied by an unflattering picture of the aging architect in his home.) Lowell Thomas saw the article, and Keefe expressed surprise that someone had sent him "a copy of the Freeman containing my life history!" and noted that, "the article was entirely unsolicited on my part tho I was pleased to have it appear in print." While the article, like the *Times* story, was unsigned, Keefe identified the author of the *Freeman* piece as "Richard Gruver, a young writer who works for the Freeman and is trying to put life in the paper by using material that is different than the usual 'Mr. & Mrs. Blank spent Sunday with their son at Mombacus.'" Gruver undoubtedly also wrote the *Times* story, as his obituary states that he wrote about Catskill resorts for the *Times*.[90]

Richard Osborne Gruver (1903–67), a graduate of Kingston High School and St. Stephen's (later Bard) College, was city editor of the *Freeman* from 1936 to 1955.   Richard's wife, **Margaret Hunt Gruver**, was, as Keefe told Thomas, the niece of Franklin Booth, a well-known illustrator. Franklin Booth's brother, Hanson Booth, also an illustrator, had a stone house in Woodstock, and in 1940 the Keefes had a dinner party at Lisnaskea, "served on the porch overlooking the flower gardens," that included the Gruvers and Hanson Booth. While Margaret was a silversmith who exhibited locally, her husband wrote not only for the *Freeman* and *Times*, but also reviews of Woodstock art shows for the *New York Herald Tribune*. In 1939 the Gruvers lived at 311 Washington Avenue, not far from the Keefe family home at 291 Washington Avenue. Richard lauded Keefe as "one of Kingston's leading professional men," and the architect felt at ease in providing interesting details about his career for the young newspaperman.[91]

So it is not surprising that Keefe would be asked to draw plans for the Gruvers' home, a one-and-a-half-story Colonial in Hurley. Keefe designed the house in 1940 (Margaret was named as the client), and Richard, Margaret, and their three children occupied it in 1941. Keefe thought well enough of the house to mount its plans and photos for exhibition, along with a text explaining the rationale for its two bathrooms (the father and children left home at the same time in the morning) and the large windows of living and dining rooms (to take advantage of the mountain view to the north). While the architect noted that the walls were

Richard and Margaret Gruver house.

Gruver house, living room.

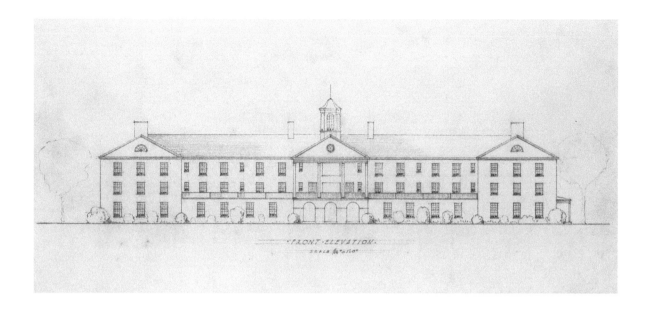

FRONT·ELEVATION·
SCALE ¼"=1'-0"

white and shutters black, he made no mention of Margaret's need for space for her craft work, and there was no designated studio.[92]

Proposed Convalescent Sanitarium.

West Hurley and Woodstock

In the 1920s Keefe had been associated with Teller & Halverson in the design of the Ulster County Tuberculosis Hospital on Golden Hill in Kingston. In 1938 Keefe made preliminary drawings for a **"Proposed Convalescent Sanitarium"** in or near West Hurley, in the vicinity of Woodstock. The client was **Edwin Burhans** (1865–1946), a veteran fruit farmer who also dealt in real estate. The proposed site was a hill composed of a mass of rock but "with beautiful scenery on every side." There was some thought of a facility with 500 rooms, but Keefe proposed a more practical and economical building of three stories and 72 patient rooms. Surrounding patients with daylight and fresh air on porches and in their rooms indicates the sanitarium was to serve tuberculosis patients. The Georgian-style central portico and cupola would have given the building a certain stately dignity like that of the earlier hospital, but Keefe's design was never built.[93]

While Myron Teller designed a number of houses for artists in Woodstock, Keefe did little work there, perhaps because he did not cultivate friendships in the artists' colony. Introduced by his client Eugene Morehouse, Keefe in 1938–39 designed minor alterations to an old stone house on Zena Road that was home for artist **Norbert Heermann** (1891–1966) and his wife, writer and novelist Elizabeth Alexander. Alf Evers recalled that Heermann "aspired to become a fashionable portrait painter," and this may explain the Heermanns' acquiring Hay Meadows, called "the finest estate in Woodstock"[94]

CHAPTER SIX

Critic of His Profession, Stock Plans, and Modernism

"A Famous Connecticut Yankee" in Pictorial Review.

Charles Keefe was not one to conceal his opinions about architectural matters, instead going straight to the point in personal letters, letters to the editor, and interviews. In 1914 he was not afraid to write James Dwyer to vigorously defend his Knights of Columbus building and make clear Dwyer's ignorance of Colonial architecture.

More significant are the letters Keefe wrote to the editors of architectural journals in the '20s and '30s that forcefully criticize those journals, the architectural profession, and the rise of modern design.

In 1924 Keefe had not yet had his work published in *The Architect*, an important journal, when he wrote a flattering letter to its editor, A. Holland Forbes, citing "the 'readability' of the text matter. . . . There is information aplenty but presented in such a way that one absorbs it without effort. Conversation with bright and well informed people is a pleasure and reading the articles in *The Architect* is like having a good old fashioned visit with just such folks."

But set against the readability of *The Architect* was:

the reading matter that is presented in many architectural magazines . . . the lack of interest displayed by most architects in this reading matter lies, I believe, in the attitude taken by the writers. So many of the writers seem to . . . make use of a choice collection of words rather than . . . be informative. They write things about a building that I am sure the designer never even imagined. To judge by the articles one would believe an architect goes into some sort of trance to commune with the Gods and the building they are writing about is the result. According to the best authorities sweat goes further than anything in securing results and so it is with the best designs. Of course this is too crude for these writers as they are a rather delicate lot when judged by their output. The profession would be better for fewer soprano voices and spats both among the practitioners and the writers for this seems to be the source of most architectural reading matter.

A FAMOUS CONNECTICUT YANKEE

Designed by Charles S. Keefe, A.I.A.

THIS delight of a house, erected in Connecticut, was the proud recipient of a medal in the Better Homes in America contest. It was entered in the story-and-a-half class. This means that the living accommodations are partly in a second story, which is actually a half story.

The object of this Better Homes in America contest is to discover and call attention to the best small houses actually constructed during the period for which the awards are made, and thus to stimulate interest in overcoming the faulty design and construction of the really small house. It is conducted in coöperation with the American Institute of Architects.

Mr. Keefe's house is a colonial, having five rooms, all of good size, the exterior lines being based on those of the early days of our country. The result is a particularly pleasing cottage which should readily appeal to those whose interest lies in the small home of really good design. The designer of this house has a national reputation for his houses of colonial origin, and it was natural for him to submit as his entry in the competition one of the type of houses for which he is famous.

The house is built of wood, with sawed-shingle walls and shingle roof. The blinds are solid except for the perforated design at the top of each. Each of the larger windows has twelve lights, and the entrance doorway, with its knocker and hardware, is patterned after those of the colonial days. The whitewashed chimney lends interest to the darker color of the roof.

On the first floor are dining room, living room, and kitchen. Off the last is a service porch, and in front of the main entrance is a small porch flanked by two attractive benches. The living room is 23 feet long and 12 feet wide, an exceptionally good size for a house as small as this. This room has five windows on three sides, providing three-way ventilation for the room. The inner wall contains the fireplace.

The dining room is on the opposite side of the house, and is

13 feet long by 12 feet wide. The kitchen is in the rear of the house and is so arranged as to provide direct entrance into both the living room and the dining room. This important part of the home is 18 feet, 6 inches long by 10 feet wide, and is well supplied with windows for ventilation and light. With an arrangement such as this, the dining room could, if desired, be used for a third bedroom, and the lower end of the living room could be arranged to include a dining alcove. The door from the kitchen would provide ample means of communication for serving if this arrangement were carried out.

The stairway rises from the small entrance hallway, which contains a clothes

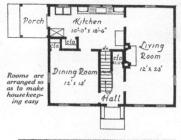

Rooms are arranged so as to make housekeeping easy

Porch

Kitchen
10'-0" x 18'-6"

clo. clo.

Living Room
12' x 23'

dn clo.

Dining Room
12' x 13'

Hall

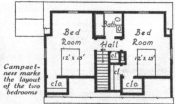

Compactness marks the layout of the two bedrooms

Bed Room
12' x 15'

Bath

Hall

cl

Bed Room
12' x 15'

clo.

clo.

closet, to a small hall on the second floor. This hall opens into both bedrooms and the bath as well, making an unusually compact arrangement of the sleeping quarters of the house. Each bedroom is 15 feet long by 12 feet wide, and is provided with two-way ventilation. Large closets have been worked in in an interesting manner, one bedroom having been provided with two. A linen closet has been arranged between the stairway and the chimney.

All in all, this house would seem to be just about ideal for the small family which seeks a home of this size and type of architecture. It is roomy without having a bit of waste space. Its room layout makes for convenience in its operation; its architecture is beyond reproach. In making the award the contest committee announced that the house "represents a fine handling of a simple structure, and shows good proportion and simple mass. The home will be easy to take care of through its simple, straightforward layout. The materials are of the simplest and well used."

This little cottage was built at Darien, Conn. The walls are white and the roof is green, the blinds being painted a lighter shade of green than the roof.

The carefully - thought - out planting plan provides a setting for the house that makes it particularly attractive. The bushes are well arranged and well selected.

It would be a simple matter to arrange an attached garage to this house if one were desired. Mr. Keefe suggests that one could be built adjoining the rear porch, leaving that there to provide means of access without making it necessary to go out of doors.

The interior of the house is also most attractive. The walls are painted a buff color, the woodwork being white. The floors are stained a dark color. Laundry tubs are provided in the kitchen, and the floor of the kitchen and bathroom is linoleum. A glance at the adjoining plans will show the complete livableness of this famous house.

THE HOME BUREAU

Forbes responded, "Naturally I agree with all you say! . . . it is good to know that our efforts are appreciated by discriminating readers like yourself."[1]

Keefe's objection to "soprano voices and spats" suggests he disliked effeminate men and fancy dressers who appeared effete.[2] Photos of Keefe show him plainly but neatly attired. Perhaps, too, this was an outburst from one who never belonged to New York's elite circle of architects, members of the Century Association and other highly selective clubs, or listed in the Social Register. The *New York Social Register 1930* included James Gamble Rogers, sometime associate of Keefe, as well as other leading New York architects whose work appeared in *The American House*—Walter D. Blair, William L. Bottomley, William A. Delano, Howard B. Major, John Russell Pope, and Mott Schmidt.

Keefe may have been favorably disposed toward *The Architect* because his former colleague James Gamble Rogers was Chairman of the Board of Forbes Publishing Co., the magazine's publisher. In any case, Keefe's letter appears to have had its effect, as *The Architect* published Keefe's buildings for Harkness and Norton in September 1926 and others by him in later years.

Stock Plans

Keefe used publication of his houses in popular magazines to secure new clients. *House Beautiful* published his Harkness cottage in November 1923, and the following May illustrated it in a circular to drum up readership among architects. The circular also quoted a letter from Keefe: "I have had forty-five inquiries from people directly interested in plans for such a house. The letters came from Oklahoma to Canada, and from Maine to California, plus one from Panama. From these inquiries I have secured three clients for houses, and these are not sales of duplicate plans." While inquiries were mainly from prospective home builders, a letter from an eighth-grade girl in Grand Rapids, Michigan, who wanted information about the Harkness cottage for an art project, so appealed to Keefe that he wrote her a long reply describing "my little house."[3]

Keefe generally disapproved of selling duplicate plans, believing that the individual needs of the client and character of the site were not well served by them. This he pointed out to J. H. Flynn, credit manager for the Malleable Steel Range Manufacturing Company in South Bend, Indiana, who not only wanted duplicate plans of the Harkness cottage, but wanted them at no cost, citing his limited budget and ending with this appeal, "Seems as though a man named Keefe might help a man named Flynn if he could." Architect Keefe was not moved by the plea from an Irishman and became annoyed when he learned that Flynn had approached Creo-Dipt Company, which featured the cottage in its advertising, for free plans: "I appreciate your desire for a good home just as you appreciate the desires of other folks for good ranges. The day ranges are free to those that ask for them will be the same day that plans are free. Be sure and let me know when that day arrives."[4]

Keefe was also upset that building material suppliers were selling inexpensive stock plans for houses, taking away business from young and small-town architects while expecting these architects would be "stupid" enough to continue ordering materials from these suppliers. He wrote *The American Architect* in 1925 that, "I came from a small town office, where moderate size residences were the meat and drink and the occasional large job the cream. It's all tommy-rot to say that the people of small towns cannot afford an architect's services when building their homes. If given half a chance to understand what an architect can do for them, they will employ one."

Moreover, he was at a loss to understand how the American Institute of Architects could endorse the Architects' Small House Service Bureau. This organization, too, offered inexpensive house plans in direct competition with small architectural offices like Keefe's, whose practitioners the A.I.A. was supposedly trying to attract as members. It seemed to Keefe that the A.I.A. was actually "limiting the members to those with large offices." The editor, W. H. Crocker, agreed with Keefe, responding that the Small House Service Bureau "acts to keep the men in small practice out of the Institute and it will never be thoroughly representative until it gets those men in."[5]

Keefe's low opinion of the Service Bureau was lowered still further in July 1930 when its magazine, *The Small Home*, published, without crediting him, a house design closely copying his Harkness cottage. Using Keefe's plan, the Service Bureau offered designs for both a brick and wood exterior. The architect penciled "CRIB" on the magazine cover and kept it in his files.

Still, in 1932 when the Service Bureau requested for publication in *The Small Home* photos of small houses Keefe had designed, the architect, desperate for work, was in no position to refuse. He sent photos of the Young cottage with garage and the Brenchley cottage, making sure that the photos and captions would appeal to people wanting to build but having very limited funds. In the case of the Young cottage and garage, Keefe had the photo cropped so that only two garage doors would appear with the cottage, and the buildings identified simply as "cottage and garage for Mrs. M. E. Young, Darien, Conn.," avoiding the wealthy estate terms "garage group" and "chauffeur's cottage." Similarly, the Brenchley gardener's cottage would not be identified as occupied by an estate gardener, but simply as Mrs. Brenchley's cottage.[6]

In 1934 the A.I.A. withdrew its endorsement of the Service Bureau, moved by arguments from members like Keefe.[7]

Pictorial Review and "A Famous Connecticut Yankee"

During the Depression Keefe was obliged to offer plans for sale both through the Architects' Small House Service Bureau and the Home Bureau of *Pictorial Review*, a popular magazine directed to women. Readers of the June 1933 issue of the *Pictorial Review* came upon full-page ads in color for Campbells' Soup, Ivory Soap, and Chesterfield Cigarettes, as well as a page with a detailed description and black-and-white illustrations of "A Famous Connecticut Yankee Designed by Charles S. Keefe, A.I.A." The text did not reveal that this was a cottage on the John J. Farrell estate, but simply as built in Darien, Connecticut, and "recipient of a medal in the Better Homes in America contest. The magazine recommended Keefe's design to its readers: "Mr. Keefe's house is a colonial, having five rooms, all of good size, the exterior lines being based on those of the early days of our country. The result is a particularly pleasing cottage . . . of really good design. The designer of this house has a national reputation for his houses of colonial origin."

By the end of October, Keefe had received about 167 inquiries, and he compiled a list identifying the number of inquiries by state and province: topping the list were New York (25), Pennsylvania (12), Wisconsin (11), Connecticut, Massachusetts, and Ohio (10), and California, New Jersey, and Virginia (8).[8] The architect composed "Letter A" to respond to the inquiries, and there assured prospective purchasers of the $50 package including three sets of blueprint plans as well as details of "the fireplace, mantel, stairs, dressers, trim, entrance doorway, cornices, etc.," and further assuring that "the plans and details are not at all like the usual stock plans but are definate [sic] and well worth the charge made."[9]

Keefe was keen to know how his stock plans compared with John Floyd Yewell's $12 plans offered via the *Pictorial Review*. (Keefe knew Yewell well as his preferred renderer.) The magazine's response suggested Keefe's plans were comparable to Yewell's, while the latter's specifications were longer.[10]

For some reason—possibly to create an historical record—Keefe carefully filed the inquiries, which came from ordinary Americans. One came from the president of Alma College in Michigan, another from the comptroller of the First National Bank of Houston who reported that his builder believed the bedrooms would be poorly ventilated in the hot Houston summers. Keefe tried unsuccessfully to convince him that Miss Tyng's second house provided a solution. A single woman residing in The Marlborough near Farragut Square in Washington dreamed of building "a tiny house . . . on a long, high hill on the upper reaches of the James River. . . . A marvelous view up and down the little valley as far as the eye can see. There are no modern improvements such as electricity, telephones, etc. but I hope to be able to get water from somewhere!" She admired a house Keefe designed for the Woolworth estate, published in *Small Home Magazine*, and the Connecticut Yankee. Keefe encouraged her in two letters, but Miss Hubard had no money to carry out her dream.[11]

A resident of Wapanucka, Oklahoma, asked about the cost of building in native stone. A young St. Louisan owned an 80-by-367-foot lot in the suburbs, and Keefe sketched his idea for building three houses on the lot. A well-written, typed inquiry on monogrammed stationery from Martin C. Miller of Cleveland received a detailed response from Keefe, including the suggestion that Miller and his wife commission an individually designed house as Dr. Lindenberger of Troy, Ohio, had done. But most inquiries were handwritten on cheap paper, and many were from women writing from their homes. May B. Murdock of Pleasantville, New York, wrote (in green ink) that the "tiny colonial cottage built in Darien" was "the most charming little place I've ever seen and I congratulate you on having such a wonderful idea." Keefe answered her question about construction cost but, as usually happened, that concluded the correspondence.[12] It appears that few of the inquiries resulted in the sale of plans, and fewer still in the construction of a house.

There were some inquiries that Keefe felt he should ignore. H. R. Rieger Company, Philadelphia, builders of cottages, sought plans of the Connecticut Yankee, but Keefe did not reply, noting Rieger was "evidently a spec builder." Keefe noted "too close" on a number of inquiries and did not respond when their writers lived near Darien, presumably to avoid offending Farrell.[13]

Still, some unlikely prospects caught Keefe's attention and he responded as if a sale and a house might actually be the result. Miss Martha Poindexter of "Ravine, Miss. Via Brooksville" typed her letter to the *Pictorial Review*:

> Have just studied carefully "A Famous Connecticut Yankee," its design and description. It is wonderful for such as I; however, I wonder if you could or have in the past, (I am not a subscriber) induced Mr. Keefe to give design of a small house in one story. I have a monthr and neither of us are exactly fond of climbing steps; we like all on one floor. . . . In my southern seclusion you may consider me very ignorant when I have asked such information of a designer and publishers as you and Mr. Keefe represent; if so, pardon it I pray, in my egerness for information without pay. However if you can afford this am enclosing addressed stamped envelope for reply.

Receiving the letter May 16, Keefe answered the same day enclosing a picture of the first Tyng house in California, with its bedrooms downstairs, and suggesting that a house of similar design might be built at less cost given lower labor and lumber costs in Mississippi. But there was no reply from Ravine to Keefe's offer to provide plans, details, and specifications for $50.[14]

MaPearle Williams used South Georgia Teachers College stationery to ask for information about Keefe's house. Apparently a student, Williams wrote that, "this house appealed so much to me that I chose it as my problem for this year in the Interior Decorating Class." Keefe went out of his way to be helpful, sending two "very rough sketches" of the ends and rear of the house and providing rare (for him) written advice on how the house should be furnished: "To appear at their best the interiors should be carried out in rather early Colonial. Simple Colonial pieces will fit in best. Folks that lived in such houses had modest means and lived accordingly. They had a few fine pieces of furniture but most of it was of the N. England farm house type."[15]

Keefe did sell plans to a few inquirers. Elbert C. Price was cashier of the First National Bank of Stuart, Virginia, a small town at the foot of the Blue Ridge plateau. Keefe agreed to include at no increased cost a drawing of a porch opening off the living room and prints of a garage. Price was conscious of the style of his house, asking for Keefe's suggestions for inexpensive hardware and lighting fixtures in "authentic Colonial patterns."[16]

John Hulbert, manager of a successful hop farm established by his father at Sardis, British Columbia, near the Washington State border, purchased the Connecticut Yankee plans for a site adjoining the hop gardens in what Hulbert described as "a very beautiful and fertile valley which is surrounded with mountains." He also sought Keefe's advice on garage design and placement, taking into account views of the mountains and "a bitter north east wind in the winter." Keefe sent rough sketches of the garage at no additional cost; presumably he was pleased to have his New England-style house built in remote western Canada.[17]

Helen Lane Thurston of Rockport, Massachusetts, purchased plans for land owned by her father, Henry H. Thurston. While serious inquiries such as hers usually involved extensive correspondence, Miss Thurston wrote minimally and never revealed that she was in the real estate business, renting suites and cottages at Rockport, a seaside community well known for its artists' colony.[18]

A young couple from Kalamazoo, Michigan, James A. and Janet R. Wise, paid $40 for plans and specifications, and Keefe sent detailed advice on minor changes to the plans as well as a rough pencil sketch of the garage in relation to the house.[19] However, after apparently consulting a contractor about the "plans and specifications for the Cape Cod cottage," James wrote in alarm that "we feel that we were somewhat deceived by the Pictorial Review article about the cottage." James now understood that costly materials and special millwork would be required that he could not afford. Keefe tried to reassure the couple: "Don't get discouraged. Evidently you have talked with a contractor that never uses any special work. People have a mistaken idea of the cost of a little special work. All you really need special are the entrance doorway & seats. Look over the details and see if you can use simpler trim. . . . You will find stock designs that will come close to those shown." Keefe, clearly upset by the accusation of "deceit," went on to defend architects, who, he argued, had "fought" to improve stock items, citing "Anderson [which] has now come out with stock window frames with narrow casings."[20] Since the file ends here, the Wises probably gave up their idea of building a "Famous Connecticut Yankee" in Michigan.

At least one aspiring owner of Keefe's cottage eventually occupied a Cape Cod, but not one as stylish as Keefe's. John W. Metcalf, Jr., of Brockton, Massachusetts, was in 1933 a recent college graduate and wrote, ordering plans "unless the price is unreasonable." In reply Keefe added to his form letter that he had no way of knowing what Metcalf considered reasonable. Metcalf then apologized, thanked Keefe for the personal letter, and admitted that "this is my first venture in choosing—anything quite so connubial. . . . I am so much pleased with prac- tically every detail of the house that I ask you to wait until I have saved up the amount needed. I assure you that I shall send for the plans at the earliest possible moment." Metcalf concluded the correspondence by praising Keefe's "apparent desire to keep the New England tradition prominent in the new fields of archi- tectural endeavor." It is unlikely that he ever did secure plans from Keefe, but by the 1950s he, his wife, and two children lived in a small, plain Cape Cod in Brock- ton that just barely recalled New England tradition.[21]

Competing with purveyors of stock plans was an issue that never disap- peared for Keefe, and by 1939 he must have concluded that his own production of stock plans had failed as a business venture. In that year he wrote a letter to *Pencil Points*, disputing an article on stock plans that suggested an architect could "help a purchaser of stock plans," when in fact "the whole idea back of selling such plans is to dispense with the architect's services, regardless of whatever hon- eyed words are used." Struggling to make a living designing houses in Kingston, Keefe argued that "stock plans are a matter of life and death to the small town architect, for the sale of such plans often makes it impossible for an architect to keep going." To add insult to injury, makers of building materials, such as Johns- Manville, were selling plans, undercutting architects, while at the same time urging architects to specify their products. Keefe could only conclude, as he had earlier, that companies like Johns-Manville believed "the average architect is dumb," for how could an intelligent architect support an enterprise that was putting him out of business. Even *Life* magazine, whose publisher also put out a professional jour- nal, *Architectural Forum*, was getting into the act, selling inexpensive house plans. Keefe believed the only way to fight back was to refrain from specifying materials and equipment from companies that promoted and sold stock plans. Instead, "use . . . other manufacturers that deal fairly with the architect. The Morgan Company, manufacturing mill work, does not sell stock plans and they say it pays. Why not others?" While not disputing his argument, the editors of *Pencil Points* advised Keefe that in publishing his letter they would delete his references to Johns- Manville, an advertiser in *Pencil Points*, and *Life*, as "we do not feel it would be politic for us to 'get down to personalities.'"[22]

Against Modern Design

In the late 1920s Keefe was profoundly disturbed by the influx of "modern" design of the kind later identified as Art Deco. As he had in 1924, Keefe wrote to express gratitude to *The Architect* for avoiding what other magazines were publishing—now in January 1930 addressing editor George S. Chappell. In addition to being a Yale and Beaux-Arts-trained architect, Chappell also wrote amusing books and, from 1926 to 1931, "The Sky Line" column in the *New Yorker* (signing himself "T-Square"). Keefe adopted Chappell's light tone in writ- ing this letter:

My dear Mr. Chappell:

I have been opening the envelope containing The Architect each month with fear and trembling. I was afraid some month I would discover that you too had gone 'modern,' but . . . these fears have been allayed. With the Architectural Record and Architectural Forum hipped on modern work and devoting most of these energies to it and the American Architect having become a cross between 'True Stories' and 'The American Magazine,' the subscriber to your magazine has something to fear. . . .

In the craze to be up to date, some of the other editors seem to have forgotten the average architect who after all is in the majority. Very few of us have a hoard of button hole makers after us to design modern buildings with more set backs and zig-zags than their competitors. . . . We are not interested in articles illustrated and written like the experiences of Miss Halitosis so popular outdoors but a 'dud' on the dance floor.[23]

. . . We go along working with things that have pleasant forms and lines and are happy doing it. We can see places where the modern work fits in well but it doesn't fit in with our work and may be we are pleased to have it so.

Keefe concluded with lines surely meant to appeal to Chappell, whose *Through the Alimentary Canal with Gun and Camera* would appear in 1930:

This is not from a fellow who has become 'set' in his ways for I am not afraid to try new things, for witness, my new teeth just received from the foundry. I rather like them for when repairs are necessary, why I go sit in chair and read while it is going on instead of listening to the hum of a drill and the command to "open wider."[24]

Chappell replied cheerfully: "I think we are in accord in our attitude toward the so-called 'modern' style. It is extremely interesting but I feel sure that many of its exponents are merely 'practicing', with the enthusiasm of the faddist rather than the serious interest of the student. In any case, most of it is rubbish. As for the decorative detail, much of it would be laughable if it were not so horribly permanent."

The editor-humorist picked up on the architect's paean to false teeth: "In reference to the new fangs, more power to them. May they bite hard and true and may good digestion wait on appetite. I am in the market for a new set which I am thinking of having made up along the modernistic zig-zag lines." But perhaps best from Keefe's point of view, Chappell invited him to submit photos of his work for publication.[25] The November issue had a fine spread of Keefe's Rice house in Pittsfield.

In 1930 the popular magazine *Your Home* was not pro-modern, instead publishing articles on traditional house design including "Just What Is a Cape Cod House?" based on an interview with Keefe. There he did not attack the modern directly, but proposed that houses should have a "pleasing personality" like that of a good family member: "they are individual and independent, and yet they belong to a recognizable type. We say of such persons that they have 'breeding.' They are built to certain broadly recognizable specifications, and withal they are subtly and distinctly themselves." Clearly by implication the modern house departed too far from recognizable types to have breeding. For Keefe the ideal client was one who had studied house types such as Cape Cod and "builds by a pattern, within whose limits he works out his personal preferences." This historically well-informed client could "point to little features all over the house and tell you what they mean and where they came from. He can tell you . . . why his chimney is situated where it is."[26]

Architectural novelty and dispensing with tradition may be said to have culminated in the late 1920s with Buckminster Fuller's conception of the Dymaxion house. In 1933 Keefe must have felt a kindred spirit when reading a letter from Stanley Cunningham, his former engineer-colleague in the Burnett office, condemning this futuristic project intended for mass production: "I suppose we shall soon all be living in 'di-maxion' houses or in some of the abortions that the steamboat architects are turning out, but I hope they will not all turn into engineers and forget beauty of mass and line."[27]

The later 1930s saw the rise of modernism in the form of the European-formulated International Style and the resurgence of Frank Lloyd Wright's residential architecture. The April 1938 issue of *House & Garden* featured on its cover Witold Gordon's illustration of a modern house designed by Perry M. Duncan, mostly in the International Style, while little photos of Keefe's Cape Cod for the MacMurpheys were hidden away toward the rear of the magazine.

By December 1938 the modernist slant of the *Architectural Forum* so bothered Keefe that he wrote directly to the offending editor, Howard Myers, but did not admit his very strong feeling against the "Modern Style":

Dear Sir:

I would like to ask a question, or, to be perfectly correct, several questions. Possibly some one on your staff will answer and try to set me right. Here goes.

Why do you publish so many of the so-called Modern Style residence designs? During my practice from an office in New York City and from my present address I never had or talked to a prospective client who was interested in such a type of house. I have questioned several of the other architects interested in residential work and their experiences are like mine. Most of the small house competitions published in architectural magazines seem to place such designs in the winning brackets. Please understand that I have no feeling against the so-called Modern Style, only a curiosity as to why architectural magazines seem to push this type of work when practically all the houses being built seem to be something else. Look through the suburban section of any of our cities and further out too. Also look through the pages of the *American Builder* and *Building Age*, a magazine used mostly by builders of small houses and the advertising pages of our metropolitan newspapers and note the type of house most people seem to want and buy. Some of these small houses are pretty poor in design but I have seen many that are very good, convenient, well-designed, making a good use of materials and with all the earmarks of a pleasant home. Are they wrong or are the architectural magazines wrong? From the sidelines it looks to me as if the magazines were trying to change the homes of the people much in the same way the crowd in Washington is trying to force us into a better life, whatever that is.

Keefe associated the architectural upheaval with the disturbing social agenda of Franklin Roosevelt's New Deal which, as a Republican, he would be inclined to oppose. Moreover, a request from the Federal Housing Administration for photos showing Keefe's alterations to the J. Albert Nelson cottage, South Norwalk, Connecticut, for FHA publicity seems to have been ineptly handled by the FHA, reinforcing Keefe's poor opinion of the federal administration.[28] The *Architectural Forum*, published by Henry Luce of *Time* and *Life* fame, loved controversy, and Keefe's letter with its forcefully stated architectural and political opinions was just the thing to stir the pot. Keefe then went on to cite the practical problems of the modern house:

> Here are some of the objections clients have to the Modern type of house. Who wants to shovel the snow off the flat roof houses and after all who wants to sit on the roof when it's hot. A porch or terrace near the ground level would be much more pleasant and cooler beside. The roof terrace cannot be screened and who wants to sit in unscreened places in most localities where the mosquitos come out at dusk? Who wants a square box, anyway? Another said, "I like to buy shoes in one of those shops and eat in one of those restaurants but live in such a place, never."

Finally, Keefe tried to show his openness to modernism for commercial and industrial uses, while opposing it for homes:

> We will all agree the Modern Style has greatly benefited the design of office buildings, factory buildings and business buildings of all kinds. No more piling one order on another, no more fat swags and plenty of goulosh to cover up deficiencies in the designers' minds. The Modern Style has stopped that but it doesn't seem to be the cure-all its devotees seem to think when it comes to the homes of the average American. He (the owner) may be wrong but after all he has to live in the house. Is he wrong?[29]

Editor-Publisher Howard Myers, a key figure in the campaign to advance the influence of European modernism and Frank Lloyd Wright in American design, himself took up the task of replying to Keefe:

> Dear Mr. Keefe:
>   Thank you for your good-tempered criticism of the modern house.

The reason The Forum publishes many modern houses (although by actual count we published twice as many traditional houses during 1938) is that there is not much that is new to be said about the traditional house. Magazines have been full of them for years; there are innumerable books on them in every architect's library. Nevertheless, The Forum will, of course, continue to publish as many well planned traditional houses as we can find, particularly if they show any refreshing note. In the case of modern architecture, however, and with particular reference to the domestic field, satisfactory solutions are only now emerging and we feel that in a period when this movement is in its formative stage there is every reason to report developments adequately.

I suppose none of us knows exactly what is ahead for the modern house but I am sure you will not condemn us if we take a little more optomistic [sic] view of its future than your letter indicates you do. We believe that there are many reasons why the modern house will prove increasingly popular with the public—chiefly because it, more than any other type of house, recognizes a new concept of living. During the next decade the home buyers are going to be recruited from the young people of marriageable age today and we feel that their attitude toward a house and toward living in general is not that of the home buyers of the 1920–25 era who made up the market during our last period of home building activity.

With reference to your remark about flat roofs, no screens and square boxes, these hardly seem to us to be the ingredients of a valid modern architecture. If they were, our lack of faith in it would match your own.

I should be delighted to explore this subject further with you if the spirit moves you to write again.[30]

Keefe was not so moved. Myers (born about 1895 and so a generation younger than Keefe) did not alter Keefe's opinion of modernism, but might the reference to young people and their "new concept of living" have caused a twinge of anxiety in the sixty-two-year-old architect? He visited the New York World's Fair, full of new concepts for living, but seems to have kept his opinions of the fair to himself.[31]

Keefe's letter was published in the *Forum*, minus his references to "small house competitions published in architectural magazines" and to the *American Builder* and *Building Age*. In his published response to Keefe, Myers condensed what he had written privately, then added that "42 per cent of the votes in the 'LIFE House' poll favored modern designs," and most *Forum* subscribers surveyed believed modern was "here to stay."[32]

One *Forum* reader, W. L. Schaeffer, advertising manager of National Tube Company (a subsidiary of U. S. Steel) in Pittsburgh, was moved to write a private, not-for-publication, congratulatory letter to Keefe. Schaeffer could not understand "why publishers . . . fill space by these excursions into the fantastic, notwithstanding the fact that human nature rejects the idea of surrendering the orthodox at every changing wind that blows. It's refreshing to see men in the profession exhibit the courage of their convictions as exemplified by your letter to the publisher."[33]

This small flurry of letters ended with Keefe thanking Schaeffer and venting still more: "I did not expect . . . [my letter] to be published for if I had it would have been much stronger. The architectural publishers seem to feel that they should tell folks what to build just as many organizations and governments are telling folks how to live. There is too damn much interference in other peoples' business these days anyway. But all the fuss won't stampede Americans into building Cucho cages when they want houses. It all bothers me at times but I find most folks pretty sensible and not prone to follow false prophets when it comes to building homes. Some day the publishers will wake up and get back to earth."[34]

Keefe, like most voters in Ulster and Dutchess Counties during the Depression and war years, was a Republican. He almost certainly never voted for Franklin Roosevelt, although in 1934 he had briefly participated in the New Deal's Historic American Buildings Survey in documenting the Sudam House in Kingston and the Bevier-Elting House in New Paltz. In 1940, with FDR running against Wendell Willkie, Keefe was admonished on November 4 by his client Ruth Taylor, a Republican, "See that you vote right tomorrow!" Keefe replied on the 7th, "We voted right here in Ulster County but we seem to be about the only ones. All we can do now is to go on, keep our fingers crossed & hope for the best."[35]

John Oldrin was likely another Republican client who enjoyed political banter with his architect. Oldrin sketched for Keefe his idea for altering the second-floor plan of the Young gardener's cottage for himself and wife Edna, noting, "copyright June 10th, 1941. John Oldrin—N.R.A.,—SAP—P.D.Q." Architects might append A.I.A. or R.A. (Registered Architect) to their signature as evidence of professional standing. Oldrin linked himself facetiously to Roosevelt's N.R.A. (National Recovery Administration), which was much maligned by Republicans.

In 1943 Keefe could feel privileged to know a leading Republican candidate for president, his client Thomas Dewey. After returning home from a winter vacation in Florida, Keefe allied himself with Dewey by reporting on Miami opinion: "The Miami Herald had a lot of good things to say about you until you came out for no change in the freight rates to the South. Then they acted as if you had cut some one's throat. Holding a job like your is like walking a tight rope, one peek right or left and you are off the wire. Your work is even worse than an architect's and that's going some."[36]

Just before election day 1944, with Dewey running against Roosevelt, Keefe received a printed letter addressed to "Dear Friend" asking for support and signed with a facsimile of FDR's signature. Not surprisingly, Keefe treated this request for his vote from "Your Neighbor" as scrap paper, making notes on the reverse for bathroom fixtures on the Morehouse job.[37]

Mid-Hudson Valley Architectural Society

In 1940 Keefe played an active role in the newly formed Mid-Hudson Valley Architectural Society composed of architects and draftsmen from Ulster, Dutchess, and Orange Counties. Myron Teller was its first president, and Keefe helped write its bylaws before being elected president in 1942. Harry Halverson, Gerard Betz, Albert Milliken, Augustus Schrowang, and John O'Connor were other members from Kingston. One of the purposes of the organization was "to advance public education in architecture," and Keefe earlier in the year had spoken to the Margaretville Rotary on "The Architect and His Work."[38]

The Architectural Society's most important educational task was putting together an exhibition of works by its members that was shown in Poughkeepsie, Kingston (at the Municipal Auditorium), and Newburgh in June and July 1941. Meeting at Myron Teller's Watson Hollow Inn in September 1941, the members decided to send the exhibit to the Syracuse convention of the New York State Association of Architects. In the Keefe Archive are panels with mounted photos and plans representing Keefe's Downer and Gruver houses that probably were prepared for this exhibit.[39] Keefe and the other architects exhibiting must have hoped to acquire new clients from exhibit attendees, but there is no evidence that he did, and the coming of the war apparently meant that the first exhibit in 1941 would also be the last.

CHAPTER SEVEN

World War II, Postwar Resurgence, Death, and Subsequent Events

*Col. Gordon and
Charlotte Reel house.*

Wartime restrictions on civilian construction—the April 1942 "Stop Building Order" eliminated private residential building unrelated to the war effort and costing more than $500—meant that Keefe had very little work, in contrast to the lean but still productive Depression years. And when there was a small job for Ruth Taylor in 1942, gas rationing made travel to Dorset difficult. Keefe felt obliged to buy "a couple of ales" for each of two men who managed to drive him to Manchester. "They left with the ales under their belts and only three eyes between them and I am still wondering if they ever did get home."[1]

Still, in 1943–44 Keefe drew plans for farm buildings at Furnace Brook Farm, South Shaftsbury, Vermont. The client was **Frederick Cecil Baker** (1889–1961), a mining engineer educated at Oxford and Harvard, a British flyer in World War I, and later an official in mining companies around the world before retiring to his Vermont cattle and poultry farm in 1945. More in the spirit of the times was Keefe's design for the **Fifth Ward Honor Roll** in Kingston. He made several sketches in April 1944, one with the tablet bearing names set into a boulder. Although the *Freeman* reported that the tablet designed by Keefe was dedicated in July 1944 on the grounds of Kingston's School No. 4, the monument on that site today differs significantly from Keefe's sketches. Nevertheless, his work on the monument is another sign of his commitment to remembering those who served America in the armed forces, best seen in his earlier American Legion Building. Keefe also contributed to his community in wartime by serving as a member of the Ulster County War Price & Rationing Board No. 2556.1. The chairman of the board was **Irving Kauder**; Keefe designed a porch for Kauder's New Paltz home in 1943.[2]

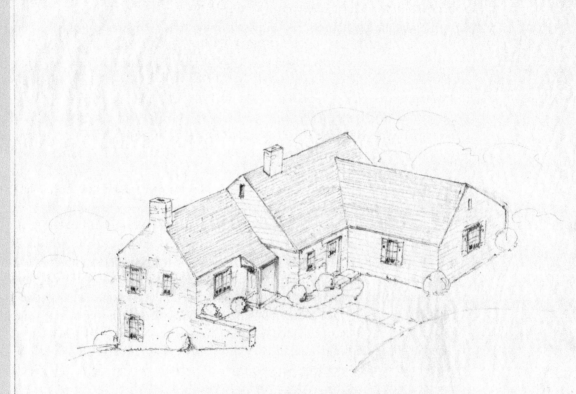

·ROUGH·SKETCH·OF·ENTRANCE·FRONT·

CHARLES S. KEEFE
ARCHITECT.

SKETCH ©
RESIDENCE FOR
COL + MRS. GORDON REEL
DRAWN MAR. 29- 1945

In December 1942 the Keefes went to Florida for the winter, as he wrote Dewey after his return to Kingston in April: "No building, because of Government restrictions, little gas and fuel oil made it seem like the right time to go away for the Winter, so we went. Mrs. Keefe has wanted to go for years, but my work carrying on thru the winters did not permit this before. This is the longest vacation I have ever had and the sun and change helped a lot. We were in Miami and Lake Worth until the middle of this month. By the way, they need a good house cleaning in Miami, such as you gave New York."[3]

Even during this period of imposed leisure Keefe remained optimistic about the architectural future, speaking to the Kingston Lions Club about "Architecture" from its early history to "post-war building plans."[4] He also had the time and proximity to make a detailed measured drawing of a "Pine Dresser from Trumpbour House, Asbury, N.Y. . . . erected 1743," two centuries later, on August 26, 1943. (The c. 1732 "Trumbour Homestead Farm" in the Town of Saugerties is listed on the National Register.) Asbury is in the Town of Saugerties, as is Flatbush, site of a proposed one-story Colonial house that Keefe sketched for **Col. Gordon Reel** (c. 1871–1951) and his wife **Charlotte Preston Reel** (1878–1956) just before the end of the war in Europe. Gordon Reel had managed a Kingston trolley line, served as state commissioner of highways, and then with army aviation in World War I. The Reels owned property in Flatbush on the Hudson, and in the 1940s he advocated cleaning up the polluted river while also proposing construction of a Kingston airport in Flatbush. Charlotte Reel had advertised as an interior decorator as early as 1920.[5] Keefe's drawings called for the use of old foundations and repair of an existing fireplace mantel in the basement to create "The Colonel's Room" with a new Dutch door opening onto the property's lower slope. Living quarters above would be surfaced with a twelve-inch stone veneer on two sections, wood on the third. Yet another of Reel's interests was local history, providing material for the *Freeman's* writer on Kingston history and lore, Sophie Miller.[6] The Reels' house, if completed, would have confirmed this interest.

With the end of the war in 1945, Keefe was nearing seventy and might have considered retirement, but in fact, after so many lean years, he welcomed new inquiries and commissions. Some were from new clients; in November 1945 Keefe drew plans for a large stone and shingle Colonial for **Ralph K. Ballard** of Kingston and Saugerties.[7] Others were from past clients.

Ever faithful **E. Hope Norton** wanted designs for buildings in Hebron as the war was drawing to a close. From May to July 1945, Keefe planned alterations to Bumble (or Bumber) Shoot, an old, story-and-a-half cottage next to Norton's house and directly on the village green. "Bumbershoot" is British slang for umbrella, so Keefe provided an outline drawing of an umbrella to be cut out of heavy copper or galvanized iron and placed over the entrance. In 2016 no umbrella motif can be found at the entrance, but the two pilasters flanking the living-room fireplace are both topped with an umbrella cutout as drawn by Keefe, July 10, 1945.[8] Charming sketches from the previous month for the cottage's

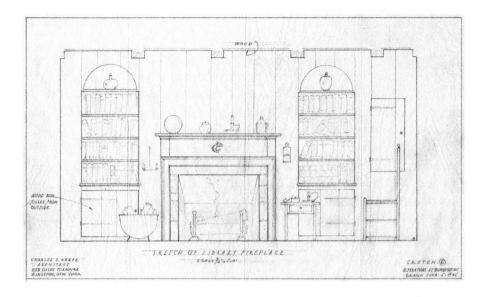

E. Hope Norton's Bumbershoot, library.

library, living-room, and bedroom fireplace walls show a variety of quaint furnishings: Windsor and ladder-back chairs, candlesticks, taper box, pipe, pewter plate, wall clock with decorative face and visible weights. Then in May and June 1946, shortly before his death, Keefe designed a garden gate and garage with guest house (and Windsor chairs on the porch) for Norton in Hebron. The garage and guest house were probably not built.

In April 1946 **John Oldrin** had Keefe prepare sketches for two rows of stores with intimate Colonial fronts lining Pomander Walk running between Railroad Avenue and Center Street in Darien. Pomander Walk and the buildings lining it were inspired by Manhattan's Pomander Walk with its rows of Tudor houses from the 1920s.

For the **Inslees'** Windy Brow Farm, Keefe in 1945–46 revisited his early specialty of farm buildings, but now planned a strictly utilitarian concrete-block apple storage building with a packing room. In 2017 the building is still in use by the current owners of Windy Brow Farms.

In his last months Keefe again went to work for **Lowell Thomas**, making sketches for a ski lodge proposed for Quaker Lake, as well as plans for the Aiken Hall caretaker's house and for *Guideposts*, a publication spreading the message of **Norman Vincent Peale**. Peale, a Protestant minister in New York with a large following well before the 1952 publication of his best-known book, *The Power of Positive Thinking*, was drawn into Lowell Thomas's orbit at Quaker Hill. *Guideposts's* offices beginning in August 1946 were located in a "colonial-type house" owned by Thomas on Quaker Hill. In early June Keefe had designed a new porch for the offices incorporating slender giant columns, the architect's favorite device for achieving some grandeur at modest cost. Keefe reported to Thomas, June 18, 1946, a month before his death, that plans for "the Guide-Post" were completed. If the porch was built, it was destroyed along with the entire building in a fire on January 12, 1947.[9]

Keefe was pleased to tell Thomas that **Eleanor Roosevelt**, of all people, wanted to consult him: "Tomorrow [July 11, 1946] I am to meet one of your old neighbors, Mrs. Roosevelt, at Esopus about some buildings for a colored school that she is interested in." Wiltwyck School, located on the former Payne Estate in Esopus, served boys sent by children's courts for rehabilitation. Eleanor Roosevelt appeared in the news as its fundraiser, and FDR on his last campaign swing through the Hudson Valley "was hailed by Negro boys from the Wiltwyck School lined up along the highway." Eleanor mentioned taking luncheon guests to see the school in her July 13, 1946, "My Day" syndicated newspaper column, but it cannot be confirmed that Keefe was among the guests.[10] Whatever feeling he may have had about working with a Roosevelt, his death soon after the appointment ended that prospect.

Between 1943 and his death, Keefe set to work for **Eugene and Florence Morehouse**, previous clients in restoring Nieu Dorp, in altering a two-story stone house with symmetrical, five-bay façade on Hurley Avenue. The façade appears to date from the early nineteenth century, but a story-and-a-half stone section at the rear may be older. Keefe, when ordering Corbin hardware, wrote that he was "restoring an old Dutch house." Keefe's changes included the removal of both a gable atop the façade and a long front porch, replaced by a small, plain Colonial porch at the central doorway, and the transformation of a room at the rear into a library with a new Colonial hearth and brick oven protruding from the north wall. Like other restoration clients, Morehouse took an active role and found an old mantel to place in the restoration, in this case after Keefe had already designed a new one. Several Dutch doors were planned, so Keefe once more approached Myron Teller: "I have an old stone house in Hurley for Gene Morehouse and need some of your hardware. Have you any latches and long or moderately long hinges for Dutch doors?" Note that Keefe, when approaching the expert on Dutch Colonial restorations, did not refer to the house as "Dutch" or his commission as a "restoration." Teller, then in Tarrytown at work on John D. Rockefeller, Jr.'s, Sleepy Hollow Restorations, responded in longhand with sketches of the limited quantity of hand-wrought strap hinges, Dutch slide bolts, Dutch drop handles, back latches, and latch handles remaining in his Kingston shop. He offered to meet Charles at the Kingston shop where he could select what he needed.[11]

Construction was delayed by shortages in building materials. But in March 1946 Keefe cheerfully told the Corbin salesman, "Business is certainly picking up for I have about twenty jobs ranging from a few thousand up to one hundred thousand. Maybe the architects and hardware men are going to enjoy life again."[12]

At the time of his death, Keefe was at work on the utterly plain, two-story **Gerald A. Gormley** house at 253 Lucas Avenue, very near and similar in basic composition to Keefe's own house, designed more than thirty years earlier with stylish details absent in the bland Gormley house. (Gormley, who died in 1988, was a salesman at Colonial City Chevrolet in 1942, and he may have sold Keefe his last car, a Chevrolet.) Death also cut short his remodeling of the home of Hurley Town Supervisor, Republican **Henry C. Battenfeld** (1893–1978). While no drawings of the Battenfeld remodeling are in the Archive, 136 Old Route 209 has been identified as the Battenfeld house, and its façade resembles Keefe's work.[13]

Among the most interesting of Keefe's unfinished projects was the alteration of the former parsonage of the German Reformed Church in Germantown, Columbia County. The parsonage, an eighteenth-century stone house treasured locally as a rare survivor of the settlement of Palatine Germans in the Hudson Valley, had been purchased by **Edward E. Ekert** (1896–c.1988), a chemist, and his wife, **Friedl Ekert** (1903–89). Both had German roots and were keen to restore the building, in poor condition after years of neglect, as their home and an appropriate setting for their collection of antique furniture. Keefe met with the Ekerts and sketched his ideas for transforming the run-down building into a pleasant home of Colonial appearance—two-over-two sash would be replaced with six-over-six, while shed-roofed dormers and a simple porch or roofed stoop with benches would be added. Keefe, as usual, did not propose a scholarly restoration. Instead the new details would blend the old stone walls with the charm of the early twentieth-century Colonial Revival.

Before working drawings were prepared and construction could proceed, Keefe died unexpectedly on July 19, 1946. John O'Connor, designing for the Keefe

Edward and Friedl Ekert house.

estate, continued work on plans into 1947, but the Ekerts were loath to proceed without Keefe's expertise. As they wrote Grace Keefe, September 10, 1946:

> We are indeed sad to have lost a very good friend. Our hopes which had been so high have faded as we do not see how we can ever get the work done as Mr. Keefe knew it should be done. For example, he pointed out to us that great care would be required to restore the outside of the stone house so that no structural harm would be done to the old walls. In particular, he cautioned against disturbing of the old slate roof which has a depression. I was of the opinion that it required straightening out and Mr. Keefe jokingly said, "A man of 80 years has no straight back and if you want to straighten his back out you would break it." Recalling this we now doubt whether it would be wise to install the dormers which you proposed.

In fact Keefe had proposed dormers himself, but the client remained unconvinced and Keefe's design was not carried out.[14]

Death, Funeral, and Burial

Keefe's death July 19, 1946, in Bennington (Vermont) Hospital resulted from head injuries after dizziness and a fall while dining in a restaurant in Manchester during a construction supervision trip.[15]

The architect did not adhere to what the twenty-first century considers a healthy lifestyle—physical exercise seems to have been avoided, while he enjoyed pipe and cigar smoking and eating heartily. He thanked E. Hope Norton for a box of cigars, which he enjoyed "after dinners at home," and he wrote John Oldrin: "Just as soon as I get a chance I'll call you up so we can go to lunch together. I can eat a turkey dinner in ten minutes so I guess forty-five minutes will be enough to eat and have time to do some talking."[16]

Keefe suffered from digestive problems and low blood pressure and had had at least one concussion. In 1917 while dining in a New York restaurant with his sister Celeste (who was training to be a nurse), he had an "attack of acute indigestion," went outside for cool air, fell and hit his head on the sidewalk, causing a concussion.[17] In 1936 he had been seriously injured while driving to the Lowell Thomas job in Pawling when his car was forced off the road by a car driven by a girl with a learner's permit. Then in October 1940 he wrote Eugene Quick, a Kingston contractor with whom he was friendly, "Am going away for a week's vacation, the first real one I have had in five years. Am all in & need a rest."[18]

The funeral on Monday, July 22, was at the Keefes' Lucas Avenue home. The *Freeman* noted a "large attendance of relatives and friends. There was a profusion of beautiful floral tributes. Mr. Keefe was a member of St. James Methodist Church and the services were conducted by the Rev. W. Wesley Williams, pastor of St. James, and the Rev. Hough Houston, a former pastor." Burial was in

Wiltwyck Cemetery, and a bugler from Colonial Camp No. 75, United Spanish War Veterans, of which Keefe was a member, played taps. The evening before the funeral the veterans met at the home "and gave their ritual service."[19]

Keefe's grave, surprisingly, remains unmarked. The story of the difficulties surrounding Keefe family burials begins well before Charles's death. When his brother, Dr. Augustus S. Keefe, died on May 12, 1934, at age fifty-four, their father Andrew was still alive but, according to Charles, "father would not have Gus' body in the house, and left it for me to find a place to bury him. Grace and Blanche [Grace's younger sister, Blanche de la Montanye Fitzgerald (1887–1969)] were kind enough to let me put Gus in their burial plot." The plot in Wiltwyck Cemetery (section Laurel 7) is identified by a vertical slab with a laurel wreath in low relief and the family names "de la Montanye" above "Keefe." Keefe's drawing for the monument is dated May 18, 1927, and the gray granite monument was fashioned by the John Swenson Granite Company of Concord, New Hampshire. The ivy wreath was carved from a model Keefe provided.[20]

In the de la Montanye-Keefe plot, low granite stones mark the graves of Grace and her sister Blanche, as well as their parents, John and Elizabeth de la Montanye, while neither Augustus nor Charles has an individual stone marker. Grace, in her will, asked to be buried next to Charles and called for markers over her, Charles's, and Augustus's graves. Charles's was to be engraved simply "Charles S. Keefe, A.I.A. 1876–1946." Why she did not carry this out herself remains a mystery.[21]

The inclusion of "A.I.A." was unusual in architects' monuments and surely reflects Charles Keefe's own pride in his membership in the American Institute of Architects—alone among Kingston architects of his time. In 1937 he told an interviewer: "Well, naturally, an architect is proud to be a member. There are only about 3,500 members out of about 16,000 professionals in the nation. Frankly, it's merely a proof of a man's architectural ability. The ethics are very strict. It's to my profession what a national fellowship is to a physician or surgeon."[22]

Closing the Practice

After Keefe's death, Grace Keefe called upon Charles's small staff—John O'Connor, trained in architecture at Pratt Institute, and Alfred P. Marquardt (1921–2011), a young draftsman and veteran—to complete unfinished jobs, including the Morehouse and Germantown parsonage alterations and work for Lowell Thomas. Grace, writing "as representative of his estate," informed clients that "Mr. Keefe left an organization capable of completing his work."[23]

O'Connor was well liked by Keefe, appearing next to Keefe in 1941 photos of meetings of the Mid-Hudson Valley Architectural Society.[24] Wintering in Florida, Keefe had expressed confidence in O'Connor's abilities in a "To whom it may concern" recommendation dated March 15, 1943:

I have known John J. O'Connor for about eight years and during this period he was in my employ for over two years. . . . Mr. O'Connor is honest, trustworthy and able in his work. While in my office he did all my structural designing as well as other work. His work was carefully done and very satisfactory in every way. He has a great deal of ability and is a hard worker. ["and is not a clock watcher" crossed out] His family background is very good and I know his wife, mother & grand parents, his father formerly organist in St. Patrick's Cathedral NY City is dead. Mr. O'Cr can be trusted to do his work well and not talk about it.

O'Connor developed the preliminary plans Keefe had prepared for the Ekerts, but they were not satisfied that O'Connor had closely followed Keefe's ideas. Other clients apparently also cut ties with Keefe's estate. In Lowell Thomas's case, Grace Keefe was obliged as late as 1952 to negotiate with Thomas and his attorneys over unpaid bills.[25]

The widow made a serious effort to preserve her husband's plans, correspondence, and library during her lifetime. When her estate was appraised in 1973, what had originally been their bedroom but transformed in the 1930s into the architect's office was still described as the "office" and contained "two draftsmans tables" and "blueprint cabinet units," the latter no doubt with the plans now in the Keefe Archive and probably others now lost. Before 1952, Grace, with the help of one or more of Charles's former assistants, created a list of the publications of Keefe's work in a notebook, "For Publishing Book of Houses designed by Charles S. Keefe," in which she inserted other notes for the proposed book. In her own will, Grace made extensive provisions for honoring Charles through publication of this book of his houses as well as through finding an institutional home for his library and office files. These provisions were not carried out.

Keefe must have convinced Grace that European travel was important for draftsmen and architects like himself without college training but with an interest in Colonial architecture, since in her will she directed that "The Charles S. Keefe Fund for deserving draftsmen and architects" be set up and administered by the A.I.A. "to assist deserving, American born, draftsmen with no college education and at least two years experience as draftsmen in Cape Cod, Federal, Southern, Dutch, or other Colonial architecture, who desire to study architecture in Europe and require financial assistance to do so." The AIA New York Chapter through the Center for Architecture offers a travel grant from Keefe and other funds.

Charles's niece Donna Keefe greatly admired her uncle, but not his wife, believing that Grace made life difficult for Charles and other family members and that Grace's devotion to Charles was only evident after his death. Donna reported that five people attended Grace's funeral and that the executors of her will refused to serve.[26] While the relationship between Charles and Grace will never be fully known, references to her in his correspondence are typically those of a bemused, harried husband who was not unkind to his wife. He noted on a May 1, 1927, royalty statement for $33.71 from his publisher: "Sent check to Mrs. K as a little present."

Legacy and Influence

There was no "school of Keefe" or substantial circle of admiring disciples. William J. Ward, Jr., a young Penn State-trained architect and architectural illustrator who had worked for the John Russell Pope and Irwin S. Chanin firms, was unusual when in 1934 he was described to Keefe as "a strong rooter for the Keefian architecture." Ward's enthusiasm was based on the quality of Keefe's designs, but also on Keefe's generosity—"you gave him a whole afternoon . . . telling him about small house plans."[27]

Writing to Hopkins from Germany in 1911, before two disastrous world wars, Keefe was struck by the number of buildings that had stood for several hundred years. The callow architect told his mentor, "I only hope I will be able, before I leave this world, to do something good that will stand a few hundred years or so."[28] As his career developed, Keefe aimed for pleasant and livable houses, mostly of wood, and so it seems doubtful that any will be valued and standing in a few hundred years. Perhaps, like Grace, Charles in later years had hope that it would be books and magazines that would carry his name and accomplishments into the future.

de la Montanye-Keefe monument. (Peter Roberts photo)

The Charles S. Keefe Archive at the Friends of Historic Kingston

The surviving Keefe drawings, prints, and correspondence referred to in this book are in the collection of the Friends of Historic Kingston unless otherwise indicated. It is my understanding that Thumbprint Antiques sold Lowell Thomas and Thomas Dewey material to other parties. The collection of drawings and prints is incomplete, and the correspondence files for many commissions are missing. The client files that do survive, e.g., the Young/Brenchley files, include financial records and correspondence with clients, contractors, and suppliers of materials as well as Keefe's pencil notes from site visits, but little relating to design decisions or architectural style.

Keefe wrote client William Rice (December 18, 1928): "I suggest your filing the prints you have of the house in some place where the light cannot get at them. If you do this they will save indefinitely." Presumably other clients also retained prints.

Abbreviations

CSK=Charles S. Keefe
Am. Arch.=*American Architect*
Arch. Forum=*Architectural Forum*
Arch. Rec.=*Architectural Record*
Arch. Rev.=*Architectural Review*
JSAH=*Journal of the Society of Architectural Historians*
KDF=*Kingston Daily Freeman*
NYT=*The New York Times*
Pic. Rev.=*Pictorial Review*
RER&BG=*Real Estate Record & Builders' Guide*

Chronological List of Clients

This list of clients is incomplete, especially from the early Kingston years and the subsequent period working with Hopkins. It derives primarily from a card file created by the author and his wife of drawings and prints acquired from Thumbprint Antiques. Not all projects resulted in completed buildings. Clients are generally listed only under the year of the earliest plans, letters, or financial records associated with them.

Richard Gruver, "Charles S. Keefe, A.I.A., Finds Small House Designing Thrilling Vocation," *KDF*, October 9, 1937, included Indiana, Michigan, North Carolina, Oregon, and Washington as states where Keefe designed "country houses," although these now have not been identified.

Undated

Brewster, George S., farmer's cottage, Brookville, (with Hopkins).

Caswell, house, garage, cottage, location?

Catskill Examiner (weekly newspaper, published 1858-1935), remodeling?

Dodge, Charles Gerard, half-timbered house sketches, Darien, Conn. Dodge (1883–1972) was a Harvard graduate and investment banker who bought a lot in Tokeneke in 1930, possibly the intended site for the house sketched by Keefe. [*NYT*, Jan. 24, 1930]

"Five Room House," designed when office at 258 Lucas Ave.

"Model House—Stucco," drawings for a simple Tudor house.

Mollenhauer, Adolph, gardener's cottage and farm buildings, Bay Shore, (with Hopkins).

"Movius Work" folder with various projects.

Secor, J. K., farm buildings, Toledo, O (Hopkins architect, CSK associate).

Stern, M. D., unknown building, Kingston.

"Stock Cottage," drawings for a Colonial house with Federal doorway.

c. 1900

Keefe, Andrew, house at 30 Lafayette Ave., Kingston.

1911

Keefe, Charles S., own house, 258 Lucas Ave., Kingston.

Winter, George A., bungalow, Kingston.

1912

Stetson, Francis L., gate lodge and farm buildings at Skylands, Sterlington (with Hopkins; Keefe's later work at Skylands for C. McK. Lewis).

1913

Knights of Columbus, Kingston.

Kingston High School Competition, Hopkins & Keefe (lost to Arthur Curtis Longyear).

1914

Court-House & Prison of Inferior Jurisdiction, Manhattan (with Hopkins).

Lewis, Clarence McK., farm buildings, Mahwah, N.J. (with Hopkins).

Sloan, Samuel, farm buildings, Garrison (by James Gamble Rogers, Keefe's role uncertain).

Stewart, Glenn, superintendent's cottage, Locust Valley (with Hopkins).

1915

Clayburgh, Albert, farm buildings, Mt. Kisco (with Hopkins); photo album of views of the landscaped grounds by Olmsted Brothers in the Olmsted Archives, F. L. Olmsted National Historic Site.

Westchester County Penitentiary & Workhouse, East View (with Hopkins).

1916

Adirondack Trust Co., Saratoga Springs (with Hopkins and Scarff).

Agnew, George Bliss, garage and chauffeur's house, South Salem.

1917

Schiff, Mortimer L., farm buildings, Oyster Bay (with Hopkins).

Thorn, Mrs. C. R., cottage altered and new farm buildings, Massapequa (with Hopkins,

Real Estate Record & Builders' Guide, Sept. 1, 8, and Oct. 6, 1917).

1918

Straus, Percy S., stable, Middletown, N.J. (with Hopkins). Straus (1876–1944) was an official with R. H. Macy & Co., as was his brother Jesse Isidor Straus (see 1928 below). [*NYT*, May 16, 1924]

Van Deusen, Charles C., major alteration of house, Saratoga Springs (with Hopkins).

1919

Fessenden Shirt Co., factory alterations, Field Court, Kingston.

Havemeyer, Horace, farm building, Islip (with Hopkins).

1920s

Carn, A. L., office, location? (early 1920s job list #60).

Carpenter, store building, location? (early 1920s job list #57).

Hartley, L. M., house, location? (early 1920s, job list #56).

"House at Middleburg, Virginia," a pencil perspective drawing, "Hallam L. Movius & Charles S. Keefe, Architects, Boston & New York." H. L. Movius served as a judge of a fox hunt at Middleburg in 1905. [https://houndwelfare.wordpress.com/tag /middleburg. Accessed Nov. 28, 2016]

Ludington, Charles Henry, cow barn addition to old stone barn, Ardmore (now Gladwyne), Penn. Ludington (1866–1927) was secretary-treasurer of the Curtis Publishing Co.

Perkins, James. Listed as a client (with Movius), by Nov. 30, 1925.

Schiff, Charles, residence, location? (early 1920s job list).

Titus, Fred, house (early 1920s job list #88). Probably identical with the Harkness estate superintendent's house.

1920

Andrews, J. H., house, Humboldt, Kan. In August 1920 Keefe drew plans for a one-story Colonial house, unusual in having the façade be the narrow side of the rectangular plan and tucking the garage into the basement. Keefe had observed in *The Amer-*

ican House (p. 21) that autos, unlike horses, could reside near human occupants at great country houses without offense.

Fessenden-Carl Co., preliminary drawings for commercial alteration and addition, 240 Broadway at Field Court, Kingston.

Joslen, Granville M., commercial building, Hudson.

"Houses at Kingston, New York," drawing published as "Housing at Kingston, New York," *American Architect*, Sept. 22, 1920, 383.

La Fleur (Lafleur), L. M., house, pencil rendering, "Residence for L. M. Lafleur, Esq.," a stucco-walled, tile-roofed house with an arched, solid-paneled front door and iron balcony of Spanish or Mediterranean inspiration for an unknown location; also an unidentified color rendering of a similar house.

Nassau County Association, jail, not built.

Shufeldt, Alexander, house, Kingston.

Standard Building Supply Co., storage building, drawing Aug. 26, 1920, perhaps the one-story brick building for cement storage at 12th Ave. and 50th St. designed by Keefe. [*NY Evening Post*, Aug. 30, 1920]]

1921

Burden, Mrs. William A. M. (Florence Vanderbilt Twombly Burden), farm buildings, Uplands, Mt. Kisco (with Burnett & Rogers).

Fessenden, Edward E., house, Kingston, preliminary perspectives and plans for president of Fessenden Shirt Co.

Frost, LeRoy, root cellar, Nyack.

Goodliffe, E. S., proposed house, Bryn Mar (Yonkers), published in *Architecture*, Oct. 1922, 320. An unusual Keefe design: façade with five low windows in the second-story frieze, a composition derived from Greek Revival houses.

Harkness, Edith Hale, buildings for estate, Glen Cove.

Iselin, Charles Oliver, house? Iselin (1854–1932) was a banker and notable yachtsman with a country home at Glen Head, Oyster Bay. [*NYT*, Jan. 2, 1932]

Twombly, H. McK., cottage and farm buildings, Convent Station, N.J. (Burnett, Keefe & Rogers).

1922

Bailey, L.P., Co., dairy and factory, location? (Burnett & Keefe. In folder with Griffis Farm Group for John Borden, Glenwild Plantation, near Grenada, Miss., by Burnett & Rogers, 1922).

Brokaw, Howard C., poultry building, Brookville. A member of the Holland, Huguenot, and St. Nicholas Societies, Howard Crosby Brokaw (1875–1960) graduated in 1897 from Princeton. He succeeded his father as head of Brokaw Brothers Clothiers, and erected an eleven-story building on Times Square where his private office was paneled in oak from a 16th-century English manor house. His country home, The Chimneys, was a 40-room brick Georgian mansion (begun c. 1917) at Brookville, L.I., by the noted architect Horace Trumbauer. Keefe's job, humbler, involved laying out a poultry building with a few Colonial details. [*NYT*, Mar. 7, 1916, Mar. 19, 1960, Apr. 30, 1961]

Evans, D. L., house, Mt. Vernon.

Farwell, Frank (or Francis) C., farm buildings, Lake Forest, Ill. (with James Gamble Rogers).

Keen, Louis, house, Phoenicia, Ulster County?

Lewis, Clarence McKenzie, farm and other buildings, Skylands Farm, Sterlington.

Price, Walter, house, Kingston.

1923

Basten, Louis Bevier, house alterations and additions, Stone Ridge.

Cate, William E., house, Long Branch, N.J. (with Crook).

Cheney, Anne W., farm buildings, South Manchester, Conn. (with McKim, Mead & White).

Morehouse, Florence, brick Georgian house, Bronx.

1924

American Legion, Kingston.

Berwin, house, location? (probably not built).

Bruce, Robert L., house, New Martinsville, W.Va.

Doyle, Gertrude M., house, Bronx.

Guinzburg (or Ginzburg), Victor, poultry houses, Chappaqua. Guinzburg, a leader in the rubber industry, with his wife Etta Kleinert Guinzburg, maintained an estate with elaborate gardens. Her philanthropies included Jewish charities. [*NYT*, June 27, 1929, Mar. 25, 1934, July 9, 1945]

Lindenberger, Dr. Lauren N., house, Troy, O.

Tyng, Elizabeth McJ., house, Palo Alto, Calif.

Ulster County Tuberculosis Hospital, proposal (with Myron S. Teller).

Winter's Sons, E., store alterations, Kingston. Keefe in 1911 had designed a bungalow for George A. Winter, an officer of this business.

By Nov. 1925

Clients with Movius: Jim Perkins, Mrs. Carlton Smith at Lewiston, and Percy Straus. [Movius to CSK, Nov. 30, 1925]

1925

Crane, F. G., Jr., garage group, Dalton, Mass. (with Movius).

Keefe farmhouse, alterations, Richmond, Vt.

Moehring, Lester and Barbara, house, Winchell's Falls, Ulster County. Not built.

Norton, Evermont Hope, various buildings, Tokeneke, Darien, Conn.

Rice, William T., house, Pittsfield, Mass. (originally with Movius).

Sainson, Eugene, house, Great Kills, Staten Island? Brick Colonial with casement windows and garage in basement. Sainson (1882–1972), born in France, was an importer and salesman of fine china. [St. Petersburg, FL, *Times*, May 22, 1972] Keefe's plans called for a large case by the living-room fireplace and two china closets in the dining room.

1926

Bachem, John H., house, probably on Long Island. Bachem worked in magazine advertising. [*New York Evening Post*, Mar. 19, 1932]

Catskill Country Club, Catskill.

House Beautiful, House #16, published *House Beautiful*, Jan. 1927.

Keefe, subdivision of land on Lounsbury Ave. at Taylor Ave., Kingston. Neither street name is in use today, but the property was probably in the vicinity of today's Lounsbury Place. A map drawn Nov. 20, 1926, by G. W. Codwise identifies three lots as "Keefe."

Matthews, Stanley, house, 61 Lounsbury Place, Kingston.

Meola, John B., house, possibly at Norwich, N.Y., where a JBM was superintendent of the New York, Ontario & Western Railroad and his wife, the former Grace Alice Ingersoll, was a member of the D.A.R. [*Albany Knickerbocker News*, Oct. 7, 1964; *Binghamton Press*, Jan. 22, 1927]

Parker, Harry, various buildings, Tokeneke, Darien, Conn.

Woolworth, Richard W., cottage and farm buildings, Northshire Farm, Salem Center.

1927

Burbank, Dr. Reginald, cottage and garage group, Dalton, Mass. (with Movius).

Condran, Walter, house, Dallas Center, Ia.?

de la Montanye-Keefe monument, Wiltwyck Cemetery, Kingston.

Drayton, Anna H., plan of house, Tokeneke, Darien, Conn. No elevations but map of property conveyed to AHD by Norton Inc., Oct. 1927. At her death in 1932, Anna Drayton was in her fourth term as president of the Darien Community Association. [*NYT*, Dec. 29, 1932]

Harring & Betts Building, commercial building remodeling, Catskill.

Hutchins, Constantine, house group, Needham, Mass. (with Movius).

Inslee, Charles L., house, "Windy Brow," Newton, N.J.

Lerner Bros. store, remodeling, Catskill.

Lerner Bros. store, remodeling, Saugerties.

Patterson, David, remodeling of old house, North Salem.

Tyng, Elizabeth, second house, Palo Alto, Calif.

Walker, house, Pembroke, Mass.?

Wheeler, Herbert and Catherine, house, Tokeneke, Darien, Conn.

Young, Minnie E. (Mrs. Albert Young) and Edna Young Brenchley, various buildings, Tokeneke, Darien, Conn.

1928

Boice, Hugh, house additions, Milford, N.J.?

Crane Museum, Dalton, Mass.

Farrell, John J., several buildings including gardener's cottage, Tokeneke, Darien, Conn.

Hofheimer, Lester, farm building, Briarcliff Hills. Hofheimer, a philanthropist especially supporting Jewish charities, purchased Dream Lake, a 125-acre estate in Briarcliff Hills in 1928. [*NYT*, May 29, 1928, Dec. 1, 1936]

Inslee, Ralph H., house, "Windy Brow," Newton, N.J.

Keefe, Charles S., office layout, 40 E. 49th St., New York.

Kirby, Gustavus Town, garage and farm group, Bedford Hills. Kirby (1874–1956) was active in Belgian relief in both world wars, served on American Olympic Committees, and was honored for his work on local history by the Village of Mt. Kisco.

Pentecost, Wyntje S., house, Tokeneke, Darien, Conn.

Pomeroy, Brenton, farm group, Pittsfield, Mass. (with Movius).

Straus, Jesse Isidor, farm buildings and cottage, Mt. Kisco (with Movius). Straus (1872–1936) was president of R. H. Macy & Co. and in 1933 was appointed ambassador to France by Franklin Roosevelt.

1929

Alliger, Lewis A., house, Katonah. Drawings for a proposed Georgian stone house with Book Room. Alliger (c. 1875–1952) was a native of Rosendale, attended Kingston schools, and in 1898 went to New York where he eventually became a partner in Whitehead & Alliger Co., paper merchants, and member of the Institute of Graphic Arts. [*KDF*, Mar. 1, 1952] The Keefe Archive has the 1931 card of Whitehead & Alliger, fine book papers, but whether he used Alliger's paper is unknown. Alliger was a leading member of the Ulster County Society, composed of successful men with roots in Ulster County who met annually over dinner in New York City.

Bellows, Charles C., house, New Canaan, Conn. Demolished.

Blanchard, Archibald, garage for summer home, Nahant, Mass. (with Movius).

Fay, E. Prescott, garage with sitting room, Cohasset, Mass. (with Movius).

Haight, Louis, stable group and house addition, Darien, Conn. Haight was a member of the New York Stock Exchange; his wife, Florence Coppell Haight, rode competitively at the Ox Ridge Hunt Club, as did another client, Mrs. John J. Farrell. [*NYT*, July 22, 1928, Apr. 27, 1940]

Mason, H. F. R., house, Mason's business address was *The Chronicle*, a newspaper in Bound Brook, N.J. Plans for the 2-story Colonial house included a "Book Room."

Mickle, Charles Chew, Jr., and Mabel M., additions to house, Darien. Mabel had studied sculpture at the Borglum School and was a member of the Ox Ridge Hunt Club, like several other Keefe clients. Keefe kept a clipping about Mabel Mickle from the *New York Sun*, Dec. 1, 1930, headed, "Distinguished Horsewoman Turns Artist . . . Darien Matron Forgoes Social Pleasures to Seek to Perpetuate Equine Beauty in Bronze." The "masters bedroom" in Keefe's plans (Oct. 29, 1929) included a specially designed "closet for riding habits." The stock market crash may have put off construction of the addition, but the file does contain a boldly penned note by Mabel Mickle, dated June 14, 1932, thanking Keefe for flowers sent her during a hospital stay.

Patterson, John F., additions to house, location?

Root, Charles Arthur, cow barns, Uxbridge, Mass. (with Movius).

Shelp, F. Leon, farmer's cottage and alterations to house, Brewster.

Smith, E. Dutilh, house, Tokeneke, Darien, Conn.

Smith, Frances S. (Mrs. George DeForest Smith), proposed cottage, Kingston.

Stevens, Hope Norton (Mrs. George E.), house, Darien, Conn .

Wheatsworth, Inc., proposed museum, Hamburg, N.J.

1930

Anderson, Robert M., house, Circleville, O.

Banks, Mrs. Henry W., Jr., beach cottage, Noroton Bay, Darien, Conn. Construction of this one-story, stuccoed beach cottage reminiscent of Bermuda cottages was certainly postponed and probably canceled because of the market crash. [CSK to Mrs. Banks, May 5, 1930] Keefe's library probably included *Bermuda Cottages* (1923) by John S. Humphreys. [Swann Galleries, Sale 993, item 26] The plan of the Banks cottage, with rooms arranged around three sides of an open court, was comparable to Cluster Cottage as illustrated, p. 27, in Humphreys's volume.

Brock, Dr. Arlie V., garage, Harvard, Mass. (with Movius).

Clark, Mrs. D. L., proposed cottage, Nashua, N.H.

Hafner, Walter A. and Millicent, extensive house alteration, Darien, Conn.

MacDonald, Alfred J., proposed house, Alpine, N.J.

Malcolm, Mrs. Percy S. D., interior house alterations, Tokeneke, Darien, Conn.?

Morse, Darwin S., fence, Pittsfield, Mass. (with Movius).

Nelson, J. Albert, complete alteration of house, South Norwalk, Conn.

Pritchett, Mrs. Martha D., house, South Cairo. Working drawings, Sept.–Oct. Also preliminary drawings, July, for a house in Ossining. Pritchett died in her home on Sandy Plains Road, South Cairo. [*Greene County Examiner-Recorder*, Jan. 5, 1950]

Tokeneke Club, Darien, Conn.

1931

McMichael, Miss Jessamine, house, Muncy, Penn. 2-story frame Colonial at 531 S. Market St.

Stapleton, Luke D., Jr., alterations and additions to house, South Norwalk, Conn. Stapleton was a Manhattan attorney; his wife, Catherine Farrell Stapleton, was the sister of Keefe's client John J. Farrell. [*New York Evening Post*, June 28, 1924; *NYT*, June 28, 1948]

1932

Branson, G. Russell, house, Grand Lake Stream, Me.

Hacker, William Hope, proposed house, location?

Hanstein, Allan L., house alterations and additions, Kingston.

MacMurphey, Robert Hyde and Ann, house, Scott's Corner, near New Canaan, Conn.

Rockwell, house, location?

1933

Hawkins, Robert F., house, Bellport? Keefe planned a Colonial house in 1933-34, but Hawkins wrote Keefe Aug. 16, 1936, from Academy Lane, Bellport, postponing building. Hawkins and his wife also lived in Massachusetts and Florida.

Heisler, Joe, house, Poughkeepsie?

Hulbert, John, Conn. Yankee cottage, Sardis, B.C.

Keefe, Andrew, proposed house with brick façade on Mountain View Ave., Kingston.

1934

Norton, Evermont Hope, house and office, Ecuador.

Ohrstrom, George Lewis, preliminary drawings for cottage from old schoolhouse and house from old barn, Greenwich, Conn. Ohrstom was a Wall Street financier who in 1927 owned 135 acres in Greenwich and intended to build a $100,000 stone house. [*NYT*, Aug. 9, 1927, Nov. 11, 1955]

Thomas, Lowell, alterations to house and other projects, Quaker Hill, Pawling.

1935

Fassett, Dr. Edwin C., minor alterations to house, Kingston.

Gedney, Earl R., house, 60 Merritt Ave., Kingston.

Norton, Evermont Hope, house alterations, Hebron, N.H.

Parrish (or Parish), Berthe, cottage, Kingston.

Sornborger, Dorothy G., house, location?

Taylor, Theodore C., sketches for house, New Rochelle. Taylor was an assistant professor of organic chemistry at Columbia when he died in 1936. [*NYT*, Apr. 21, 1936]

1936

Carroll, James F., house, location?

Fair Street Reformed Church, Kingston, alternate designs for new windows, diamond vs. rectangular glass.

Geneva Development and Construction Co., plans for Cottages #1 and #2, location?

O'Connor, Francis E., M.D., house, Kingston.

Schwenk, Fred W., minor house alterations, (141 Clifton Ave.?), Kingston.

TeBow, George Burton, cottage (or house,

1940), Kingston area? TeBow (1880–1968) resided in Kingston most of his life and had been an official with the Kingston Consolidated Railroad. [*KDF*, Jan. 8, 1968]

Thornburg, Raymond and Pherbia, house, Quaker Hill, Pawling.

Winnell, Paul W., proposed house, Hartsdale.

1937

Aiken Hall, addition of Georgian cupola, Quaker Hill, Pawling.

Arnold, Charles, house, Kingston.

de Posch (or de Posh), Lionel, house, New Canaan, Conn. A two-story Colonial with maid's and man's quarters, dog room, and library; possibly extant at 172 Dans Highway according to Janet Lindstrom e-mail to author, July 25, 2016.

Poley, Philip P., house and veterinary office, Kingston.

1938

Burhans, Edwin, proposed convalescent sanitarium, Ulster County.

Dickson, house alterations and cottage, location?

Downer, Mortimer B. and Carol, house and office, Kingston.

Heermann, Norbert, house alteration, Woodstock.

Morehouse, Eugene, house alteration, Hurley.

Schuchhardt, Robert, house, probably at Saugerties. One-and-a-half-story Colonial. Robert Schuchhardt, a graduate of Saugerties High School and Rensselaer Polytechnic Institute, was an engineer with the New York State Department of Architecture. In 1928 he married Mildred Massino in the Asbury home of her aunt and uncle, Mr. and Mrs. W. Grant Trumpbour. [*KDF*, July 7, 1928, Jan. 13, 1960] In 1943 Keefe drew a pine dresser from the Trumpbour House in Asbury.

1939

Baxter, T. R., house, in New Jersey?

Dewey, Thomas E., house alterations, Pawling.

Eaton, Henry T., Colonial garage (with Guy H. Lee, Landscape Architect).

Marsh, Olive M., house, Kingston.

1940

Conro, William F., minor alterations to c. 1852 Greek Revival house, Hurley.

Gruver, Richard and Margaret, house, Hurley.

Herbert, Mrs. John W., various plans including garage group and cottage, Dorset, Vt.

Murphy, Nicholas D. J., alterations to row of apartments, Kingston. Murphy (1871–1941) was a funeral director and charter member of the Kingston Knights of Columbus. [*KDF*, June 30, 1941]

Taylor, Ruth Moore, house, Dorset, Vt.

Whiteman, Glen L., house, Quaker Hill, Pawling.

1941

Bosco, preliminary drawing of a two-story Colonial house with symmetrical façade, location?

Fessenden, Elizabeth Carl, house alteration, Kingston.

Mason, Frank E., house, Pawling (not built).

Oldrin, John, cottage alterations, Tokeneke, Darien, Conn.

Whitney, Edwin M., house, Quaker Lake, Pawling.

1942

Griscom, sketches for house addition? location?

Keefe, Christopher, M.D., monument, Wiltwyck Cemetery, Kingston.

Kent, George C., store addition, Hurley.

Shady Lane Farm, addition to studio, location?

1943

Baker, F. C., Furnace Brook Farm, farm buildings, South Shaftsbury, Vt.

Kauder, Irving, porch added to mid-19th-century house, Springtown Road, New Paltz. Kauder ran a boardinghouse (*Greene County Examiner-Recorder*, June 23, 1949) and poultry farm described by the *New York Sun*, Nov. 12, 1938, as a "poultry metropolis" operated with a "vision . . . almost utopian." The property was later the home of boxer Floyd Patterson (*New Paltz Independent*, Sept. 1, 1965).

Morehouse, Eugene, house alteration, Hurley Ave., Hurley.

1944

Fifth Ward Honor Roll tablet, Kingston (not completed to Keefe's designs).

Lattin, N. L., commercial building alterations, Margaretville. Large, ground-story window fitted with small Colonial panes. Sketches in 1930s for interior alterations for this furniture and undertaking business.

1945

Ballard, Ralph K., house, Saugerties?

Erpf, measured drawings of existing c. 1900 Queen Anne house, location?

Hurley Reformed Church, outdoor Colonial signboard.

Reel, Col. and Mrs. Gordon, house, Flatbush, Ulster County.

Ritch, Janet (Mrs. Wilson, Jr.), minor house alterations, Kingston.

1946

Aiken Hall Association, house alteration, Quaker Hill, Pawling.

Battenfeld, Henry, house alteration, Hurley.

Ekert, Edward and Friedl, Germantown parsonage alteration.

Elmendorf, minor house alteration, Port Ewen, by CSK Estate.

Gilder, alteration of a c. 1900 Queen Anne house (Frank Smith house?).

Gormley, Gerald A., house, Kingston.

The Guidepost, alterations to commercial building, Pawling (destroyed by fire).

McGinniss, Mabel, stable to house alteration. Alfred Marquart, Feb. 9, 1985, phone conversation, identified the location as Ulster Park.

Nelson, C. Albert, two-story, symmetrical façade Colonial house, location? June drawings by Keefe; August drawings by his estate (relation to J. Albert Nelson, 1930?).

Newcombe, drawings of existing house by Keefe estate prior to alteration, Catskill.

Oldrin, John, store group, Darien, Conn.

Smith, Howard W., minor house alterations, Pawling. Smith, like Raymond Thornburg, was an Ohio Wesleyan graduate involved with the rubber industry.

Ward, Ronald Leslie, house, probably not built but proposed for Pawling or Patterson.

Publications of Keefe's Works

This list stems mainly from the notebook, "For Publishing Book of Houses designed by Charles S. Keefe," created for and perhaps by Grace Keefe after Charles's death. Not all these items have been verified. It also stems from Michael Lynch's very accurate 2013 list of Keefe's magazines which he donated to the Friends of Historic Kingston, and from other sources. Only a few of the many newspapers relating to CSK are listed here.

American Architect. June 1918. "Development of the American Doorway." p. 818.

American Architect. Sept. 1920. "Housing at Kingston." p. 382.

American Architect. Sept. 1920. Store Building at Hudson, Carlton & Co.

American Architect. Aug. 1922. Review of Keefe's *The American House.*

American Architect. Nov. 1924. Ad for 2nd ed., *The American House.*

American Architect. Feb. 1927. George Stevens House, Tokeneke, Darien. p. 193.

American Architect. May 1927. Twombly House at Madison. pp. 611, 613, 614.

American Architect. May 1927. American Legion Memorial Building, Kingston. pp. 611, 612.

American Architect. May 1927. Mrs. W.A.M. Burden House at Madison. pp. 613, 614.

American Architect. Nov. 1927. Alterations to the façade of a store front, Catskill, N.Y. p. 687.

American Architect. June 1932. Grace Keefe noted: "Crib by architect Marshall H. Foote for his own house. Of CE's Harkness Garden House."

American Architect. Aug. 1932. Young (Brenchley) Estate, service group: gardener's cottage, garage, and laundry, at Darien. pp. 57–60.

American Architect. Oct. 1932. J. Albert Nelson Alteration. p. 55.

American Architect. May 1933. Charles C. Bellows, New Canaan, Conn. pp. 77–82.

American Architect. July 1933. Favorable review of Newcomb, *The Colonial and Federal House,* with no mention of Keefe, p. 130.

American Architect Arch. Review. June 1922. House Mrs. L. Cahn. CXXI.

American Architect Arch. Review. July 1922. Gate Lodge (Hyde). CXXII.

American Architect & Architecture. Nov. 1936. Zenas Crane Memorial Tablet. p. 75.

American Architect & Architecture. Mar. 1937. Stevens's entrance and columns; Lowell Thomas porch; measured drawings Rice children's entrance.

American Architect & Architecture. Aug. 1937. Sundial (Brenchley Gardener's Cottage). Portfolio vertical sun dials.

American Builder & Building Age. Mar. 1933. Farrell. p. 27.

American Legion Monthly. American Legion Memorial Building.

Architectural Forum, Sept.1922. Write-up on *American House.*

Architectural Forum. Oct. 1923. CSK letter to American Radiator Co. in ad.

Architectural Review. Mar. 1916. New York City Prison and Court House of Inferior Jurisdiction.

Architectural Review. Nov. 1924. Ad for 2nd ed., *American House.*

Architecture. Jan. 1912. CSK, "The 'Mellowness' of Old Brick, Can It Be Obtained in a New Building?" pp. 18–19.

Architecture. Oct. 1922. Small Houses. A. B. Shufeldt, E. S. Goodliffe, Burden Farm Cottage at Madison (CSK and Burnett). pp. 318–320.

Architecture. April 1923. Review of *The American House.* ". . . book of exceptional value in the field it covers."

Architecture. Mar. 1924. Shufeldt House. pp. 93–94.

Architecture. Oct. 1924. Skylands, Sterlington, laundry & laundry yard, tool house, garage. p. 343.

Architecture. Oct. 1924. Harkness Cottage. p. 344.

Architecture. Dec. 1928. Herbert Wheeler, Tokeneke, Darien. pp. 357–358.

Architecture. Jan. 1929. Burbank Cottage and Garage, Dalton, Mass. pp. 33–34.

Architecture. Feb. 1929. p. 94. Suggestions for architect's working library included Keefe's book. Compiled by Marcelle Frebault, under direction of John Cotton Dana, Librarian, Public Library, Newark, N.J.

Architecture. Sept. 1929. David Patterson restoration, North Salem. pp. 165–168.

Architecture. Apr. 1930. Burbank Summer House, Dalton, Mass. p. 254.

Architecture. Nov. 1930. Norton Guest House & Farrell Gardener's Cottage, Darien. pp. 289–292.

Architecture. Mar. 1931. Crane Museum, Dalton, Mass. pp. 157–158.

Architecture. June 1933. Hutchins guest room mantel. p. 339.

Architecture. Sept. 1935. Hutchins Guest House. pp. 161–163.

Architecture & Building. Aug. 1924. Shufeldt. p. 78.

Art & Decoration. Oct. 1934. Hafner mural in entrance hall. p. 49.

*Better Homes & Garden*s. Aug. 1925. Grace Keefe noted: "Crib by *Better Homes & Garden*. Her letter re. it & Ce's answer to her."

Better Homes & Gardens. Nov. 1932. Nelson, South Norwalk, Conn. remodeling. pp. 16, 34.

Better Homes & Gardens. May 1936. Grace Keefe noted: "Crib E. Stanley Elwood of 1st Tyng. Tyng Letter re Crib of 1st House."

"Better Homes in America" Architectural Competition. Apr. 1931. Prize-winning small houses. Norton Guest House. Honorable Mention. Reprint Am. Building Assn. News. By Better Homes. p. 6.

Bruce Pub. Co. May 1931. Grace Keefe noted: "(paid for) rendering Woolworth Cot. in perspective drw."

Building Age. Mar. 1920. CSK, "Before & After." p. 37.

Building Age. July 1924. Shufeldt. p. 77. Grace Keefe noted: "good article for book."

Building Modernization. Feb. 1934. J. Albert Nelson House, South Norwalk. pp. 12–13.

Building Modernization. Apr. 1934. Harring & Betts.

Building Modernization. June 1935. Stapleton. S. Norwalk. pp. 10–11. Also Nelson. South Norwalk. p. 27.

Bulletin Board. Better Homes in America Awards. May 1932. p. 15.

Cement Age combined with *Concrete Engineering*. Aug. 1911. 5 Room Concrete Bungalow.

Charm. May 1931. R. Inslee. p. 31.

Country Life. July 1913. Winter bungalow.

Country Life, supplement. Sept. 1922. Note about *The American House.*

Franklin News (Franklin Society for Home Building & Savings). Apr. 1930. Woolworth Cottage. Cover page.

Garden & Home Builder. Oct. 1924. Harkness Cottage. p. 93.

Glidden Co. June 1931. Woolworth Cottage. Courtesy of Charles S. Keefe & Small Home Magazine.

Glidden Brighter Homes. Aug. 1932. Woolworth Cottage. p. 8.

Good Housekeeping. July 1931. Patterson. Grace Keefe noted: "Remodeling & Restoring an Old House for $6,000. 66, 67, 219. Pictures & article by C. S. Keefe (for book)." [Harry Halverson sent CSK a clipping from the *Middletown Record*, Feb. 29, 1932, with a picture and story re this remodeling. CSK to Halverson, Mar. 8, 1932, thanked him for the clipping.]

Herald Tribune. Sunday, Mar. 8, 1931. Woolworth Cottage. Grace Keefe noted: "Photographs upstairs & in metal cabinet cellar. Picture, plans, & fine article by Charles S. Keefe."

House & Garden. Aug. 1926. Harkness Garden House. p. 85.

*House & Garde*n. Aug. 1931. "A Stone and Shingle Cottage in Connecticut" for Mrs. E. Y. Brenchley. Tokeneke, Darien, Conn. p. 74.

House & Garden. Feb. 1933. Bellows. New Canaan, Conn. pp. 40, 41.

H*ouse & Garden*. Jan. 1937. Lowell Thomas House. 47+.

House & Garden. Apr. 1938. MacMurphy House. pp. 97, 115, 116. [This is the only item for 1938 in "For Publishing Book of Houses," and no others until 1945.]

House & Garden. May 1945. Morehouse. In the Dutch Tradition. pp. 86-87.

House Beautiful. Dec. 1922. Fessenden.

House Beautiful. Mar. 1923. Grace Keefe noted: "(For Book) CE's designs interprets [sic] beauty in terms of utility and utility in terms of beauty. And both in terms of human life. Never employed adventitious ornament nor academic formulas that had survived their use. . . ."

House Beautiful. June 1923. Keefe House. p. 604.

House Beautiful. Nov. 1923. Harkness Cottage. pp. 468–469.

House Beautiful. Jan. 1924. Harkness Tool House. p. 48.

House Beautiful. Apr. 1925. Farm Bldg for Small Place Their Planning & Grouping. pp. 368-369, 420. "Perspective, Plans & Fine Long Article by C.S.K."

House Beautiful Building Annual. Sept. 1925. Miss Tyng's 1st house. p. 212. Ad. p. 514.

House Beautiful. Jan. 1927. Stock house designed for *House Beautiful.* pp. 38–39, 84. Grace Keefe noted: "Cut out of magazine & clipped to Miss Tyng's letter. . . ."

House Beautiful. May 1927. E. Hope Norton Garage Group. Written by V. C. Salomonsky. "An Exemplar of Old & New Colonial Details."

House Beautiful. June 1927. W. L. Harkness Green House. p. 817. Written by V. C. Salomonsky. "An Exemplar of Old and New Colonial Details."

House Beautiful. Feb. 1928. Wm. Cate. p. 176.

House Beautiful. Nov. 1928. Woolworth Cottage. p. 556.

House Beautiful. June 1929. Tyng 2nd House. p. 816.

House Beautiful. Sept. 1931. Guy Lee, "A Collaborative Problem." Hutchins Group, Needham, Mass. pp. 199–204.

House Beautiful. Aug. 1933. Charles C. Bellows, New Canaan, Conn. pp. 48–49.

House Beautiful. Nov. 1937. Charles C. Bellows. Grace Keefe noted: "Good Description (For Book)." pp. 46–47.

Kingston Freeman. Apr. 1935. Restoration David Patterson. Grace Keefe noted: "Photo by C.S.K."

McCall Decorative Arts and Needlework. Summer 1932. Article by C.S.K. Wallpaper in Early American Manner. Farrell & Hutchins interiors. pp. 4–5.

New York Times Book Review. Aug. 1924. ad.

Painter's Magazine. June 1934. Bellows Dining Room as cover and p. 22. See *American Architect*, May 1933, p. 80.

Painter's Magazine. Aug. 1934. Bellows, New Canaan, interior. 14.

Pencil Points. Mar. 1934. Details of bay window, Bellows residence.

Pencil Points. July 1939. CSK, "Competing with Stock Plans." sup. 20.

Pictorial Review. July 1932. Young Gardener's Cottage. p. 40.

Pictorial Review. Nov. 1932. Hutchins Guest House. p. 38.

Pictorial Review. Apr. 1933. Woolworth. Modified Dutch Colonial. p. 48.

Pictorial Review. June 1933. Farrell. A Famous Connecticut Yankee. Honorable Mention. p. 40.

Pictorial Review. May 1934. Robert M. Anderson, "I Got the House I Wanted." p. 38.

Small Home. July 1930. "crib" on p. 31.

Small Home [?]. Dec. 1930. Woolworth Cot. pp. 16–17.

Small Home [?]. May 1932. Norton Guest. p. 13.

Small Home [?]. June 1932. Young Garage Cot. pp. 2-3.

The American Home. Sept. 1929. Patterson. Harriet Sisson Gillespie, "Roof Trees." pp. 663–666, 698, 700.

The American Home. Feb. 1930. Hooked Rugs. p. 444. Grace Keefe noted: "(My Home Bureau Work)."

The American Home. Sept. 1930. House designed for *The American Home* by C.S.K. p. 571.

The American Home. Jan. 1931. Norton Guest House. p. 282.

The American Home. Aug. 1934. J. Albert Nelson. pp. 146–147.

The American Home. Jan. 1935. Walter Hafner alteration. pp. 87–89, 122c, 122d.

The Architect. Nov. 1925. Letter (Testimonial) by CSK.

The Architect. Sept. 1926. Harkness and Norton. pp. 699-701, 725–730.

The Architect. Sept. 1927. Cate House. p. 759.

The Architect. Nov. 1930. Wm. T. Rice, Pittsfield, Mass. pp. 63–71.

The Architect & Engineer. May 1933. Farrell. p. 32.

The Architectural Record. Nov. 1923. Harkness Superintendent's House, Glen Cove. p. 484.

The Architectural Record. Nov. 1926. Harkness Garden House. pp. 478–479.

The Architectural Record. Apr. 1929. Hutchins, Needham, Mass. pp. 34–351.

The Architectural Record. Feb. 1931. George E. Stevens House, Darien. pp. 109–115.

The Architectural Record. Apr. 1932. Norton Guest House, Darien. Better Homes Competition. pp. 245–246.

The Architectural Record. July 1932. Hutchins Guest House, Needham. pp. 27–29.

The Architectural Record. Mar. 1933. Farrell House, Darien. Better Homes Competition. pp. 200–201.

The Architectural Record. Dec. 1946. CSK obituary. p. 13.

The Octagon. Oct. 1942. CSK listed in A.I.A. membership directory. p. 39.

Williams Saylor Inc. Awnings. July 1929. Woolworth Cottage.

Your Home. Mar. 1929. Young Gardener's Cottage. pp. 36–37.

Your Home. Apr. 1929. Herbert Wheeler. pp. 22–23.

Your Home. Mar. 1930. Woolworth Cottage. p. 30 and cover.

Your Home. Mar. 1930. Interview. Wainwright Evans, "Is Your Builder Working for You or Himself?" pp. 13–14, 59.

Your Home. May 1930. Interview. Wainwright Evans, "Risks in a Homemade House." pp. 18, 48, 50, 51.

Your Home. Aug. 1930. Interview. Wainwright Evans, "Some New Homes Are Too Original." pp. 12–14, 57.

Your Home. Sept. 1930. Interview by Evans with Verna Cook. p. 16.

Your Home. Oct. 1930. "A True Connecticut Yankee." Farrell Cottage. p. 15.

Your Home. Dec. 1930. Interview. Wainwright Evans, "Just What Is a Cape Cod House?" pp. 9–11, 66.

Your Home. Jan. 1931. Interview. Wainwright Evans, "Building an Authentic Dutch Colonial House." pp. 13–14, 61–62.

Your Home. Mar. 1931. Cate House. p. 21.

Your Home. Apr. 1931. E. Hope Norton's Homewood Guest House. p. 15.

Books including buildings by Keefe:

Eberlein, Harold Donaldson and Donald Greene Tarpley. *Remodelling & Adapting the Small House.* Philadelphia: Lippincott, 1933. Patterson House.

Hopkins, Alfred. *The Adirondack Trust Company: How We Built It.* Saratoga Springs: Adirondack Trust Company, 1916 [1917].

_____. *Modern Farm Buildings.* New York: McBride, Nast, 1913. Small Stable for Horse and Cow.

Newcomb, Rexford. *The Colonial & Federal House: How to Build an Authentic Colonial House.* Philadelphia: Lippincott, 1933. Two houses for Tyng, Farrell Cottage, Norton Guest House.

Power, Ethel B. *The Smaller American House: Fifty-five Houses of the Less Expensive Type Selected from the Recent Work of Architects in All Parts of the Country.* Boston: Little, Brown, 1927. Harkness Cottage and first Tyng House.

Reiff, Daniel D. *Houses from Books.* University Park: Pennsylvania State University Press, 2000. Harkness Cottage and Keefe's own house.

Rhoads, William B. *Kingston, New York: The Architectural History & Guide.* Delmar: Black Dome Press, 2003. Arnold, Keefe, Matthews, and Shufeldt Houses.

_____. *Ulster County, New York: The Architectural History & Guide.* Delmar: Black Dome Press, 2011. Drawings of the Van Deusen and Spy Houses.

Walsh, Harry J., ed. *Home-Owner's Handbook.* New York: McFadden, 1930. Chapter II. Five Rooms in Shingle (Young Cottage). Chapter III. A House that Has Room to Grow (Woolworth Cottage).

Books by Keefe

The American House: Being a Collection of Illustrations & Plans of the Best Country & Suburban Houses Built in the United States during the Last Few Years. New York: U.P.C. Book, 1922, 1924.

The Georgian Period: Colonial Details of Measured Drawings (edited by Keefe). New York: U.P.C. Book, 1922.

Keefe's Library and Book Collection

Charles Keefe's life centered around architecture. As a practicing architect he maintained an office library of periodicals and books directly useful in design and construction. This office library has been dispersed, and no catalog survives. Keefe published his buildings in the *American Architect, Architecture, Architectural Record*, and other professional journals, as well as *House Beautiful, Your Home*, and other popular magazines (see Appendix I), and so it can be assumed that he subscribed to a number of these journals and magazines. He maintained a complete run of the *White Pine Series of Architectural Monographs*, valuable for its photos and drawings of Colonial landmarks, and when his copies of volume IV (1918) were "soiled by water," he paid for replacements. [CSK to Ruth A. Maginnis, Nov. 19, 1937] Three issues of *Landscape Architecture* are in the Archive. Keefe marked an article, "Old Cape Cod Fence-Posts," in the Oct. 1922 issue. His office library certainly included books comparable to his own *The American House* and *The Georgian Period* whose illustrations might inspire new designs. His reference books included a *Cyclopedia of American Agriculture* and Mansfield Merriman's *The Strength of Materials* (New York: Wiley, 1903), both in the Keefe Archive, the latter with his signature and date, "2-16-03". In 1925 he ordered *The Bible in Iron* by Henry Chapman Mercer from the Bucks County Historical Society at the recommendation of Myron Teller. [CSK to Bucks County Historical Society, Oct. 6, 1925]

Keefe apparently had no hobbies outside architecture and books—he enjoyed visiting old houses, and he enjoyed collecting books about old buildings, as well as old books interesting for their age and appearance whether or not their contents were architectural and might be used to inspire designs. He especially sought antiquarian books from English dealers. (Letha Gedney, in a Jan. 24, 1985 phone interview, was almost right in recalling that her friend, neighbor, and architect had no hobbies beyond designing and studying houses in the area.)

A few months before the stock market crash, Keefe wrote Harry Halverson, the young partner of his Kingston friend and rival Myron Teller, giving advice on book collecting from English dealers:

April 3, 1929

Dear Harry:

Here is the list of old book dealers in England. You can write them asking to have your name put on their mailing lists. Looking over these lists is a lot of fun (to me at least) and unless one is careful, it gets to be what one of my clients calls a vicious habit. When he told me this in February, he had used up all his book money for the year. So be warned.

Wm. C. Elly, 17a Sweeting Street, Liverpool, England.

C. Howes, 485 Old London Road, Hastings, England.

James Rimell & Son, 6 Duke Street, St. James, London, S.W.1, England.

Reginald Atkinson, 188 Peckham Rye, London, S.E. 22, England.

George Gregory, 8 Green Street, Bath, England.

Hope you get as much kick out of reading these catalogs as I do.

The origins of Keefe's love of book collecting are uncertain, but one was surely the example of Alfred Hopkins, who guided Keefe to English booksellers on his only trip abroad in 1910. In 1933, years after Keefe left Hopkins, Hopkins wrote a florid tribute to his own search in shops from Naples to Paris for old volumes bound in gilt-decorated leather: "For there is no beauty quite like the beauty of old leather and burnished gold." [Alfred Hopkins, "Old Leather and Burnished Gold," *The Colophon*, Part 14 (New York, 1933), unpaged. "Fine bindings, rare books and manuscripts, including the collection of the late Alfred Hopkins" composed the May 19, 1964, Parke-Bernet auction. *NYT*, May

10, 1965] All indications are that Keefe cared less about the bindings of the books he collected than about their contents, and especially their illustrations or plates whether useful to the architectural designer or of purely artistic interest.

An informal list of books Keefe ordered from English booksellers according to surviving correspondence and bills ("sold" indicates that the item was sold before his order could be completed; "Swann" and an item number refer to the sale of Keefe's books believed to have occurred June 12, 1975, at Swann Galleries in New York):

Bell's *Poets of Great Britain*. 20 vols. 1777. From W. Heffer & Sons, Cambridge, 1928.

Cooke. *Book of Dovecotes*. 1920. From C. Howes, Hastings, 1928 (Swann 45).

Daniel. *Rural Sports*. From W. Heffer & Sons, Cambridge, 1928 (sold).

Daniel. *Rural Sports*. 1801–02. From R. Atkinson, Bookseller, London, 1929.

Haghe. *Sketches in Belgium*. From George Gregory Bookstore, Bath, 1925 (Swann 72).

Holbein's *Portraits*. 82 tinted plates. 1828. From Dulau & Co., London, 1925.

Ireland. *Views on Thames*. 2 vols. 1792. From W. Heffer & Sons, Cambridge, 1928 (Swann 78).

Miniature Bible. 1896. From R. Atkinson, Bookseller, London, 1929.

Morrison. *Haddon Hall*. From George Gregory Bookstore, Bath, 1925.

Muller's *Sketches*. From George Gregory Bookstore, Bath, 1925 (sold).

Nicholson. *British Scenery*. From George Gregory Bookstore, Bath, 1925.

Old Cottage in Kent & Sussex by Davis. From James Rimmell & Son, Bath, 1925 (sold).

Old Lombard St. by Price. 1890. From James Rimmell & Son, London, 1925 (sold).

Paris Moderne. c. 1840. From C. Howes, Hastings, 1928 (Swann 104)

Price. *Interiors etc. in Venice*. From George Gregory Bookstore, Bath, 1925.

Roberts. *Sketches in Holy Land*. 6 vols. From W. C. Elly, Liverpool, 1925.

Sketches in France by Prout. Folio. 1839. From James Rimmell & Son, London, 1925.

Sketches in Spain by Lewis. 26 colored lithos. 1834. From James Rimmell & Son, London, 1925. Noted in Grace Keefe's 1954 will.

Sketches of the Age of Francis I. Folio. 1841. From James Rimmell & Son, London, 1925.

Timbs. *English Eccentrics*. 1890. From C. Howes, Hastings, 1928.

[unidentified] Fifty lithographic plates. From George Gregory Bookstore, Bath, 1925 (perhaps Swann 128, "Spanish Lithographs").

Views in India. 48 lithos, Folio, 1832. From C. Howes, St. Leonards-on-Sea, England, 1925.

Weaver. *English Leadwork*. From W. Heffer & Sons, Cambridge, England, 1928 (Swann 148).

White. *Natural History of Selbourne*. From W. C. Elly, Liverpool, 1925.

Wilkie. *Sketches*. 2 vols. From George Gregory Bookstore, Bath, 1925.

The architect made a habit of giving books and prints to favored clients. Keefe purchased four lots from R. Atkinson's catalogue no. 81, including the Daniel, *Rural Sports*, and miniature Bible noted above. His pencil notes indicate that the two vols. of Daniel, *Rural Sports*, were given to Mrs. Brenchley, a Connecticut client, and the miniature Bible to Mrs. K. (his wife). A third lot consisted of 16th- and 17th-century engraved title pages; he gave one to client Lew Alliger of Whitehead & Alliger, sellers of fine book papers, and another to New Jersey client Mrs. Ralph Inslee. The fourth lot consisted of six 18th-century portrait prints; he gave two to Mr. Norton and one (framed) to Mrs. Charles Inslee, both important clients. Raymond Thornburg to Keefe, Jan. 3, 1937, expressed thanks for Keefe's gift at Christmas of "the beautiful colored lithographs," but their artist and subject are unknown. A fragment of an undated and possibly unsent letter from Keefe to client Charles Bellows, in the Thornburg file, reads: "I am not sure that you are interested in books about your family but I ran across an"—indicating that Keefe encouraged his clients to collect books and prints.

Clarence McK. Lewis had Keefe design and install a sundial on the Lodge at his Skylands estate, and he collected books on the topic. Keefe gave Lewis a "little book on dialling," which the recipient noted "has the decided attraction of being short, which may lead to its being read (!), and in addition it exemplifies your particular skill at picking out books that, in spite of the considerable number which I have just acquired on this subject, yours should not be among them, and is therefore a doubly-prized possession." [Lewis to CSK, June 24, 1924]

Given his love of books, Keefe must have found the design of the museum for Crane & Co., paper makers, a congenial commission. In 1934 he sent his client, presumably as a gift, a book printed in nearby Pittsfield by Phineas Allen in 1806. Keefe and his friendly contact at Crane, C. J. Kittredge, believed the book's paper had been produced at the Crane mill, the only paper mill in the vicinity in 1806. [C. J. Kittredge to CSK, June 8, 1934]

In the case of Lowell Thomas, Keefe sent his client extracts from "an old history" relating how, in August 1776, Mrs. Phebe Thomas of Quaker Hill had been robbed by a gang of 180 silver dollars and other valuables. Keefe pointed out "that some branch of the Thomas family was on Quaker Hill even in those days. Apparently the family trait of finding a fine place to live still holds good for there you are right now." He concluded: "If another war comes along I hope you will have as many pounds in your sock as the old time Mrs. Thomas did." [CSK to Thomas, Dec. 7, 1937, Thomas Papers, Marist College] Thomas then passed along the extracts to the Pawling newspaper, which published them along with Thomas's note identifying his source as "Charles S. Keefe, the famous colonial architect" who designed his sister Pherbia's home. [*Pawling News-Chronicle*, Dec. 16, 1937]

In 1921 Keefe wrote his Kingston contemporary, New York State Senator Charles W. Walton, in search of two New York State publications, *Birds of New York* and *Wild Flowers of New York*. It isn't known whether Keefe wanted them for his library or perhaps as a gift, but whatever the case Keefe noted apologetically: "Usually I am not in the habit of troubling a busy man with such trifles, but I know of no other way of going about it." In fact, for Keefe ordering books was not such a trifling matter.

Keefe's practice of making friendly gestures via gift books is recorded in his letter to noted architect and bibliophile Bertram G. Goodhue, who in 1920 had been unable to accept Keefe's invitation to have his work illustrated in *The American House*. [Goodhue to CSK, Nov. 19, 1920] Goodhue's portrait photograph by F. Holland Day shows the handsome architect with books on a table and on shelves behind [James F. O'Gorman, *Some Architects Portraits* (American Philosophical Society, 2013), 64]; early in his career he had been a book designer and then, as a highly successful architect, a leading member of the Grolier Club, New York's prestigious club of bibliophiles. [Romy Wyllie, *Bertram Goodhue: His Life and Residential Architecture* (New York: Norton, 2007), 37]

May 22nd, 1923

My dear Mr. Goodhue:

I am sending with this letter an old copy of the Brickbuilder which I ran across the other day and I would like to have you accept it with my compliments. On looking thru it I noticed some of your drawings that you very likely have forgotten, and it occurred to me that it might bring to your mind some pleasant memories of the days before clients worried you.

I have a habit of reading catalogs of second-hand books and sometimes I buy the books. This is what one of my clients calls a vicious habit. At times I get so that I buy books for other folks when I think the books might interest them. This is my only excuse for sending the book and I trust if you have not some similar failing, you will at least have some charity for another's weakness.

To which Goodhue good naturedly replied at once before departing for Lincoln, Nebraska, where he was designing the state capitol:

May 22nd, 1923

My dear Mr. Keefe:

It's really very good of you indeed to send me the old copy of the Brickbuilder. Little amenities like this are not any too common in the profession—or in life either for that matter—and I am glad of the chance to thank a brother architect for his thoughtful kindness.

As for the book itself, I have just finished looking it over—in rather a rush it must be confessed, for I am leaving this afternoon for 'Gopher Prairie,' in other words Lincoln, Nebraska—and am amused by the balance of it even more than by my own sketches of an imaginary place. These are not so unfamiliar to me because they were re-reproduced in a book of my drawings that came out ten or twelve years ago and, bad as they are, are a darnside better than anything I can do now. In fact I think I had about the best fun in all my life when I was doing these. Let me recommend the process to you: its the only way I know of to get entirely rid of clients and their absurd requirements. The rest of the book is indeed strange. Of all the names of the contributors only a few have managed to keep their heads above water and, Lord! how they are changed! I am going to chaf some of those I know about their efforts in this book when I next see them.

Lawrence Grant White, Stanford White's son and a McKim, Mead & White partner in the twenties, was the recipient of another of Keefe's gifts, a photograph of William R. Mead and Charles F. McKim, which again indicates Keefe's interest in the recent history of his profession and probably, too, his instinct to maintain good relations with leading firms. [Lawrence Grant White to CSK, Jan. 11, 1929]

One of the few published photographs of Keefe appeared with a 1937 *Freeman* article celebrating his career and recent work for Lowell Thomas. Keefe is pictured at home in his "library," surely a sign of the importance books held for the architect. In *The American House* (p. 14) Keefe wrote, in reference to Bottomley's Townsend House on Long Island, "The little library with its panelled walls is just the proper home for good books," and further, regarding a Georgian house by Pope in Baltimore (p. 17), "In the library the wood work is American walnut which forms a fine setting for the brighter colored books." Several of the houses Keefe designed had a room designated "library." Keefe must have regretted that he never could enjoy such a handsome and expensive room as Bottomley and Pope had created, nor even a simpler library such as he had planned for others. (Similarly, he may have regretted not belonging to the Grolier Club, the elite club of bibliophiles in New York, whose leaders included Bertram Goodhue.) Many Keefe houses, including his own, incorporated book shelves in the living room, and it was probably there that Keefe posed for his *Freeman* photo. [*KDF*, Oct. 9, 1937] Frank Lloyd Wright was among the architects of Keefe's generation who were devoted to books and libraries. [See Elaine Harrington, "Books and Libraries in Frank Lloyd Wright's Oak Park Days," in *American Architects and Their Books, 1840–1915* (Amherst: University of Massachusetts Press, 2007), 231-256.]

Grace Keefe retained her husband's office files and his books through her lifetime. In her 1954 will, Grace directed that Keefe's plans and specifications be given to "architectural colleges." A few, not-rare, architectural books were to be given to former draftsman Isaac Reuben. She bequeathed to the Kingston City Library "the rare books and collector's items which are in the library in my home" (a "black note book, in which all our library books are listed" has been lost) along with $5,000 for the building of a room at the city library to house the collection. She mentioned three books dated 1492, 1552, and 1588, without giving their titles or authors. However, the 1492 volume was probably printed May 28, 1492, by Peter Drach in Speier according to a paper with typed description of this incunabulum with penciled notes by Keefe. Also mentioned were three folios—"Lewis of Spain, Roberts of Spain and Lear of Rome, all in color," presumably the Sketches in Spain listed above, David Roberts's *Picturesque Sketches in Spain*, and Edward Lear's *Views in Rome and Its Environs*. A tablet at the room's entrance would memorialize "Charles S. Keefe, Architect, Artist and Author." The room should be designed by Royal Barry Wills, the notable Boston designer of Colonial houses, or Robert Hutchins, A.I.A. President, and be "paneled in conformity with my husband's designs."

Each book was to have a bookplate inserted reproducing a pen-and-ink sketch by the late architect with the legend, "Charles S. Keefe, his book." Keefe had sketched in pencil and pen several ideas for his bookplate, all simply picturing books. Two pencil sketches are on the back cover torn from a catalogue of The Caxton Head, a famous antiquarian bookshop in London. (On the same cover he also sketched the center of his house, doubtless for the Christmas card design.) Oddly, the bookplate sketches show a book resting on the edges of its front and back covers, with spine up, a position likely to, over time, break the spine. No printed bookplate has been found.

Sadly, by the time of Grace's death in 1971, there were insufficient funds to carry out her wishes. Robert H. Palmatier and Fredric Misner of Thumbprint Antiques purchased a heavy van-load of books from the Keefe estate. Palmatier had appraised the books inventoried in the "black note book" at $800. The more valuable books from Keefe's library were sold at auction at Swann Galleries, probably in their June 12, 1975, sale of "Architecture & Allied Arts" with 156 items in the catalogue. Several of the items included a number of individual books. A few of the books could not have belonged to Keefe, namely those published after his death, and more than likely those by Frank Lloyd Wright whose modern houses Keefe disliked. [Fredric Misner, phone conversation, Nov. 10, 2014. Swann Galleries has not answered an inquiry regarding the sale of Keefe books.]

A box of miscellaneous books owned by Charles and Grace was sold by Thumbprint Antiques to the author and his wife, Oct. 25, 1975. Dorothea Hamilton Fyfe's *Oxford* (New York: F. A. Stokes, n.d.), illustrated with pen-and-ink drawings by L. Russell Conway, provided Keefe a visual and historical record of Oxford's landmarks, just as Frank H. Taylor's *Valley Forge* (Valley Forge: Daniel J. Voorhees, 1922) did for the Pennsylvania park. Similarly Charles, the artist and printmaker, presumably chose E. R. Pennell's *The Art of Whistler* (New York: Modern Library, 1928) and Curtiss Sprague's *How to Make Linoleum Blocks* (New York: Bridgman, 1928), although no linoleum

block prints by Keefe are known. Charles, the Spanish-American War veteran, wrote "Charles S. Keefe, 258 Lucas ave." on the flyleaf of Erich Maria Remarque, *All Quiet on the Western Front* (Boston: Little, Brown, 1929)—a "first printing." Also war-related was Charles Vince, *England in France: Sketches Mainly with the 59th Division* (London: Constable, 1919). The Cape Cod travelers had Henry Beston's *The Outermost House: A Year of Life on the Great Beach of Cape Cod* (Garden City: Doubleday, Doran, 1928), where the writer-naturalist made his observations from a self-designed two-room house. Charles, student of New England's frame Colonial houses, inscribed his name, New York City address (40 East 49th St.), and 1929 on the flyleaf of Jane De Forest Shelton, *The Salt-Box House: Eighteenth-Century Life in a New England Hill Town* (New York: Scribner's, 1929; copyright 1900), which was illustrated with a photo and drawings of Connecticut saltboxes. Keefe signed his name in script in *All Quiet*, for his home library, while he printed his name, as he would on an architectural drawing, in *Salt-Box House*, for his office library. One book, T. Morris Longstreth's *The Catskills* (New York: Century, 1918), inscribed with Keefe's name and 247 Park Avenue, remained with the owners of Thumbprint Antiques until after their deaths when it was sold at Flannery's Auction, Pine Bush, August, 29, 2016. Among the other books in the box sold to us in 1975: Walter Pater, *The Renaissance* (New York: Boni & Liveright, 1919); Anna R. Sheldon and M. Moyca Newell, *The Medici Balls: Seven Little Journeys in Tuscany* (New York: Charterhouse, 1904); and Thomas Anthony Wilson, *Weekends at the Farm* (New York: N.L. Brown, 1925).

Just as clients and associates received books from Keefe as friendly gestures, the author has benefited from the generosity of Michael Lynch, who in the 1970s purchased, from Thumbprint Antiques, Keefe's collection of journals and magazines in which his designs were published. Lynch, an engineer, architect, and preservationist, presented them to the Friends of Historic Kingston in 2013.

Christmas Cards by Keefe

Grace Keefe wrote to Dorothy Hoffman, stepdaughter of Grace's sister Blanche and named co-executor in Grace's 1954 will, describing Charles's creation of their Christmas cards. "Each year Charles S. Keefe, A.I.A. made a pen and ink sketch of a house, or scene, of historical interest, from which prints were made for our Christmas cards, sent out both from the N.Y. office to clients & business friends, also from our home to personal friends. A precious few remain." She enclosed a "pen and ink sketch . . . of the Old Spy House entrance" and "our Christmas card of the Van Deusen House."

Perhaps the most appealing of Keefe's cards portrayed his and Grace's Lucas Avenue home as the idyllic setting for Christmas cheer. About 1930, as the Depression began and Prohibition was still in force, Keefe sketched a kitchen with old-fashioned cook stove, cat, and mouse along with lines composed for a card: "SOMETHING'S COOKING/IT'S GOING TO BE/CHRISTMAS SOON/AND NEW YEAR'S TOO/DOWN THERE THE XMAS SPIRIT IS ALL IN BOTTLES/UP HERE IT'S IN THE AIR." The sketch with "Something's Cooking" is on a sheet of rough architectural sketches for the Lewis Alliger house.

Alliger's firm sold fine paper, and Keefe may have intended to use its paper for the card. With the reference to "Xmas spirit in bottles down there," might the card have been intended for Norton and Oldrin in Ecuador? No "Something's Cooking" card is known to exist. As the Depression lingered, Keefe told a client, Robert M. Anderson, January 2, 1935, that business was so bad he had had to close his New York office and even stop sending Christmas cards in both 1933 and 1934.

By 1938 he resumed the practice of sending a personally designed card, although not one centered around a building. The 1938 card (of which 300 copies were printed) showed a child on a Victorian sofa, identified by Keefe as: "a picture of Graces dad [John de la Montanye, 1848–1931] made frm a daguerreotype taken 87 years ago when he was three. A swell fella, I say."

That Keefe's clients appreciated his cards is suggested by an acknowledgment penned by Robert Bruce, January 4, 1930, for the 1929 version: "We were so happy to be remembered by you at Christmas time and we have come to looking forward, each Christmas, to your card, which carries such a personal touch."

Keefe's Renderers and Photographers

Keefe had sufficient skill as a draftsman to make his own renderings or perspective drawings intended to give the client an understandable and visually attractive representation of the completed building, but for some commissions he engaged a professional renderer to make large, bold drawings, to increase the appeal of the design as the client decided whether to build. In the case of the Rices of Pittsfield, the rendering was also made in the hope that their friends, admiring the perspective, would commission designs from Keefe and Movius, and renderings generally had publicity value. On renderings in the 1920s, see Arthur L. Guptill, *Sketching and Rendering in Pencil* (New York: Pencil Points Press, 1922), 78, 109.

From the signed renderings retained in the Keefe Archive—of the Crane Museum and Inslee, MacDonald, and Patterson Houses (the last titled "Rendering for Remodelling the Old House")—all by **J. Floyd Yewell** (1885–1963), it can be inferred that Yewell was Keefe's favorite renderer. Yewell employed stronger contrasts of blacks and whites than Keefe did in his drawings. Winner of the Architectural League's Birch Burdette Long Memorial Prize for architectural rendering in 1942 [*New York Sun*, Mar. 20, 1942], Yewell was also a residential architect, and the Keefe Archive has Yewell's 1927 plans for Mrs. H. Bellavignor's brick Georgian house in Flushing, Queens. As noted previously, Keefe was curious to learn how his stock plans for the *Pictorial Review* compared with Yewell's.

Photographs of completed buildings published in professional journals and popular magazines were important to Keefe as a means of establishing his reputation and garnering commissions. Therefore Keefe took care in choosing photographers and selecting from their photographs.

In 1923, Keefe had **Antoinette Rehmann Perrett** (Mrs. Galen J. Perrett, 1880–1952) photograph the superintendent's cottage at the Harkness estate on Long Island. Mrs. Per-

rett, both a photographer and writer, was a 1901 graduate of Vassar College and was located at 492 Mt. Prospect Avenue in Newark, New Jersey. [*NYT*, May 1, 1952] Keefe approved two photos—a general view of the front and end, as well as one of the entrance porch. Her photos were to be published in *House Beautiful* [CSK to Miss E. B. Power, July 23, 1923], and Keefe explained to *House Beautiful's* Ethel Power his arrangement with Mrs. Perrett, who was working on her first job for Keefe: "Mrs. Perrett photographs the building and submits the pictures to me and I pay her for the ones that are acceptable. Mrs. Perrett has my permission to sell copies of the pictures that I O.K. to any good magazine, preferably one like *The House Beautiful* or an architectural magazine. As you know, all pictures are not successful and I requested Mrs. Perrett to sell only the ones I considered satisfactory." Keefe feared the photographer "desires to sell other pictures than those I approve. I remember a rear or side view that was submitted, which was out of perspective and generally a poor view of the house." [CSK to Power, Aug. 15, 1923] Keefe copied Mrs. Perrett on this. Indignant that Keefe accused her of breaking their agreement, she demanded an apology for the insult. Ultimately Keefe and Perrett both apologized for their misunderstanding. [Perrett to CSK, July 31, 1923, and received Aug. 20, 1923; CSK draft to Perret, Aug. 20, 1923; Perrett to CSK, Aug. 21, 1923] Generally satisfied with Mrs. Perrett's work, Keefe had recommended her to his client, C. McK. Lewis, who needed photos of his place in Mahwah, New Jersey, before its sale was concluded: "Mrs. Perrett makes good pictures and is well up in all landscape work." [CSK to Lewis, Aug. 3, 1923; CSK to Mrs. Perrett, Aug.3, 1923]

However, in 1931 Keefe enthused to client William Rice that **Paul J. Weber** (1881–1958) of Dorchester, Massachusetts, in photographing a house in Needham for Keefe, had produced "the best pictures I have ever had made of my work and are really pictures not photographs. [CSK to Rice, Feb 28, 1931] Keefe's Constantine Hutchins house in Needham had been photographed by **Louis H. Dreyer** (1873–1952) for the April 1929 *Architectural Record*, and Dreyer's photos of the David Patterson house in North Salem appeared in *Architecture*, September 1929. But Weber did photograph the later Hutchins guest house, and it must have been these, in *Architectural Record*, July 1932, that Keefe so admired. Rice then had Weber photograph his Pittsfield house. Keefe and Rice were both very pleased with Weber's photos, and Keefe wrote Rice: "With the planting and the garden as they are, the place looks as if it had been there a long while. The interiors are good and bring out Mrs. Rice's furnishings and decorations. . . . Weber can certainly find the right points to take his pictures. Many places are charming as one sees them, but when photographed in the ordinary way they are disappointing. They lack the composition

and color that Weber gets into his pictures. Did you ever see such cloud effects?" [Rice to CSK, Aug. 27, 1931; CSK to Rice, Sept. 10, 1931] Keefe wrote Weber, September 10, 1931, "The pictures are really wonderful. I never saw such gorgeous cloud effects anywhere or anyhow." Between 1929 and 1931 Weber was employed by Harvard University's News Office to photograph the university's buildings and grounds. [oasis.lib.harvard. edu/deliver/~16011]

George H. Van Anda (c. 1891-?) was also a talented photographer. His views of the Bellows house were published in the May 1933 *American Architect*. On a blueprint plan Keefe drew, probably to guide Van Anda, are yellow arrows to "suggest shots inside of house." In response to Julius Hoffman's request from Stuttgart, Germany, Keefe wrote Van Anda, September 10, 1938, for photos of the Bellows dining-room fireplace for a book on fireplaces.

APPENDIX VI

Keefe's New York Offices and Staff

By March 1920, Keefe departed from Hopkins's office at 101 Park Avenue and set up his own office at 368 Lexington Avenue. His office addresses in the city were: 368 Lexington Avenue (1920–21); 331 Madison Avenue (1921–23); 247 Park Avenue (1923–28); and 40 East 49th Street (1928–33).

Keefe's undated plan, "Alterations to offices at 331 Madison Ave.", shows a small "reception room," slightly larger "office," and largest "drafting room" with four drafting tables and "books" shelving. Murphy & Dana, architects, were also located in the building. [*NYT*, Feb. 8, 1915] Keefe sent out an attractively printed announcement, dated July 1, 1923, of "the removal of his office from 331 Madison Avenue to the New Park-Lexington Building at 247 Park Avenue. Telephone number Murray Hill 3373."

The Park-Lexington Building rose twenty stories between 46th and 47th Streets; Benz autos leased ground-floor space in 1923. Keefe's office was Room 1419, apparently on the 14th floor. The year 1923 was Keefe's most successful to date [CSK to Harry Kendall, Jan. 9, 1924], and 247 Park was probably Keefe's most prestigious office address. [*NYT*, Mar. 1, 1923] The building was razed about 1963. [*NYT*, Apr. 4, 1963] Hallam Movius paid a fraction of the office rent, apparently $5 a month in 1925. [Movius to CSK, Dec. 18, 1925] Keefe sent an announcement dated May 1, 1928, similar to the 1923 announcement, of "the removal of his office from 247 Park Avenue to 40 East 49th Street Between Park and Madison Avenues. Telephone number Vanderbilt 7876." The announcement in the Keefe Archive has the pencil note, "Room 904."

Keefe's plan, "Office for Charles S. Keefe Architect at 40 E. 49th St. N.Y.C.", is dated April 2, 1928, and indicates a small "reception room", larger "conference room" with circular table and two sets of "book shelves", and largest "drafting room"—with one desk (presumably for Keefe), three files, and four tables. Only the drafting room had windows.

Keefe designed a bookcase for this address, May 7, 1928. Keefe wrote Hallam Movius, May 8, 1928, that his larger office had a better clients' room and anteroom, and that he would have Movius's name put on the door when his own went on.

Keefe's office staff was small, and he took on men and women as needed for specific jobs. Information about Keefe's draftsmen and other staff survives in recommendations he wrote for those seeking employment after departure from his office. About 1920 Keefe composed this letter "To whom it may concern":

> Miss Marguerite L. Powers was employed for five years in the office of Alfred Hopkins with whom I was associated until recently. As I had charge of the office I am familiar with her work. I have found Miss Powers to be loyal, honest, faithful and a hard worker. She is a competent stenographer, a very fast typewriter and a good dictaphone operator. She is thoroughly familiar with the routine of an Architect's office and is competent to install a special book keeping system. . . . She has initiative and executive ability and handled all the accounts when contracts were let on a percentage basis. Her work in the office was varied. In addition to her regular work she answered correspondence, ordered materials, made up payrolls and checks, did our banking and made up income tax reports. I can highly recommend her. . . .

Miss Powers had worked with Keefe in preparing "Suggestions for List of Duties of Office Boy," including "Answer telephones . . . Filing . . . Errands." It noted that "All duplicates of Mr. Hopkins' letters are be put on C.S.K.'s desk, and vice versa." Her special suggestion: "Appearance. It should be the duty of the office boy to look as neat and clean as possible. Clean nails, blackened shoes, etc. help." Miss Powers had also given Keefe, with whom she clearly had good relations, a typed copy of "Standard Specifications for Contractors . . . (compliments of

H.D. Willis)" along with the penciled note: "Mr. Keefe: You might enjoy reading this when you are not too busy. It's humorous. M.L.P." A typical clause: "ENGINEER: The term 'engineer' herein appearing, shall be understood to mean the engineer or any uncivil and unsanitary engineer that he may foolishly employ to assist in making trouble for the contractor." Keefe described a "Mr. Seelye" as "the engineer that does my work" in relation to a concrete slab for the Lewis feed room. [CSK to Lewis, May 8, 1926]

In 1926 Keefe wrote on behalf of Carl C. Herter, who was seeking employment as an expediter for Bing & Bing, Inc., a real estate and building construction firm. Herter had worked in Keefe's office about three years: "he took care of all the detail work and when I turned a thing over to him I could forget it with perfect safety. . . . He is posted on the details of construction and mechanical equipment. . . . I can say he is one of the best men that ever worked for me." [CSK to L. M. Zach of Bing & Bing, May 11, 1926] Herter may have been the draftsman who sketched "Doyle" and "D" for the "Enitial for Doyle knocher, Sept. 15, 1924." Herter resided in the German-American district of Yorkville in the 1930s. [*NYT*, Mar. 20, 1934]

Isaac Reuben attended Kingston High School and received a B. Arch. degree from Cornell University in February 1928. George Young, Jr., the Cornell architecture professor and old school friend of Keefe, recommended Reuben to Keefe, who in fact employed him as an "architectural draftsman and designer" from just after graduation until September 1929, shortly before the stock market crash. During the Depression, when jobs for draftsmen were few, Reuben applied for a position with the New York State Education Department, and Keefe recommended him, as "his work was very satisfactory." Keefe and Reuben had become friends, and Charles admitted to him upon returning to his office after a "vacation" (doubtless partly a result of few commissions) and being "very glad to be working once more. Mrs. Keefe said that my disposition, while never too good, was getting worse so I guess it was time to go to work." In 1934 Reuben assisted Keefe in making measured drawings of the Sudam House in Kingston for the Historic American Buildings Survey, and the two were among the Kingston architects who made measured drawings of New Paltz's Bevier-Elting house for HABS. [*Cornell Daily Sun*, Mar. 31, 1928; obituary of Isaac's wife Anne Reuben, *KDF*, Apr. 17, 2012; George Young, Jr., to CSK, Feb. 9, 1928; CSK to Young, Feb. 15, 1928; CSK to New York State Education Department, Mar. 11, 1932; CSK to "Dear Rube", Mar. 11, 1932] Reuben remained a friend of Charles and Grace and was mentioned in her will.

Baltimore architect Lawrence Hall Fowler in 1932 wrote inquiring about John G. Hironimus, who had given Keefe as a reference. Fowler had "a small hall of records to do in Annapolis, so before long shall need a draughtsman who is capable at working drawings and also has some ability and taste in design of a colonial character." Fowler was probably aware of Keefe's own preference for Colonial design. Keefe responded that, "John Hironimus would be a good man for the work you have in mind. He is well acquainted with

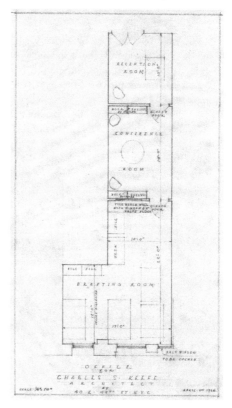

"Office for Charles S. Keefe Architect at 40 E. 49th St. N. Y. C."

colonial work and you will find him industrious and capable of turning out his work quickly. Also, he is perfectly capable of carrying a job thru from start to finish. He is far from being like the usual New York draftsman who generally knows one thing and that not very well." [Fowler to CSK, June 1, 1932; CSK to Fowler, June 2, 1932] Hironimus had grown up in Evansville, Indiana, attended architecture classes at Columbia (1925–27), and worked for a number of New York architects in the 1920s and 30s before returning to Evansville and establishing a successful practice. [https://sites. google.com/site/modernevansville/architects/individuals/john-hironimus]

Few job applications survive. An especially telling one is a letter from Marian S. Walker to Keefe, March 8, 1931, seeking an interview for a place in his office and referring to her training at the Cambridge School of Domestic Architecture, the first American school devoted exclusively to educating women architects. [Sarah Allaback, *The First American Women Architects* (Urbana: University of Illinois Press, 2008), 25]

My dear Mr. Keefe,

It may be that this beautiful spring weather has reawakened the all but hopeless feeling I have had about getting a job this year, but whatever it is, I am inspired to make another effort to-day.

I graduated at the Cambridge School of Domestic Architecture last year and in the Fall I was so fortunate as to be called upon by a country architect to help him with some extra work that had come to him. That work finished, I came to my home here in New York [333 East 68th St.] and in high spirits I set out to find any sort of opening in an architect's office. I was prepared to empty scrap baskets if that would provide the entering wedge—the business situation being what it was (and is!) After applying at various offices with such credentials as I could bring from my school and my short time employer, I found to my dismay that not only was my appearance considered an annoying intrusion but that my long cherished hope of just winning a very ordinary job was more or less of a presumption.

I cannot believe that there is not a place for me as there is for countless thousands of other young hopefuls and in my refusal to relinquish my effort to win a place, I am taking the liberty of writing you. Is there the slightest chance that you will give me an appointment? I can work hard and conscientiously and I have had excellent training. I am prepared to make no pretentious claim, but I bid for the "entering wedge."

Keefe replied, March 11, 1931:

Dear Madam:

I read your rather unusual letter with a great deal of interest. Unfortunately I have no opening at present for a draftsman and none in sight. Some offices will not consider a woman in the drafting room, but I have no such prejudices. I had a young woman in such a capacity but was obliged to drop her on account of business conditions. Your best opportunities will be with architects specializing in residential work and I suggest your trying those in the suburban towns near New York where there seems to be less objections to having a woman in the drafting room.

If you can work as well as you can tell your story you ought to get along.

In 1933 the *Times* announced that "Miss Marian Walker of New York" had been appointed to a fellowship in the American School of Classical Studies at Athens, although she is not listed among the fellows and students of the school, nor does she appear in A.I.A. directories. [*NYT*, Apr. 27, 1933; www.ascsa.edu.]

It is not surprising that Keefe was open to hiring a woman, as he enjoyed a good professional relationship with Verna Cook Salomonsky, one of the few women architects in New York. He involved her in the revised edition of the *Georgian Period*, and it was she who passed along R. F. Bach's opinion of *The American House*. She also helped Keefe keep in touch with an important editor, Ethel Power of *The House Beautiful*, which published several of his houses. [CSK to Power, June 8, 1926] In 1938 Robert Irving Carter, a former Salomonsky employee, when asking Keefe for a recommendation, added a P.S.: "I saw Mrs. Salomonsky last week. She is going to take a rest away from the office for awhile." [Carter to CSK, Oct. 30 and Nov. 16, 1938] VCS's architect husband Edgar Salomonsky had committed suicide in 1929.

Keefe is not known to have hired any African American or other minority, if any applied for a position. He held the racial prejudices and insensitivities common in his time. In a letter to client William T. Rice, June 26, 1928, he explained his willingness to change design details to please the client. One woman had "thought the columns at her entrance porch were too thin . . . that they always reminded her of a little colored girl with very thin legs who worked for her once. While there is no nigger in your wood pile this is an example showing there are more ways than one of looking at a thing."

Keefe relied less on the telephone than on written communications. Still, in the Norton file there are numerous yellow slips with telephone messages from 1925-26 signed "Sam," while in 1928 "Andy" was taking messages for Keefe, in the Young/Brenchley file. Keefe himself rarely invited correspondents to phone him.

Wills

Notes Regarding Charles S. Keefe's Will, October 3, 1922, and Selected
Items Listed in Grace Keefe's Will, June 29, 1954, with Values from Robert
H. Palmatier's Appraisal of her Estate, August 20–26, 1973

Charles Keefe's will named Grace Keefe as his sole beneficiary and executrix. If she did not survive him, a trust with Rondout National Bank should be created with income to Grace's mother and father, Elizabeth and John de la Montanye.

Grace Keefe's will directed that Charles's plans and specifications be given to "architectural colleges" and that his rare books be preserved at the Kingston City Library in a room built for that purpose. Her will also listed many items of jewelry, silver, furniture, and household items. While Charles seems not to have inherited family heirlooms, among the antiques listed in Grace's will are several that she proudly noted had descended in her family.

"I direct that the old Dutch shelves in Dining Room be sold or given to a Museum with the understanding that it be on exhibition as being from the collection of Charles S. Keefe, A. I. A." The old Dutch shelves were valued at $450, the second most valuable item in the 1973 appraisal.

"ANDREW KEEFE, Dr. Augustus Keefe's fraternity ring and my husband's open face gold watch; my husband's two bronze medals (in top chiffonier drawer in office)." The two bronze medals were valued at $10.

"EDWARD REMMERT, . . . etching 'Woodstock Fair' by André Smith."

"JAMES AND LEONA DE LA MONTANYE, de la Montanye coat of arms and crest framed over my desk, replica of vase (wrought by Gorham) designed by Charles S. Keefe." The original vase was probably for floral memorials in the American Legion Building.

"EILEEN KEEFE, Italian pitcher on old Dutch shelves, also Japanese print in guest room. . . ."

"CELESTE KEEFE, Photo of oil painting of Martha Hoffman and snapshot etching 'Old Age' by Gustave Adolphe Hoffman." Hoffman (1869–1945) was a German-American artist active in Connecticut.

"ISAAC REUBEN, Books, Architectural graphic standards and Architectural Digest in office closet." Isaac Reuben had been a draftsman and designer in Keefe's office in 1928-29.

"DOCTOR AND MRS. ED. PERKINS . . . etching by Gustav Adolphe Hoffman, 'The White Cloud.'"

"MY SISTER, BLANCHE FITZGERALD, great grandmother's dining room table, 5 side and 1 arm chair, and buffet, and grandmother Montanye rush bottom ladder back painted black chair." The dining room table ("Mahogany Drop Leaf Table") was valued at $150.

"I give and bequeath to the Senate House Museum, Kingston, New York, three pieces of furniture that were buries [sic] in underbruch [sic] in Jacob's Valley (S. Clinton Avenue) during the burning of Kingston, consisting of stretcher table, rush bottom blue ladder back chair and small pine chest painted red, all from the Hotaling-Schempmoes family. I also give and bequeath to the Senate House Museum, Kingston, New York, 4 small solid silver teaspoons from great-grandfather Isaac de la Montanye; 2 solid silver teaspoons from grandmother Margaret Phillips Montanye, one engraved M.P. and the other engraved M. Montanye; large solid silver tablespoon, engraved J.D.L.M.; 2 solid silver salt spoons from grandmother de la Montanye." The stretcher table (described as an "18th Cent. Drop Leaf Table") was valued at $750, the highest amount in the appraisal.

"I give and bequeath to D. A. R. of Kingston, New York, fireplace tongs and shovel (old-late 1700) from the Hotaling-Schepmoes family."

Mrs. Dorothy Fitzgerald Hoffman of 245 East Chester Street, Kingston, was named an executor (along with Mrs. Leona de la Montanye of Woodstock), but declined to serve. Mrs. Hoffman's stepmother was Grace's sister, Blanche de la Montanye Fitzgerald. Mrs. Hoffman's son, Joseph, as a young boy was befriended by Grace. She wrote him about her 1930 trip to Holland: "Since you are a Hoffman you too are likely part Holland Dutch and . . . I'll let you have my guide book (filled with pictures) of Holland. Maybe someday you'll take me again, will you? Love, Aunt Grace of the Holland Dutch Hoetaling-Schepmoes family! Let's shake Joey!!!" [Grace Keefe to "Master Joseph Hoffman," n.d.] She willed him her automobile and a gold watch. The auto, a 1941 Chevrolet, was in poor condition (partly from various accidents Grace had had) when Joe received it. [Phone conversation with Joseph E. Hoffman, Dec. 15, 2014] The new car is mentioned in an undated letter from Ruth Taylor to CSK.

Donna Keefe told the author, Nov. 28, 1984, that the Keefe house was in disorder after Grace's death, and that a number of items were stolen.

Keefe on Handling Ideas Brought by Clients

In 1928 *House Beautiful* asked for Keefe's opinion of an article that had appeared in Printers Ink, written by an architect who complained about clients "riding rough shod" over his advice about materials. The architect blamed advertisers for convincing clients that a particular product was essential. Keefe's long response gives a nice summary of his experience dealing with clients and discusses not only clients set on having a specific material or product, but also clients wanting to take over major design decisions, and then concludes with a complaint about cheap plans offered by suppliers of building materials:

Aug. 28, 1928

Mr. W.C. Griffing
c/o The House Beautiful
Fifth Avenue Building
New York City

My dear Mr. Griffing:

I have read with a great deal of interest the article from Printers' Ink . . .

In a way the writer is right in what he says of these clients. I have noticed a tendency on the part of clients to arrive for the first conference with a mass of clippings and booklets showing all sorts of building materials and devices. Others come prepared with a series of clippings showing doorways, staircases, mantels and all kinds of details. If I am dealing with reasonable people I do not object to this as it gives me an idea of what they are thinking about. Generally, a talk will straighten out all these matters and as they come to me for a certain type of house they are willing to be guided by my advice. It is perfectly reasonable for a client to ask for certain materials & for the architect to incorporate them in the plans or specifications if the materials are suitable. When it comes to matters of design, I believe I am best qualified to decide such matters and find I can satisfy the client without copying any designs they have brought in. This in general is the way things work out, but now we come to a different type of client, the one described in the article. . . .

You would be surprised to know how many people believe they are perfectly competent to design a house. A great many believe they know as much, if not more than the architect. Why any of them ever engage an architect is more than I know. . . . They have always been in existence and probably always will be. You can explain a certain thing is not suitable but they will insist on having it. You can tell them the various devices they insist on will make the house more expensive than they want it to be. Then they will quote so and so's house that has all these things and costs less than their house is to cost. You cannot make them understand that conditions even a few miles apart are totally different and so on and on. They just know and you are wasting your time talking with them. They come to you for advice and yet do not want it. They are just as foolish as a man who collects a lot of patent medicines and takes them to a doctor, telling the doctor to cure his ills with the mass of junk he has collected.

This type of client is certainly on the increase, whatever the cause may be. The best thing for an architect to do is to refuse to work for them because all he will get is trouble. If the house turns out well after a lot of study on the part of the architect trying to make things jibe, they say, "We designed our own house and only had an architect put our ideas on paper." If it turns out badly they blame the architect.

Once in a while I read articles in household magazines about just such folks describing how they did this and that. If they truthfully tell where they have made mistakes, as some do at times, you will find these errors just the things architects are paid to avoid. Often in these articles they mention the troubles they have with their architects. Sometimes they ignore him altogether, believing they did it all. I remember one particular article in your magazine. The owner described how she remodeled an old house, speaking feelingly of her talks with the carpenter each day. How she insisted on certain things against the contractors will and so and so for many words. However, she neglected to mention the architect. I know one was employed for I know the house and the architect.

I believe I can truthfully say that more and more prospective owners are influenced by the consumer advertising. They do not all go to the extremes noted in the article, but never the less this advertising does affect their ideas. The people with the smaller houses seem to be influenced most and often demand materials far beyond their pocketbooks.

I know the editorial staff of your magazine never even suggests to its readers that they not abide by their architect's advice. In fact magazines of its class have done a great deal to teach people the value of better architecture and better furnishings and have in this way helped the architects. I must say, however, some associations by direct consumer advertising of cheap plans have made it very difficult for architects in small towns. If they want to do business this way, alright, then they should not try to get the architects to specify their materials on the other hand. Some have the gall to work both sides.

This is quite a long story, longer than I intended in fact. I have wandered a bit from the subject but I hope there is some little point that may be of value to you.

Not surprisingly, Griffing was not able to find in Keefe's letter a useful rebuttal to the Printers' Ink article. [W. C. Griffing to CSK, Aug. 29, 1928] Still, *House Beautiful* continued to publish Keefe's houses.

Keefe's Description of the Proposed Basement Common Room, Rice House, Pittsfield

March 31, 1932

Mr. William T. Rice
43 South Street
Pittsfield, Mass.

Dear Mr. Rice:

Enclosed are sketches for your proposed room in the basement. I have kept this work all along early lines and have shown beams in the ceiling. These beams will be like the sample sent to you today under separate cover. The larger ones are half round and the smaller ones about like the sample sent only the edges will be square instead of grooved. The walls are shown as being covered with boards put on horizontally which was done in some early houses. All the folks that use boards today put them on vertically so we will be different but still correct. The ceiling would be plastered in uneven but not rough plaster an oyster shell white in color. The floor would be of slate slabs along the lines of the slate shown on the enclosed card but without sawed edges.

I placed the counter where it is shown so the pipes could be concealed in the shelving behind. The upper part is of round bars with one part that swings out for serving purposes. There is a low door at the further end of the counter and a door also opening into the other part of the cellar for supplies. There is a primitive type of foot rail shown, this is authentic. All the doors are batten doors with wooden latches and H hinges of iron. The sconces and lamps are stock examples of Colonial reproductions. These can be for candles or fitted with electricity. I used seats at the end somewhat along the lines of the picture Mrs. Rice gave me as this made room for some cabinets useful in storing cards, score pads, toys, cups, saucers, etc.

The drawing of the fire place shows the fittings that can be used there as you get them. The spit rack can hold little bars for toasting marshmellows, etc. The long handle frying pan can be used for bacon and eggs if your guests stay long enough to need sustenance. In making such drawings bottles seem to fit in nicely but please understand this is as far as the suggestion goes. A little trivet and a kettle are shown as suggestions for dressing up the fire place and also for use.

The present wood storage place has been left as there are pipes in there that would affect the head room. The only pipes that come in the room we have shown are on the east and west walls and these can be boxed in.

I have tried to keep the larger space clear so it can be used for dancing if desired. Also note that small swinging windows are shown on the inside of the cellar windows. They help the appearance and will be warmer in winter. As laid out the room should be a pleasant place for everyone young and old. Turn the boys loose in there, all they will do is to antique the place. Let me know what you and Mrs. Rice think of the sketches and if they are along the lines you have had in mind.

Notes

All correspondence cited here is in the Keefe Archive at the Friends of Historic Kingston unless otherwise indicated.

Introduction

1 *NYT*, July 20, 1946; *Arch. Rec.*, Dec. 1946, 13; Keefe's obituary also appeared in *Empire State Architect*, Sept.-Oct. 1946, 53.

2 On Wills, see Richard Guy Wilson, *The Colonial Revival House* (New York: Abrams, 2004), 179–189.

Chapter One

1 Kingston City Directories; *KDF*, Nov. 28, 1949; CSK to Mr. Higgins, Dec. 12, 1932, providing biographical information at the request of *House & Garden*.

2 Andrew Keefe obituary, *KDF* Aug. 15, 1935; Mattie Pultz Keefe obituary, *KDF*, Nov. 28, 1949; *Poughkeepsie Daily Eagle*, Jan. 18, 1894; Ruth P. Heidgerd and William Mercer Shoemaker II, comp., *The Schoonmaker Family*, Part III (Huguenot Historical Society, 1979), 158, 287; conversation with Charles Keefe's niece, Donna Keefe, daughter of his brother Andrew, Nov. 28, 1984; *KDF*, Mar. 7, 1944, and July 20, 1946; phone interview with Letha Gedney, Jan. 24, 1985; *Kingston Leader*, about May 30, 1931.

3 Snapshot of CSK smoking a pipe while playing with kittens: "First trip to Vt. with Overland car Aug. 1919"; CSK to W. T. Rice, Mar. 18, 1932; *KDF* Oct. 21, 1939.

4 *KDF*, July 20, 1946.

5 *KDF*, June 6, 1952; William B. Rhoads, *Teller & Halverson* (Kingston: Friends of Historic Kingston, 2005); CSK to Mrs. MacMurphey, Apr. 13, 1933*KDF*

6 William B. Rhoads, *Ulster County, New York: The Architectural History & Guide* (Delmar, N.Y.: Black Dome Press, 2011), 64-65. Before attending the Academy, Keefe probably was a student at School No 11, as a December 1926 note from George Young, Jr., to Keefe asked whether he remembered him from No. 11.

7 Clara Norton Reed writing for the series, "Our Neighbors Whose Fame is International," *KDF*, Aug. 26, 1936. Keefe placed a long history of the Academy by Edward L. Merritt, published in the *KDF*, June 7, 1938, in his clipping file.

8 Donna Keefe to author, Nov. 17, 1985; *KDF*, Oct. 9, 1937; Rhoads, *Ulster County*, 50–51, 142.

9 Certificate of New York State Adjutant General's Office, Sept. 21, 1916; Theodore A. Dreis to CSK, Dec. 30, 1930, with Keefe's note: "Joined, Life membership, Jan. ? 1931 - 5.00."

10 Author's interview of Donna Keefe, Nov. 28, 1984, at her home, 30 Lafayette Ave., Kingston; *KDF*, Mar. 1, 1961; city directories. In 1933 Charles designed a story-and-a-half Colonial house with brick façade and sides for his brother Andrew, but the house, to be erected on Mountain View Avenue in Kingston, was almost certainly not built.

11 For a comparable photo of Hudson architect Henry S. Moul in his office about 1900, see Mary N. Woods, *From Craft to Profession* (Berkeley: University of California Press, 1999), 113.

12 James F. O'Gorman, *Some Architects' Portraits in Nineteenth-Century America* (Philadelphia: American Philosophical Society, 2013), 62, has found that by 1900 leading architects were no longer being portrayed with drafting tools, but instead often with books, as a sign that the architect was a lawyer-like professional who relied on assistants to make drawings. So the photos may indicate that Kingston was behind the times, or record the young men as hired draftsmen not yet fully in charge as architects.

13 Father Andrew and stepmother Mattie occupied 291 Washington Avenue until their deaths in, respectively, 1935 and

1949, after which it was the home of Charles's sister Celeste (Mrs. Adam K. Porter); Kirkland plans by Teller are in the possession of Kingston architect Robert Milliken.

14 *KDF*, Sept. 26, 1905; Andrew S. Hickey, *The Story of Kingston* (New York: Stratford House, 1952), 90–91; *KDF*, Feb. 6, 1928; "Charley" to the Hoffman family, n.d., courtesy of Joseph E. Hoffman. John de la Montanye's funeral was held at the Keefe house. Obituaries of grandfather John and father John, *Rondout Courier*, June 12, 1868, and *Kingston Leader*, about May 30, 1931, clippings courtesy of Joseph E. Hoffman.

15 *KDF*, Nov. 14, 1903, and Nov. 9, 1935; in her 1954 will, Grace listed a 1903 Kingston Academy graduation pin and 1904 Teachers Training School pin.

16 *KDF*, Nov. 9, 1935; Oct. 7, 1912; Oct. 18, 1915; Jan. 23, 1918; Dec. 11, 1923; Dec. 6, 1916; Sept. 26, 1923. In 1922, when the club's theme was Japan, she spoke on its art and architecture. Olympian Club, 1922–23, p. 5. The Friends of Historic Kingston preserves the club's annual booklets from 1913–14, 1922–23, 1923–24, 1924–25, all of which include Grace's club activities.

17 *KDF*, Oct. 19, 1925; Dec.19, 1922; Jan. 5, 1928; *KDF*, Jan. 11, 1935.

18 CSK to George J. Schryver, June 9, 1919; *KDF*, Feb. 16, 1925, and May 3, 1941; CSK to F. Lawrence Goldschmidt, July 3, 1928.

Chapter Two

1 1907 Kingston directory: CSK removed to New York City; *KDF*, Sept. 2, 1907: CSK, of New York, was spending several days in Kingston. On Burnett, see *Biographical Dictionary of the United States Congress*, bioguide.congress.gov., and Taya Shoshana Dixon, "Edward Burnett: An Agricultural Designer on Gentleman's Estates," M.A. thesis, University of Pennsylvania, 1998, http://repository.upenn. edu/hp_theses/290. On Hopkins, see *NYT*, May 6, 1941.

2 *The Field Illustrated*, July 1920, 630.

3 Sometime before April 30, 1915, Keefe made notes about garden plants for his Kingston home on stationery headed "Charles S. Keefe, Architect, 11 East 24th Street, New York City." And occasionally he reconnected with Burnett; in 1916 and again in 1921, Burnett and Keefe were responsible for plans of a garage, chauffeur's house, and dairy for George Bliss Agnew in South Salem, New York.

4 *Stables and Farm Buildings. A Special Number of The Architectural Review*, Sept. 1902, 239–241; Harvard College Class of 1901. Second Report, Cambridge, 1907; Cunningham to CSK, Nov. 5, 1925.

5 Keefe also seems to have retained, at least for a time, Burnett's office employee, Miss Hughes, whom Burnett also held in high regard. Cunningham to CSK, Nov. 5, 1925 and July 17, 1933; CSK to Cunningham, July 19, 1933.

6 Richard Guy Wilson, "Mysticism, Alchemy, and Architecture: Designing Laurelton Hall," in *Louis Comfort Tiffany and Laurelton Hall* (New York: Metropolitan Museum of Art, 2006), 72; Hopkins, *Modern Farm Buildings*, 128. The other Burnett clients represented by negatives are: Chanler; Morgan; (Mortimer L.) Schiff (Oyster Bay, L.I., illustrated in Hopkins, *Modern Farm Buildings*, 152); Sloane; (James) Speyer (Scarboro, N.Y., Hopkins, 132, 134); Charles Steele (Westbury, L.I., Hopkins, 136); (Francis Lynde) Stetson (Sterlington, N.Y., Hopkins, 16); and the Massachusetts Agricultural College.

7 *Stables and Farm Buildings*, 243.

8 On the qualities of A.I.A. members, see Mary N.Woods, *From Craft to Profession: The Practice of Architecture in Nineteenth-Century America* (Berkeley: University of California Press, 1999); *A.I.A. Historical Directory of American Architects*; Architectural League of New York, *Catalogue*, 1908 and 1920.

9 Hopkins to CSK, Dec. 12, 1910; Hopkins to CSK in London, Nov. 30, Dec. 12, 1910.

10 *KDF*, Dec. 3, 1910. For Hopkins's proposal for the Tudor-style residence of James H. Perkins in Greenwich, Con-

necticut, see *Architecture*, Jan. 1918. Keefe pasted a clipping of Hopkins's proposal in his blank-page binding of *The American House.*

11 CSK to Hopkins, Dec. 11, 1910.

12 CSK to Hopkins, Dec. 18, 1910.

13 CSK to Hopkins, Jan. 9, 1911.

14 CSK to Hopkins, Jan 1, 1911.

15 CSK to Hopkins, Jan 1, 9, and 15, 1911. Several German postcards acquired by Keefe have been added to his archive by Michael Lynch.

16 *AIA Architectural Guide to Nassau and Suffolk Counties* (New York: Dover, 1993), 140; Federal Writers' Project, *New York City Guide* (New York: Random House, 1939), 213.

17 Keefe's notes indicate he was considering the White Star ship *Celtic* sailing on February 18 and Cunard's *Caronia* sailing the 17th. The last charge on his Naples hotel bill is dated February 17, so he probably took the *Caronia*. The European trip is documented by undated "Itinerary" by Hopkins; Hopkins to CSK, Nov. 30, 1910; CSK to Hopkins, Dec. 11, 1910 (from Oxford), Dec. 18, 1919 (from London), Jan. 1, 1911 (from Brussels), Jan. 9, 1911 (from Heidelberg), Jan. 15, 1911 (from Venice), Jan. 27 and Feb. 3, 1911 (from Rome).

18 Hopkins to CSK, Nov. 30, 1910; CSK to Hopkins, Jan. 9 and 15, 1911.

19 *American Architect & Architecture*, May 19, 1915, 322.

20 The print of St. Stephen's Cathedral was by "O. Strache" according to an old label, although the signature appears to be "Strauhe"; it was framed for Keefe in the 1920s when his office was at 247 Park Ave. Janine Burke, *The Sphinx on the Table: Sigmund Freud's Art Collection and the Development of Psychoanalysis* (New York: Walker, 2006), 177. Charles Moore, *The Life and Times of Charles Follen McKim* (Boston: Houghton, Mifflin, 1929), 276.

21 *NYT*, Mar. 11, 1915, and Apr. 14, 1929.

22 CSK to Marjorie A. Prevost, June 18, 1926; Hopkins to CSK, July 1, 1915.

23 Among the couple's earlier homes was one in Kingston at the corner of Franklin and Pine Streets where Grace gave an engagement shower. *KDF*, Feb. 21, 1907.

24 *KDF*, Feb. 25, 1915, and Sept. 13, 1940.

25 *KDF*, July 12, 1912.

26 Dixon, "Burnett," 71.

27 CSK to George J. Schryver, June 9, 1919.

28 *KDF*, Dec. 6, 1916.

29 Charles S. Keefe, *The American House* (New York: U.P.C. Book Company, 1922), 14.

30 Another collie is mentioned in a June 29, 1926, letter from Keefe to John Oldrin: "Our white collie, 'Lady Bug' died suddenly last Saturday during a thunder storm and we believe the scare she had caused the trouble."

31 Bingee was a female, and apparently was briefly preceded by a male chow puppy also the gift of Lewis. Soon after he arrived in Kingston, Keefe wrote Lewis: "The little fellow seems to feel at home with us, and he is greatly admired. Mrs. Keefe has been waiting to write and thank you until she could give you some definite news about the young man's attitude toward life in Kingston." (CSK to Lewis, Jan. 11, 1924) A little later Keefe could report that "the young fellow . . . is one of the family now. He just belongs and wants everybody to know it." (CSK to Lewis, Jan. 29, 1924) That same day Lewis wrote a long letter to Mrs. Keefe in response to questions she had about the discipline of the male puppy, which Charles chose against Lewis's recommendation of a female. It seems the attempt at discipline failed, and the male was replaced by Bingee.

32 CSK to Lewis, Sept. 19, 1929. Note on a sheet of paper headed "American Kennel Club Stud Book." CSK to Lewis, Nov. 21, 1932. Lewis replied to Keefe, Nov. 28, 1932: "Too bad about Bingee, but losses like that are the price we have to pay for the pleasure that dog love and companionship can bring us." He recommended getting attached quickly to another dog and regretted that he had no puppy available to offer Keefe at the moment. Keefe was chagrined that Lewis interpreted his letter

as seeking the gift of another dog. CSK to Lewis, Dec. 9, 1932.

33 Marjorie A. Prevost to CSK, June 4, 1926; CSK to Prevost, June 8, 1926; CSK to Fielding, June 8, 1926.

34 *NYT*, Oct. 8, 1933. The Berkshires were actually well out of sight.

35 Branson to CSK, July 4, 1932; CSK to Branson, July 27, 1932.

36 *KDF*, Aug. 26, 1911; *KDF*, Oct. 6, 1908. In 1940 George Winter was quartermaster and Charles Keefe trustee of Colonial Camp, 75, United Spanish War Veterans. *KDF*, Jan. 9, 1940.

37 In 1937 Keefe remained proud of his design for the Winter bungalow and was especially pleased with how he had been able to separate living and sleeping rooms on the single floor. *KDF*, Oct. 9, 1937.

38 "A Concrete Bungalow," *Cement Age*, August 1911, 71.

39 *New York Press*, Feb. 8, 1914.

40 In 2016 the Knights of Columbus building became the Abundant Life Tabernacle.

41 *KDF*, July 14, 1913; Apr. 24, 1913; May 21, 1912.

42 *KDF*, July 14, 1913; CSK, "Mellowness of Old Brick," 18–19.

43 CSK to Dwyer, Jan. 6, 1914.

44 Joseph F. Sullivan, "Kingston Council, No. 275," *Burning of Mortgage, Knights of Columbus Home, Kingston, N.Y.*, January 6, 1921. Cashin was superintendent of the Hudson River Bluestone Co.

45 *NYT*, Oct. 26, 1913; *KDF*, July 14, 1913; *KDF*, April 18, 1914; W. B. Rhoads, "The Colonial Revival and the Americanization of Immigrants," in *The Colonial Revival in America* (New York: Norton, 1985), 350–353; *KDF*, Feb. 23, 1915.

46 Myer to CSK, Dec. 30, 1936; on the Thornburg mill see below; *KDF*, Dec. 5 and 8, 1938.

47 John J. Klaber, "The Grouping of Farm Buildings: Examples from the Work of Alfred Hopkins," *Arch. Rec.*, Apr. 1915, 341; Robert B. MacKay, *Long Island Country Houses and Their Architects* (New York: Norton, 1997), 216.

48 William O'Brien to CSK, Oct. 29, 1918; *NYT*, Apr. 8, 1944.

49 Hopkins repeated a portion of the chapter in "The Superintendent's Cottage," *The Field Illustrated*, June 1920, 546–547, 592.

50 Alfred Hopkins, *Modern Farm Buildings* (New York: McBride, 1920), 217–237.

51 *NYT*, June 5, 1931; MacKay, 184; *Arch. Forum*, Mar. 1919, 75–76, pls. 37-38; *RER&BG*, May 5, 1917, 643. In 1997 the Schiff farm buildings were "relatively unaltered." MacKay, 217–218.

52 *NYT*, Oct. 12, 1935; *Arch. Rec.*, Apr. 1915, 340, 345, 349-352; *Arch. Forum*, Mar. 1919, 75, pl. 36; Hopkins, 218, 236, pl. adjacent to 218; *Arch. Rev.*, Oct. 1919, 105–106; Keefe, pl. 82.

53 *NYT*, Oct. 12, 1935; *RER&BG*, Feb. 22, 1919; MacKay, 44.

54 *NYT*, Oct. 22, 1914; June 26, 1935; May 3 and 26, 1955; Hopkins, pls. opposite 226, 227.

55 *NYT*, Oct. 22, 1914; Keefe, 16, pl. 81; *Arch. Rec.*, Apr. 1915, 353-357; *Arch. Forum*, Mar. 1919, 75; Hopkins, pl. adjacent to 231. Among the "small jobs" Keefe listed in his Mar. 19, 1918, "Notes on Filing System" was "Glenn Stewart's log cabin." There is no further information about the log cabin.

56 Klaber, 351. It would seem reasonable to assign Keefe some credit for farm buildings (mostly white frame Colonial cottages) by Hopkins represented in clippings that Keefe pasted in his blank-page binding of *The American House*. These include the Schiff, Mollenhauer, Burchard, and Stewart farm buildings already discussed, and also farm and estate buildings for: J. K. Secor, Toledo, Ohio; J. Watson Armour, Lake Forest, Illinois; Effingham Lawrence, Cold Spring; and Clifford Brokaw, Locust Valley, Long Island, whose farmer's cottage chimney bears the date 1912.

57 Field Horne, *With the Strength of the Adirondacks: A History of the Adirondack Trust Company, 1901-2001* (Saratoga Springs: Adirondack Trust Co., 2002), 51, 225-229; Alfred Hopkins, "The Adirondack Trust Company," *Am. Arch.*, Nov. 14, 1917, 347-351.

58 *KDF*, Oct. 9, 1937; Hopkins, "Adirondack Trust," 350.

59 CSK, "Before and After: A Brief Story of the Remodeling of an Old-Fashioned House," *Building Age*, Mar. 1920, 37–38, 44–45; "Preservation Matters: An Evolution of Design: 658 North Broadway," *The Saratogian*, Nov. 1, 2014. In 2014 the Van Deusen House was owned by Charles Wait, Chairman and CEO of the Adirondack Trust.

60 *NYT*, Sept. 6, 1914 and July 27, 1948; *Arch. Rev.*, Mar. 1916, 38-39, pls. 21–28; "East Village/Lower East Side Historic District. Designation Report," Oct. 9, 2012, NYC Landmarks Preservation Commission. Keefe cited his role as "associate architect" of the building when providing credentials to the Chicago Tribune competition. CSK to Howard L. Cheney, July 5, 1922. Since 1988 the building has functioned as the Anthology Film Archives. Barred windows remain from the original holding cells, but the interior of the building reveals few traces of its original use. The courtroom appears in Robert Downey, Sr.'s, underground film, *Chafed Elbows*, from 1966 when the courthouse was no longer in use by the city. John Mhiripiri, Director of the Anthology Film Archives, e-mail to author, June 14, 2017, and conversation at the building, Sept. 12, 2017.

61 *NYT*, July 4, 1915; Hopkins, "Prisons and Prison Building," *Arch. Forum*, Feb. 1918, 49-57, pls. 26-30; Hopkins, "Westchester County Penitentiary and Workhouse," in *Plans and Illustrations of Prisons and Reformatories* (New York: Russell Sage Foundation, 1922), 47–54.

62 *NYT*, Feb. 28, 1918.

63 *KDF*, Oct. 9, 1937 and July 20, 1946; *NYT*, May 9, 2004.

Chapter Three

1 *Arch. Forum*, Mar. 1920, 134; *The Field Illustrated*, July 1920, 630.

2 Receipted hospital bill, Jan. 7, 1918; CSK to Hopkins, Apr. 26, 1920; *American Architects' Directory*, 1956, 485; Scarff, as a token of friendship, gave Keefe a watercolor he had painted of the Boboli Gardens in Florence with the pencil inscription, "Boboli Gardens/C.S.K. from J.H.S./May 1917." The watercolor is owned by Sarah R. Bruce, Vienna, Va.

3 CSK to Cunningham, Apr. 8, 1925.

4 CSK to Movius, Jan. 6, 1926, in regard to client William T. Rice; CSK to Hopkins, Oct. 26, 1926; W. L. Hopkins's obituary in *New York Herald*, Oct. 10, 1926, Keefe's newspaper clippings file; Hopkins to CSK, Oct. 28, 1926; CSK to Hopkins, Nov. 3, 1926. The next item in the file is Alfred Hopkins's clipped obituary, *NYT*, May 6, 1941.

5 Crocker to CSK, July 23, 1920.

6 Richard M. Bates was the architect who completed the bank between 1922 and 1924. S. Allen Chambers, Jr., *Buildings of West Virginia* (Oxford University Press, 2004), 217.

7 *Hempstead Sentinel*, Apr. 1, 1920; *Brooklyn Daily Eagle*, Apr. 30, 1920. Keefe reported to Hart on his inspection of the current jail and plans proposed by others. CSK to Hart, Mar. 12, 1920. CSK to Harry Kendall, July 5, 1923; CSK to E. S. Hall, June 25, 1938.

8 CSK to Howard L. Cheney, July 5, 1922; Cheney to CSK, July 8, 1922; *International Competition for a New Administration Building for the Chicago Tribune* (Chicago: Chicago Tribune, 1923).

9 Dixon, "Burnett," 65–66; *NYT*, Jan. 12 and 16, 1910. Another pallbearer was Francis L. Stetson, attorney for J. P. Morgan & Co. (*NYT*, Dec. 6, 1920), whose gate lodge at his estate in Sterlington was designed by Hopkins (and Keefe) in 1912.

10 Wilson, *McKim, Mead & White, Architects* (New York: Rizzoli, 1983), 154–159. The mansion and some of the 800-acre estate now form a campus of Fairleigh Dickinson University. The farm cottage is now the campus's wellness center. The Twomblys' daughter Florence married **William A. M. Burden**, and between 1921 and 1923 Keefe, with Burnett and sometimes Rogers, designed farm buildings and workers' housing on the Burden estate, Uplands, in Mt. Kisco.

11 "Harvard College Class of 1902," www.mocavo.com, accessed Oct. 23, 2015; *Harvard Alumni Bulletin*, 1914; CSK to Rice, Dec. 17, 1925.

12 *KDF*, Apr. 10, 1930; Halverson interviewed by author, Nov. 7, 1984. The hospital was demolished in 1984, although the nearby nurses' home was spared.

13 Halverson to CSK, Mar. 10, 1931; CSK to Halverson, Mar. 8, 1932.

14 *New York Evening Post*, Aug. 30, 1920; CSK to Taylor, Mar. 11, 1926; CSK to Cunningham, Apr. 8, 1925; Movius to CSK, Nov. 30 and Dec. 2, 1925.

15 *Dalzell, Homes*, 4–6.

16 "New Books for the Architect," U.P.C. Book Company brochure, c. 1923.

17 CSK to William A. Boring, Mar. 10, 1925.

18 CSK, *American House*, 13, 15.

19 Ibid., 13–15.

20 Ibid., pls. 42–44, 27–30.

21 Ibid., pls. 58, 81.

22 Ibid., pls. 15, 45.

23 Ibid., 24.

24 Ibid., 17–18.

25 CSK to Saul Haber, May 10, 1924; CSK, *American House*, 20.

26 CSK, *American House*, 21, 22.

27 Ibid., 22.

28 Teller to CSK, May 12, 1922; Baum to CSK, Nov. 20, 1920.

29 Rogers to CSK, June 18, 1923; Scarff to CSK, May 13, 1922; after CSK's death, Scarff's review in the *Baltimore Evening Sun*, June or July 29, 1922, was copied in pencil in the notebook, "For Publishing Book of Houses Designed by Charles S. Keefe."

30 *American Architects' Directory*, 1956, 625; Young to Keefe, n.d.; Young to CSK, Sept. 6, 1927.

31 Sarah Allaback, *The First American Women Architects* (Champaign: University of Illinois Press, 2008), 230; Helen Binkerd Young to CSK, Sept. 5, 1927.

32 CSK to Bach, Oct. 10, 1922.

33 Bach to CSK, Oct. 13, 1922. Edgar and Verna Salomonsky had designed Bach's Riverdale residence in the Dutch Colonial style of Long Island. *Building Age*, Aug. 1920, 36.

34 CSK to Boring, Mar. 10, 1925.

35 Saul Haber to CSK, Oct. 23, 1923; CSK to Boring, Mar. 10, 1925.

36 Haber to CSK, Oct. 23, 1924. Keefe was paid $400 for his editorial work on the first edition and received royalties of 10 percent on sales of the second edition. He took an active role in pushing sales. CSK to Haber, May 10 and Oct. 24, 1924.

37 CSK to Boring, Mar. 10, 1925; *Architecture*, May 1925, 174. The paper of the second edition is not significantly lighter than the original edition's, and the contents are identical.

38 CSK to Rice, Dec. 17, 1925.

39 Arnold to Judge D. T. O'Brien, Sept. 10, 1929.

40 WWF to CSK, Sept. 26, 1934.

41 Allaback, 214. Salomonsky's "An Exemplar of Old and New Colonial Details. IX. The Interior Door and Its Types," *House Beautiful*, Sept. 1927, 265-266, included drawings and photos of old Ulster County doorways, with contributions by Myron S. Teller, as well as drawings of two doors in Richmond, Vt., probably contributed by Keefe, since he had family ties to Richmond. This issue of HB is among the magazines from Keefe's office presented by Michael Lynch to the Keefe Archive.

42 *Am. Arch.*, July 18, 1923, 16; *Arch. Rec.*, Aug. 1923, 197.

43 S. A. Jones of Botsford-Constantine Company to CSK, Sept. 10, 1926.

44 Rhoads, "The Colonial Revival and American Nationalism," *JSAH*, Dec. 1976, 239– 254.

45 CSK to Botsford-Constantine Company, Oct. 7, 1926; S. A. Jones to CSK, Nov. 3, 1926. The Keefe Archive does not have material showing that his endorsement and photos were published.

46 Architectural League of New York, *Catalogue*, 1920 and 1930; CSK to Howard Cheney, July 5, 1922.

47 Edward C. Kemper to CSK, May 12, 1924, and Keefe's membership certificate, same date, signed by William Baker Faville, President, and Edwin Hacker Brown, Secretary.

48 Andrew M. Shanken, "Breaking the Taboo: Architects and Advertising in Depression and War," *JSAH*, Sept. 2010, 406–426; Spencer Vanderbilt to CSK, Nov. 9, 1923.

49 CSK to Rice, Dec. 17, 1925.

50 Taylor to CSK, Dec. 14, 1925; CSK to Taylor, Mar. 11, 1926; CSK to Young, Dec. 21, 1926; CSK to Taylor, Feb. 1, 1935.

51 CSK to Dorothy Fielding, June 8, 1926; CSK to Young, Dec. 21, 1926. Framer's notes on the mat of Keefe's drawing, "An English Yard," indicate it was "sent to Mrs. Charles S. Keefe, 152 Dyckman St., N.Y.C." Trow's New York City directory lists CSK residing at this address in northern Manhattan, c. 1917–20.

52 *KDF*, Sept. 21, 1920; CSK to Automobile Blue Book Publishing Co., Oct. 13, 1920; CSK to Lewis, Sept. 27, 1922; CSK to Rice, Jan. 6, 1926.

53 *NY Evening Post*, Aug. 3, 1923; *KDF*, Sept. 26, 1923.

54 On his return, Keefe told client William Rice of his vacation on "Cape Cod where they have the nicest little houses in the world as you know." CSK to Rice, Sept. 13, 1929. The hand-colored card was given to the author Feb. 17, 2015, by Joseph E. Hoffman. Grace Keefe sent the card to him in the early 1960s with the inscription, "Cape Cod Entrance. Original pen & ink sketch by Charles S. Keefe A.I.A."

55 CSK to Rice, Apr. 18, 1930.

56 Lewis to CSK, Jan. 26, 1925; CSK to Lewis, Jan. 27, 1925.

57 Written on the back of a typed catalog description of incunabulum, Gregorius IX, printed 1492 Speier by Peter Drach.

58 CSK interview with Wainwright Evans, "Just What Is a Cape Cod House?" *Your Home*, Dec. 1930, 11, 66-67.

Chapter Four

1 MacKay, 379. Edward Harkness was William's cousin and an even greater benefactor at Yale and patron of James Gamble Rogers. Aaron Betsky, *James Gamble Rogers* (Cambridge: MIT Press, 1994), 32.

2 *NYT*, Jan 15, 1947; CSK to Mrs. Harkness, July 31, 1924; Mrs. Harkness to CSK, Sept. 22, 1924.

3 CSK to Ethel Power, Aug. 17, 1923.

4 CSK to Power, July 23, 1923; "A Very Small House," *House Beautiful*, Nov. 1923, 468–469; Ruth Wendell to CSK, Dec. 26, 1923; CSK to Wendell, Jan. 7, 1924. The cottage was also published in Ethel B. Power, *The Smaller American House* (Boston: Little, Brown, 1927), 10.

5 CSK to Fred Titus, Jan. 7, 1926; CSK to Mrs. Harkness, Nov. 10, 1925; Salomonsky, "An Exemplar of Old and New Colonial Details," *House Beautiful*, June 1927, 817– 819.

6 *Architect*, Sept. 1926, pls. CXXV and CXXVI; CSK to William Leavens & Co., Dec. 18, 1925. Inquiring here about oak chairs, Keefe ordered two in birch stained gray.

7 CSK to Mrs. Harkness, Aug. 31, 1926; Mrs. Harkness to CSK, Sept. 13, 1926. *Cythera* was turned over to the Navy in both world wars and was sunk by U402 in 1942. *NYT*, Jan. 15, 1947.

8 CSK to Rogers, Aug. 31, 1926; Rogers to CSK, Sept. 3, 1926.

9 CSK to James B. Sipe Company, Sept. 28, 1925. The offending blotter remains with the correspondence.

10 CSK to Mrs. Harkness, Mar. 24, 1927 and Nov. 6, 1931; CSK to Mrs. Ingalls, undated (1931); Mrs. Harkness to CSK, Nov. 8, 1931; CSK to Mrs. Harkness, Nov. 10, 1931.

11 CSK to Stanley Cunningham, Apr. 8, 1925; CSK to Botsford-Constantine Company, Oct. 27, 1926; Power, *Smaller American House*, 11.

12 "Palo Alto House Wins Nat'l Honor," unidentified newspaper clipping in CSK's Scout file with Harkness material; castilleja.org; *House Beautiful*, Sept. 1925, 212; Rexford Newcomb, *The Colonial and Federal House: How to Build an Authentic Colonial House* (Philadelphia: Lippincott, 1933), pls. 69–70.

13 The current owner, Dennis M. Donnelly, reports (Mar. 17, 2015) that the letters, carved into wood blocks, are still in place. In an October 1925 drawing of

the entrance porch of the Eugene Sainson house, Keefe placed an "S" in two blocks above the door.

14 Elise Howland Lindenberger to CSK, Dec. 26, no year.

15 Judy Deeter of the Troy Historical Society e-mails to author, Feb. 16–18, 2015, with obituaries of Dr. and Mrs. Lindenberger, *Troy Daily News*, Feb. 25, 1963 and May 21, 1971; also *Troy Daily News*, Jan. 4, 1963, and other information mailed Feb. 23, 2015; phone conversations with Dennis Donnelly, Mar. 17 and Oct. 12, 2015; photos and information from Tyler George, grandson of the Lindenbergers, forwarded to me by Donnelly, Nov. 15, 2015.

16 politicalgraveyard.com; CSK to Robert Bruce, Dec. 20, 1923, and Dec. 11, 1924.

17 Bruce to CSK, May 10, 1925.

18 Bruce to CSK, Feb. 10, 1930; CSK to Bruce, Feb. 12, 1930.

19 Mrs. Bruce to CSK, May 31 and June 20, 1931; CSK to Mrs. Bruce, July 2, 1931.

20 CSK to Mrs. Bruce, Dec. 13, 1930; Mrs. Bruce to CSK, May 31, 1931.

21 Donald M. Schlegel, "Robert Marshall Anderson," *Bulletin of the Catholic Record Society—Diocese of Columbus*, May 2004.

22 CSK to Anderson, July 15, 1930 and Sept. 29, 1931.

23 CSK to Anderson, Jan. 2, 1935. The 250 letters are lost, but the Keefe-Anderson correspondence (Dec. 13, 1929, to Jan. 2, 1935) and Anderson's drawings survive in the Anderson Family Papers, The Huntington Library, San Marino, California, which provided me copies. Keefe's plans are in the Keefe Archive.

24 foskett-genealogy.co.uk; *Harvard Alumni Bulletin*, June 24, 1920; *Register of the Wellesley College Alumnae Assn.*, 1917–18; *Library Journal*, Feb. 15, 1922; Donna Keefe to author, Nov. 27, 1985; Marlene Pultz Kirby to author, Nov. 11, 1985. In 1940 Ethel Pultz sought and received advice from Keefe on building a house, from choosing a lot to financing, as well as a description of charges for his architectural services. CSK to Ethel Pultz in Long Branch, Jan. 13 and Feb. 10, 1940.

25 Photocopies of the Cate interiors with Marlene Pultz Kirby to author, Dec. 11, 1985.

26 *Princeton Alumni Weekly*, Sept. 18, 1959; *NYT*, Jan. 8, 1947, and Apr. 13, 1959; *New York Evening Post*, Sept. 6, 1929; CSK to Woolworth, Sept. 2, 1926, Dec. 12, 1927, and June 21, 1929; mottschmidt.com.

27 Elsie M. Rushmore to CSK, Nov. 20, 1928; the Woolworth cottage was also published in the Architects' Small House Service Bureau's *The Small Home* (Dec. 1930, 16), which inspired an inquiry to publish it yet again in a book, *General Mechanical Drawing: A Course Based on the Junior High-School Movement*, by R. A. McGee and W. W. Sturtevant. Robert T. Jones to CSK, May 13, 1931; Kozlowicz of Bruce Publishing Company to CSK, June 3, 1931. A reproduction of a rendering of the Woolworth cottage is identified as being published in the *Pictorial Review*, Apr. 1933, as a "Modified Dutch Colonial."

28 *Skylands: The Garden of the Garden State* (Ringwood: New Jersey Botanical Garden, 2011), 32; blueprints for Lewis in Mahwah that remain the Keefe Archive include "Proposed Greenhouse for Mr. Clarence Lewis, Mahwah, N.J. Charles S. Keefe, Architect, 368 Lexington Ave., N.Y.C. Hitchings & Co., Elizabeth & N.Y.C., Feb. 13, 1920."

29 Samuel B. Parsons, Jr., designed the grounds for Stetson. *Skylands*, 27.

30 CSK to Lewis, Mar. 1, 1923; Lewis to CSK, Mar. 3, 1923; CSK to Harry Kendall, Jan. 9, 1924.

31 *Skylands*, 22. The Swimming House was completed but no longer exists. Author's phone conversation with Rich Flynn, Sept. 2, 2016; photos e-mailed by Flynn, Sept. 14, 2016.

32 CSK to Lewis, July 17 and 19, 1923; CSK to E. L. Wagner, Aug. 16, 1923.

33 "Skylands Farm, The New Jersey Estate of Clarence Lewis," *Country Life*, Aug. 1937, 36; Lewis to CSK, Mar. 17, 1930; CSK to Lewis, Mar. 18, 1930.

34 CSK to Lewis, Jan. 13, 1931.

35 *NYT*, June 5, 1934, and Feb. 19, 1925.

36 *NYT*, Mar. 29, 1928. It is uncertain whether either brother's residence as designed by Keefe was erected. Conversation with Jim Hunt, current owner of Windy Brow Farms, Jan. 5, 2017. For "Misses Inslee," probably Caroline and Dorothy Inslee, sisters of Ralph and Charles, Keefe in 1929 designed cabinets for existing bookcases in their New York apartment.

37 *NYT*, Apr. 6, 1961.

38 Ken Reiss, *Tokeneke* (Darien, Conn.: Darien Historical Society, c. 2010), 18. CSK to Mrs. E. Y. Brenchley, Apr. 18, 1930, noted that "a set of plans for the greenhouse addition . . . have been approved by Norton Inc. . . . This approval is necessary according to your deed."

39 *Tokeneke*, published by the Tokeneke Association, 1928; Lisa Prevost, "Like Stepping into a (Very Expensive) Painting," *NYT*, May 15, 2005; Maggie Gordon, *The Gilded Age on Connecticut's Gold Coast* (Charleston: History Press, 2014), 113–117.

40 "Tip from Harry Parker," May 19, 1925; *House & Garden*, May 1932, 39–41.

41 CSK to Norton, May 21, 1925; CSK to Nuno, Apr. 8, 1930; CSK to Norton, Jan. 20, 1926.

42 *KDF*, Oct. 9, 1937; *Architecture*, November 1930, 291–292.

43 James Ford to CSK, Jan. 7, 1932; Ray Lyman Wilbur to CSK, Feb. 8 and May 6, 1932; CSK to Ray Lyman Wilbur, May 11, 1932. Keefe's bronze medal is not in the Keefe Archive. He had also submitted photographs and plans of two one-and-a-half-story houses, the Hutchins Guest Cottage and Brenchley Gardener's Cottage. Pencil notes by CSK added to James Ford to Members of the American Institute of Architects, May 1, 1931; CSK to Ford, Feb. 16, 1932.

44 CSK to Knobel Brothers, Dec. 8, 1925, and Feb. 11, 1926; "The House with the Be-at-Home Air," *Your Home*, April 1931, 15.

45 CSK to Blanche Halbert, Mar. 8, 1932.

46 *Your Home*, April 1931, 15; *The American Home*, Jan. 1931, 282, in an article directed to women, recommended the guesthouse as "an extremely compact and comfortable little bungalow"; James Ford, "The 1931 'Better Homes' Small House Architectural Competition," *Arch. Rec.*, April 1932, 243–248, 255.

47 S. Serota, Early American Antiques, to Norton, Oct. 8, 1929; Norton to CSK, Apr. 24, 1930. The architect also presented Norton with two inexpensive 18th-century portrait prints acquired from a London dealer. CSK notes on copy of April 22, 1929, bill for books and prints from R. Atkinson, London.

48 Photos of Norton's Homewood in *Pictorial Darien* 1939-40, available at the Darien Historical Society.

49 *NYT*, Dec. 31, 1924; Norton to CSK, Oct. 18, 1929; Keefe to Norton, Oct. 23, 1929. In August 1928 Keefe completed drawings for Norton of a two-story brick house with giant portico modeled after Homewood's in Baltimore. The subject of a large, professional rendering, it was probably intended for Hope and George Stevens, since it included a nursery and two bedrooms for children, as well as a library and servants' quarters comparable to the plan of the stone-veneer house actually built for the couple.

50 CSK to Norton, Oct. 11, 1929; *Arch. Rec.*, Feb. 1931, 109-115; *NYT*, Nov. 19, 1938; *Nuestra Arquitectura* to CSK, Mar. 21 and June 9, 1932.

51 Oldrin to CSK, Jan. 1, 1928, on Quito Tramways Company stationery. Keefe identified his work for Norton in Ecuador as "a country house, also an office building, at San Miguel . . . as well as a group of model dairy buildings for blooded cattle at Guayaquil." *KDF*, Aug. 26, 1936.

52 *KDF*, June 9, 1938; the *Freeman* noted that Keefe had also designed "for Mr. Norton . . . an office at Guayaquil, Ecuador . . . of Spanish architecture."

53 *NYT*, Jan. 13, 1942; *Architecture*, Dec. 1928, 357-358; *Your Home*, April 1929, 23.

54 *NYT*, Apr. 23, 1966, and Feb. 28, 1929. Farrell's residence and the listed improvements have been demolished. Kenneth Reiss in conversation with author, June 7, 2017.

55 *Your Home*, Oct. 1930, 15; *Better Homes and Gardens*, Nov. 1932, 34; *Your Home*, Apr. 1931, 15, and Dec. 1930, 66.

56 James Ford to CSK, Dec. 21, 1932, and Feb. 24, 1933; *NYT*, Feb. 8 and 26, 1933; *Herald Tribune*, Feb. 8, 1933. The Farrell cottage was published in the professional journal, *Architecture*, Nov. 1930, 289-290, as well as a magazine read by builders, *American Builder and Building Age*, March 1933, 27, a copy sent with B. L. Johnson to CSK, Mar. 18, 1933. George Wilisch of Cincinnati, Ohio, to CSK, Aug. 3, 1933, inquired about the cost of working drawings and specifications. The cottage was also included in Rexford Newcomb's *The Colonial and Federal House*, pl. 17, and *American Country Houses of Today* (Architectural Book Publishing Co., 1935), 118, which pictured the Borglum medal, dated 1931 and titled "The Home," showing a woman reading to a child. When featured in a popular magazine, the June 1933 *Pictorial Review*, dozens of readers inquired about securing plans.

57 CSK to Norton, Dec. 13, 1927; *NYT*, Oct. 20, 1908; Nov. 13, 1931; Aug. 19, 1990; Sept. 29, 1991. See Reiss, *Tokeneke*, 18, for photos of the house before and after alterations. The house, grounds, and owners over the years are the subject of a meticulously documented and illustrated history, *The Story of Round Meadows*, 2014, written and compiled by Belinda Bowling Metzger, Nancy Bowling Gramps, and Stephanie Bowling Ziegler, daughters of the present owner, Ann Jones Bowling. The privately printed book may be consulted at the Darien Historical Society. In 1920 Keefe had designed a similar Italian- or Spanish-style house for L. M. Lafleur at an unknown location.

58 *Your Home*, March 1929, 36-37; *Am. Arch.*, Aug. 1932, 57-60.

59 *House & Garden*, Aug. 1931, 74. CSK to Mrs. Young, Dec. 5, 1929, sent his bill for work on the two cottages, which he called the "garage cottage" and the "gardener's cottage."

60 Edna Brenchley to CSK, Aug. 15, 1931.

61 CSK to Brenchley, Apr. 9 and June 18, 1930.

62 CSK notes, Norton file, Sept. 22, 1925; CSK to Oldrin, Dec. 13, 1927, and Jan. 22, 1930.

63 *KDF*, Aug. 31, 1935, and Oct. 9, 1937; e-mails from John Oldrin's son, John Wood (Woody) Oldrin, to author, Sept. 2016.

64 Pentecost to CSK, Sept. 22, 1927; CSK to Pentecost, Oct. 17, 1928.

65 Young to CSK, Feb. 1938, in Thornburg file; tokenekeclub.clubhouseonline-e3.com.

66 *Brooklyn Daily Eagle*, Aug. 17, 1930, and Mar. 8, 1934.

67 Doris R. Bellows to CSK, no date, enclosing a copy of the plan of the "old house"; *House Beautiful*, Aug. 1933, 48; cslib.cdm host.com; *KDF*, Dec. 17, 1937.

68 CSK to Charles Bellows, Dec. 12, 1929; CSK to Doris Bellows, June 21, 1929.

69 CSK to Doris Bellows, Oct. 16 and 24, 1929.

70 Janet Lindstrom of the New Canaan Historical Society e-mail to author, July 25, 2016; *House & Garden*, Feb. 1933, 40-41; Morrison to CSK, Mar. 30, 1933.

71 *Am. Arch.*, May 1933, 77-82; *NYT*, Oct. 31, 1933, and Feb. 8, 1939. Keefe himself enjoyed a drink—his list of expenses for a trip to the Taylor house in Vermont in May 1941 included a 30-cent cocktail. In his archive are undated notes and blueprints relating to wine racks and cellars.

72 Alexa Brazilian, "Spatter Dash," *New York Times Style Magazine*, May 17, 2017, 54.

73 Harold Donaldson Eberlein and Donald Greene Tarpley, *Remodelling and Adapting the Small House* (Philadelphia: Lippincott, 1933), 61.

74 The Patterson House was also published in *Architecture*, Sept. 1929, 165-168. Louis H. Dreyer's photos of the dining

and living rooms show them full of Colonial Revival furnishings: painted blanket chest, slip-covered wing chair, pewter plates, candlesticks, and fireplace bric-a-brac. For a time in the 1930s, the house functioned as an inn, Bubble Brook Lane, serving meals prepared by a "Southern darky cook" and recommended by Duncan Hines, *Adventures in Good Eating*. Susan J. Thompson, Historian, Town of North Salem, furnished information about the Patterson house, Jan. 4, 2013.

75 *Harvard College, Class of 1905, Fourth Report*, 1920; *NYT*, July 8, 1932. The Hutchins property was also featured in Guy H. Lee, "A Collaborative Problem," *House Beautiful*, Sept. 1931, 199–204. Lee was a Harvard-trained landscape architect.

76 Lee, 200-204; photos by Weber and plan of the guesthouse in *Arch. Rec.*, July 1932, 27–29.

77 Lee, 202, 260; Appleton to CSK, Apr. 19, 1929; CSK to Appleton, Apr. 25, 1929.

78 Mumford, *Roots of Contemporary American Architecture* (New York: Reinhold, 1952), 434; Whitaker to CSK, Apr. 10 and 16, 1930. Whitaker knew the Hutchins house from the photos in the April 1929 *Architectural Record*, which also published LeCorbusier's Villa in Vaucresson and Mumford reviewing Henry-Russell Hitchcock's book on Frank Lloyd Wright.

79 CSK to Whitaker, Apr. 14, 1930.

80 CSK to Whitaker, Apr. 21, 1930; CSK to Whitaker, Apr. 17, 1931; Whitaker to CSK, May or Oct. 21, 1931; Donald L. Miller, *Lewis Mumford: A Life* (New York: Weidenfeld & Nicolson, 1989), 428-429; Behrendt, *Modern Building* (New York: Harcourt, Brace, 1937), 31, 106.

81 CSK to Rice, July 1, 1931; *New York Evening Post*, July 5, 1930; Movius to CSK, Oct. 26 and Dec. 2, 1925; Rice to CSK, Mar. 22, 1932; CSK to Rice, Mar. 23, 1932. Another member of this club and Keefe client in Dalton was Dr. Reginald Burbank.

82 CSK to Movius, Sept. 17, 1925; Movius to CSK, Nov. 4, 1925; Rice to CSK, Nov. 10, 1927; CSK to Rice, Dec. 9, 1927.

83 CSK to Movius, Apr. 4, 1928; CSK to Pike, May 8, 1928; Movius to CSK, June 4, 1928; CSK to Rice, Aug. 16, 1928; Rice to CSK, Dec. 12, 1928; CSK to Pike, Dec. 18, 1928.

84 CSK to Rice, Apr. 2, 1928, and Nov. 9, 1928; CSK to Movius, Oct. 25, 1928.

85 Rice to CSK, July 18, 1928; Cleota Reed, *Henry Chapman Mercer and the Moravian Pottery and Tile Works* (Philadelphia: University of Pennsylvania Press, 1987), 195-216.

86 CSK to Rice, Aug. 14, 1928; Rice to CSK, Aug. 3, 1928; CSK to Rice, Aug. 17, 1928. That "better hardware" included brass; in 1932 Keefe advised George R. Branson (July 27, 1932) that for his wood frame Dutch Colonial house in Maine he would "use small Colonial brass knobs, etc. Houses of this period are a little past the crude wrought iron hardware and are entitled to better hardware."

87 Rice to CSK, Aug. 22, 1928, and Nov. 21, 1929; CSK to Rice, Dec. 19, 1929; Rice to CSK, Jan. 9, 1930; CSK to Rice, Jan. 15, 1930.

88 Rice to CSK, Mar. 5, 1931, and Apr. 8 and June 26, 1932. In the April letter Rice also cited a seating "arrangement of pleasant memory in college."

89 CSK to Rice, Mar. 31, 1932, and Dec. 19, 1929.

90 CSK to Pike, Apr. 10, 1931; Rice to CSK, May 11, 1932. Other work contemplated for Rice included a guesthouse in the Cape Cod manner (sketches, Mar. 24, 1932), and a "Farm Group" for horses, goats, chickens, and geese designed in 1933. Rice decided against building the farm group. Keefe, greatly disappointed and in dire straits, wrote Rice asking for payment for preparing plans and specifications: "Most of the architects I know are out of business and I want to stave this off as long as I can. Any way, I'll go down fighting." CSK to Rice, July 12, 1932.

91 Taylor to CSK, Dec. 26, 1939, and May

4, 1941; *Troy Times,* June 10, 1918; *Troy Times Record,* Aug. 27, 1938, May 2, 1939, and May 11, 1940; Tyler Resch, *Dorset: In the Shadow of the Marble Mountain* (Dorset Historical Society, 1989), 219.

92 CSK to Taylor, Mar. 14, 1941; CSK to Pike, Jan. 5, 1939; Pike to CSK, May 27, 1940.

93 Taylor to CSK, Oct. 21 and Nov. 12, 1940, and received Dec. 23, 1940; CSK to Taylor, Nov. 15, 1940.

94 CSK to Taylor, Apr. 24, 28, and June 9 and 30, 1941; Taylor to CSK, Apr. 27, 1941; Drysdale to CSK, Jan. 14, 1941; CSK to Drysdale, Jan. 25, 1941; Taylor to CSK, Mar. 29, 1941. Drysdale designed the Outdoor Classroom on the Vassar campus in 1939. Karen Van Lengen and Lisa Reilly, *Vassar College: The Campus Guide* (New York: Princeton Architectural Press, 2004), 111; CSK to Taylor, Oct. 30, 1940.

95 Taylor to CSK, Sept. 13, 1940; CSK to Taylor, Sept. 20 and Nov. 20, 1940.

96 Taylor to CSK, undated but probably December 1941. Earlier that year Keefe included these lines in the Taylor file along with notes on a trip to Manchester and Dorset, Vt., Jan. 26–28, 1941:

"a bloody bloomin sparrow
lived in a bleedin spout
There came a bloomin bloody rain
and drove the beggar out
The bloomin bleedin sun came out
and dried the bloody rain
and the bloody bloomin blighter
Went up the spout again"

A variant of "The Sparrow and the Spout" appeared in Collier's, Nov. 1, 1913, 12. Perhaps Keefe meant to pass the cockney lyrics along to Miss Taylor.

97 *NYT,* Aug. 27, 1934; CSK to Taylor, Oct. 23, 1940; *Manchester Journal,* Aug. 23, 1945; Taylor to CSK, June 2, 1940.

98 CSK to Taylor, Oct. 17, 1940; Taylor to CSK, Mar. 29, 1941; CSK to Taylor, July 24, 1941.

99 CSK to Taylor, Nov. 15, 1941. On the role of friendship with clients in a small architectural practice, see Henry H. Say-lor, "Progressive Practice in the Small Office," *Arch. Rec.,* Sept. 1941, 74.

100 CSK to Taylor, Feb. 13, 1941; Taylor to CSK, Feb. 14, 1941; CSK to Taylor, Feb. 15, 1941.

101 Taylor to CSK, Nov. 12, 1940; Taylor to CSK, Oct. 21, 1940; CSK to Taylor, Oct. 23, 1940; Taylor to CSK, Dec. 15, 1940; CSK to Taylor, Dec. 20, 1940, and Mar. 26 and Apr. 14, 1941.

102 C. P. Sadler of American Radiator to CSK, June 10, 1942; Taylor to CSK, Mar. 5, 1942.

103 Federal Writers' Project, *The Berkshire Hills* (New York: Duell, Sloan and Pearce, 1939), 239-241.

104 Federal Writers' Project, *Massachusetts* (Boston: Houghton Mifflin, 1937), 539; printed invitation to the formal opening of the museum, Oct. 27, 1930; CSK to F. H. Bennett, Jan. 7, 1931; R. E. Toucey to CSK, June 7, 1929; Calkins in Wikipedia; *Berkshire Evening Eagle,* Oct. 5, 1929.

105 CSK to Crane, Oct. 23, 1928; Olmsted Bros. to CSK, Oct. 29, 1929; CSK to Toucey, Nov. 1, 1929.

106 Keefe's notes for the proposal, Nov. 12, 1928.

107 Crane to CSK, Nov. 19, 1928.

108 *Berkshire Evening Eagle,* Oct. 5, 1929. R. A. Wight to CSK, Dec. 10, 1928, indicates that Keefe loaned him a book with illustrations of the Old Ship Meeting House gallery at the Metropolitan Museum, and that Wight has carefully studied the gallery at the Met itself. The Crane files include a photo of the Met's gallery based on the Old Ship Meeting House, sent by Pratt & Lambert, Inc.

109 Thomas Andrew Denenberg, *Wallace Nutting and the Invention of Old America* (New Haven: Yale University Press, 2003); CSK to Nutting, June 7, 1929, identified the tables as #610 and chairs as #491 in Nutting's catalogue. See *Wallace Nutting Checklist of Early American Reproductions* (Watkins Glen: American Life Foundation, 1969).

110 CSK to Nutting, Sept. 19, 1929; Donnelly to CSK, Sept. 20 and 30, Oct. 17, 1929; Denenberg, 150.

111 Toucey to CSK, July 22, 1929; CSK to Toucey, July 24, 1929; *Berkshire Evening Eagle*, Oct. 5, 1929; color printed advertising for Crane's Extra Superfine Quality in Crane file.

112 Bill for $53.50 from Myron S. Teller, Colonial Wrought Iron Hardware, to Crane & Co., July 31, 1929; Teller Colonial Wrought Iron Hardware bill for $115, Aug. 6, 1929; Teller to CSK, Aug. 6, 1929; Teller's blueprint for "False Strap" received Aug. 7, 1929. Keefe again went against Teller in designing false strap hinges for the face of garage doors for Charles C. Bellows (drawings dated Apr. 7, 1930).

113 *Handbook of Architectural Practice* (Washington: American Institute of Architects Press, 1920), 109.

114 Crane to CSK, Jan. 24, 1930. CSK to Crane, Jan. 23, 1930, thanked "all the executives with whom I worked for their helpful suggestions and co-operation. . . . I have had a fine time doing this building and I hope you all will get as much pleasure out of its use as I did in erecting it."

115 *Am. Arch.*, Nov. 1936, 75; CSK to C. J. Kittredge, May 22, 1931.

116 Flyer advertising the Castle in Keefe Archive.

117 CSK to Bennett, Apr. 19, 1929; CSK to R. A. Wight, May 15, 1929.

118 *Sussex Independent*, May 17, 1929, in Keefe Archive; CSK to Tyng, Sept. 9, 1929.

119 Keefe planned stairs and porch at the entrance, May 29, 1929, and CSK to Bennett, Jan. 15, 1930, advised on interior plastering, lighting, and heating, while asking whether outside repairs had been completed.

120 hamburgschool.com; "10 Most Endangered Historic Places in New Jersey 2012," preservationnj.org; Marion Wood, President, Hamburg Historical Society, e-mail to author, Aug. 12, 2015.

121 Kingston Directories, 1916, 1922; *KDF*, Sept. 30, 1938.

122 *KDF*, Oct. 9, 1937; *Architecture*, Mar. 1924, published Pennington photos of the house dated 1923.

123 *KDF*, Apr. 26, 1932.

124 *KDF*, Jan. 8, 1951, and June 31, 1922.

125 *Our Own Number, Kingston Post American Legion*, Dec. 1922, 2; Eugene B. Carey, "History of Our Memorial Building," *Our Own Number*, Aug. 1926, 6–16.

126 *KDF*, Aug. 26, 1936.

127 *Our Own Number*, Dec. 1922, 2; *KDF*, Jan. 20, 1926. Keefe originally proposed a large auditorium at the rear of the building, but this was not built. *Our Own Number*, Dec. 1922, 2.

128 *KDF*, Jan. 20, 1926; Rhoads, "Colonial Revival and American Nationalism," 239-254; *KDF*, May 12, 1925.

129 *KDF*, Sept. 16, 1926; *Am. Arch.*, Apr. 27, 1927; Rhoads, "The American Legion Building on West O'Reilly Street," *Kingston Times*, May 31, 2012.

130 *KDF*, Dec. 28, 1916, and Oct. 19, 1927.

131 *KDF*, May 20, 1944, July 30, 1921, and Sept. 14, 1925.

132 *NYT*, Apr. 12, 1947; *Poughkeepsie Eagle-News*, Feb. 19, 1935.

133 Obituary of Ella Winchell Darling, *Proceedings of the Ulster County Historical Society*, 1940–44, 73. The Moehring property is today The Ashokan Center. The graves of Lester and Barbara Moehring are marked by a boulder monument in Wiltwyck Cemetery.

134 Keefe's rendering was published in *Am. Arch.*, Sept. 22, 1920. Its editor, W. H. Crocker, July 23, 1920, sought Keefe's permission to also use the drawing as "a bully cover" for another magazine, *Building Age*, but it was not used, at least through December 1920.

135 Information from Tom D'Onofrio and John A. Clark of the Hudson Area Library History Room, Jan. 31, 2015.

136 *Catskill Daily Mail*, June 3 and 25, 1927, and Oct. 19, 1928. With his drawing of the Main Street Elevation dated March 23, 1927, Keefe penciled color notes: "Brick painted red with joints striped white-white trim-dark green door-sign in red letters."

137 *Albany Times Union*, Oct. 27, 1926, and June 15, 1927; *Catskill Recorder*, Dec. 24, 1926; *Catskill Daily Mail*, June 18, 1927. Keefe's clubhouse resembles the Twaalf-

skill clubhouse in Kingston designed by Gerard Betz, apparently by April 1926: *KDF*, Apr. 26, 1926. Thanks to the late Ray Caddy for bringing this to my attention. By 1984 the Catskill clubhouse had had its porches enclosed and hardly resembled Keefe's design. A Catskill newspaper in Keefe's newspaper clipping file, probably the *Daily Mail*, on Feb. 10, 1933, publicized Keefe's honorable mention in the Better Homes in America contest and noted that he had designed the Catskill Country Club and other unnamed buildings in Catskill where he "has many friends."

138 CSK to Rice, Aug. 14, 1928.

Chapter Five

1 Talbot Faulkner Hamlin, "The Architect and the Depression," *Nation*, Aug. 9, 1933, 152.

2 Lewis to CSK, May 14, 1930; CSK to Lewis, May 16, 1930; CSK to Paris Office, Guaranty Trust Co., July 28, 1930; Grace Keefe to Master Joseph Hoffman, n.d.

3 *KDF*, Oct. 15, 1930; CSK to Robert Troidl, Dec. 19, 1930.

4 CSK to Bellows at 52 William St., New York, April 30, 1931; CSK to Rice, July 12, 1932. Pleas for payment went from Keefe to Alfred J. Macdonald and H. F. R. Mason, July 15, 1932.

5 CSK to American Radiator Co., May 20, 1932; CSK to H. L. Withington, July 15, 1931.

6 CSK to MacMurphey, Feb. 15, 1933; CSK to Ann MacMurphey, Mar. 10, 1933. She acknowledged that "the winter has been exceedingly dreary," but now in mid-March "we felt the first touch of spring," and she pressed sprigs of clover in her note. MacMurphey to CSK, Mar. 18, 1933.

7 CSK to Cunningham, July 1933.

8 "Is Your Builder Working for You or Himself?" *Your Home*, March 1930, offprint in Keefe's Archive.

9 CSK to Mr. Higgins, Dec. 2, 1932.

10 Newcomb and Keefe exchanged five letters between Oct. 10 and Nov. 1, 1932.

11 CSK to Meginnis, Nov. 19, 1937; CSK to Kittredge, June 5, 1931; CSK to Rice, July 1, 1931.

12 William Knust, Advertising Manager, National Lead Co., to Ralph Reinhold, Oct. 31, 1936; Reinhold to CSK, Nov. 12, 1936.

13 CSK to Meginnis, Nov. 19, 1937; Gedney phone interview by author, Jan. 24, 1985; *Pencil Points*, Jan. 1933, 34–35.

14 Meginnis to CSK, Nov. 18, 1937; CSK to Meginnis, Nov. 19, 1937; *KDF*, June 23, 1945.

15 CSK to Mother (Mattie), Dec. 13, 1937; CSK to Robert Keefe, Sept. 26, 1934; CSK to Adam Porter, undated; Walter H. Gill, Attorney at Law, "For Services rendered and disbursements made in relation to sale of . . . 292 Washington Ave.," July 17, 1941.

16 *KDF*, Dec. 31, 1959, and Jan. 25, 1958.

17 Ian MacAlister, Secretary, RIBA, to CSK, Jan. 30, 1935; Levi to CSK, June 20, 1934; CSK to Levi, June 26, 1934.

18 *NYT*, May 22, 1926, Aug. 28 and Dec. 24, 1931; Burbank to CSK, Sept. 1, 1934; H. S. Goodhart Rendel to CSK, Aug. 14, 1936.

19 *International Architecture 1924–34. Catalogue of the Centenary Exhibition of the Royal Institute of British Architects*, London (1934).

20 CSK to Taylor, Feb. 1, 1935. Here Keefe mentioned that he kept a "postal address" in New York.

21 *KDF*, Aug. 26, 1936, Apr. 8, 1938, and Reed's obituary, *KDF*, Jan. 12, 1946. Richard Gruver, "Charles S. Keefe, A.I.A.," *KDF*, Oct. 9, 1937, exaggerated the quantity of Keefe material in the RIBA exhibit.

22 CSK to Branson, May 6, 1932. CSK to Branson, May 27, 1932, reported that the design had been constructed by a man on Long Island for about $6,800.

23 Branson to CSK, June 22, 1932; CSK to Branson, Aug. 10 and 11, 1932.

24 Branson to CSK, Aug. 4 and 22, Dec. 10, 1932.

25 Ann MacMurphey to Brenchley, Mar. 1, 1932; CSK to contractor William Young, June 9, 1933.

26 *NYT*, June 29, 1976; R. MacMurphey to CSK, Mar. 5, 1933.

27 A. MacMurphey to CSK, May 30, 1933; R. MacMurphey to CSK, July 20, 1932; Teller to CSK, June 12, 1933.

28 Janet Lindstrom e-mail to author, July 25, 2016; A. MacMurphey to CSK, received Apr. 13, 1933; CSK to A. MacMurphey, Apr. 13, 1933; R. MacMurphey to CSK, Apr. 13, 1933; CSK to R. MacMurphey, Apr. 14, 1933.

29 R. MacMurphey to CSK, Oct. 11, 1932; A. MacMurphey to CSK, Oct. 17, 1932; CSK to R. MacMurphey, Oct. 18, 1932.

30 A. MacMurphey to CSK, Mar. 18, 1933.

31 A. MacMurphey to CSK, Oct. 17, 1932; R. MacMurphey to CSK, Apr. 13, 1933; Keefe wrote in pencil on the back of a copy of his letter to Ann MacMurphey, May 31, 1933: "I heare mayebee youe goe to gaye Paree that is Paris tooe those whoe knowe. I bene get edgicate in Francee so I putte youe wise to thate place. Youe keep lefte wen you git there or you gette boomped. Doan forgette thate one thinge. Nuthere one is putte letter e on ende of alle worde whene you rite, theme peupul thinke you get edgicate there tooe. Theye thinke soe but I knoe bettere. Iffe you meete anye one there doane saye you knoe mee. I doane wante theme to knoe wher I ame nowe. Besite they not knoe thatte. Doane drinke anne thinge greene. I am IRISHE butt greene doane worke sowe welle in Francee. Nuther thinge doane goe out alone take youre wift witte youe. Thate ish saftee firste. Two muche advishe youe saye. All rite youe seeeeeeeeeeee."

32 CSK to R. MacMurphey, Oct. 18, 1932; R. MacMurphey to CSK, Oct. 30, 1932; A. MacMurphey to CSK, Oct. 26, 1932.

33 R. MacMurphey to CSK, May 15, 1933; CSK to R. MacMurphey, July 21, 1933; Hawkins is not identified.

34 A. MacMurphey to CSK, April 5[?], 1933; CSK to A. MacMurphey, Apr. 7, 1933; *KDF*, Jan. 11, 1936.

35 *Am. Arch.*, Oct. 1932, 55–56; *Better Homes and Gardens*, Nov. 1932, 16; James S. Taylor to CSK, June 19, 1934; W. Ward Mohun to CSK, Aug. 1, 1934.

36 1940 census; *NYT*, May 9, 1973; *New York Sun*, Jan. 20, 1938; CSK to Forster, May 1, 1930; Millicent Hafner to CSK, June 18, 1930.

37 Hafner to CSK, May 12, 1930; Ernest Eberhard to CSK, Dec. 29, 1934.

38 Eberhard, "A Two-Step Alteration," *American Home*, January 1935, 87-89.

39 CSK to plumber Albert M. Punzelt, Oct. 9, 1930; contractor William Young to CSK, Aug. 23, 1930; Hafner to CSK, June 9, 1930; CSK to Hafner, June 12, 1930. The artist was Major Felten (1904–75), better known as a book illustrator than muralist. "Mural in an Entrance Hall," *Arts and Decoration*, Oct. 1934, opposite 48.

40 W. Hafner to CSK, received Feb. 10, 1931; CSK to Weidner, Feb. 5, 1931; CSK to M. Hafner, May 28 and Sept. 23, 1931; Young to CSK, Feb. 19, 1938; CSK to Young, Feb. 22, 1938.

41 *House & Garden*, Jan. 1937, reprinted *KDF*, Oct. 9, 1937; "Dewey's Pawling," *Life*, Sept. 11, 1944, 48. By 2016 alterations to the house at 400 Quaker Hill Road included fully enclosing the porch.

42 *KDF*, Aug. 26, 1936.

43 *KDF*, Oct. 9, 1937, reprinted by Betsy Boice in *The Catskill Daily Mail*, Nov. 8, 1937. In 1945 Thomas moved out of the frame house at Clover Brook into the more solidly built, Georgian-style mansion nearby on Hammersley Hill. Thomas, "27 Years at Quaker Hill," undated typescript in Thomas Papers, Marist College.

44 CSK to E. L. Hubbard, Sept. 12, 1941.

45 Thomas, "27 Years at Quaker Hill," Pherbia Thornburg, "Historical Footnotes of Quaker Hill and Vicinity," July 1, 1965," at Christ Church; CSK to Mrs. Thornburg, Dec. 9, 1936. William Young to Keefe, Oct. 9, 1937, in Thornburg file, also refers to moving "the church . . . and the church was on its foundation January (1937)." A bill, in the Thornburg file, from William Young to Lowell Thomas with copy to Keefe, Jan. 23, 1937, $3,187 contract price with

extras for digging, stonework, and concrete for total of $3,680.85.

46 CSK to Thomas, Dec. 16, 1937, Thomas Papers, Marist College, inquiring whether Thomas would accept Young's estimate for building the cupola.

47 "Quaker Lake, Dutchess County, Pawling, N.Y.," copyright 1938 by R. L. Johnson, Inc., New York City; *NYT*, Oct. 5, 1941, and June 6, 1957. Vitalle and Geiffert, Gilmore D. Clarke were the development's landscape architects.

48 *Pawling Chronicle*, Nov. 2, 1967; *KDF*, Dec. 10, 1940; CSK to Thomas, Sept. 15, 1941, Thomas Papers, Marist College.

49 Ellen Mason to CSK, July 25, 1941; CSK to E. Mason, Aug. 8, 1941; E. Mason to CSK, Aug. 15, 1941; CSK to Thomas, Aug. 20, 1941; CSK to E. Mason, Sept. 2, 1941; CSK to Thomas, June 12, 1941, Thomas Papers, Marist College. Keefe had tried but failed to interest Thomas in commissioning designs for economical, conveniently planned houses at Quaker Hill to be built on speculation. CSK to Thomas, Mar. 22, 1938, Thomas Papers, Marist College. The houses announced in 1938 as "early American-style country homes in Lowell Thomas's 2,000-acre Quaker Lake community," while resembling Keefe's work, were designed by Phillips Brooks Nichols of White Plains, *NYT*, Sept. 17 and 18, 1938, and Jan. 27, 1942; *Pencil Points*, Apr. 1939.

50 *NYT*, Nov. 5, 1943; *Pawling News-Chronicle*, Jan. 22, 1981; *New York Post*, June 19, 1936; "Guest Preachers of Christ Church on Quaker Hill," 1976, unpaged.

51 CSK to P. Thornburg, Nov. 14, 1936; CSK notes from meeting with Thornburgs, Oct. 25, 1936; CSK to contractor Young, June 3, 1937; *KDF*, Oct. 9, 1937.

52 P. Thornburg to CSK, Sept. 21, 1936; CSK's notes from meeting with the Thornburgs, Nov. 1, 1936; CSK to P. Thornburg, Sept. 25, 1936. Thomas helped the Thornburgs financially in altering the house, P. Thornburg to CSK, Jan. 6, 1937.

53 P. Thornburg to CSK, Mar. 9, [1937]; R. Thornburg to CSK, Jan. 17, 1939. The log has not come to light. Unusually, Keefe drafted an inscription for the house: "_____BUILT THIS HOUSE IN 1936. CHARLES S. KEEFE WAS THE ARCHITECT." CSK on back of Sept. 10, 1937, notes re Thornburg job.

54 P. Thornburg to CSK, Oct. 3, 1937; CSK to P. Thornburg, Oct. 8, 1937.

55 CSK to R. Thornburg, Apr. 22, 1937; CSK to P. Thornburg, May 13, 1937; P. Thornburg to CSK, May 12 and 15, 1937.

56 Thornburg to CSK, Jan. 27, 1937; C. H. Vanderlaan, Inc. to CSK, May 18, 1937; CSK to R. Thornburg, Nov. 15, 1937; CSK's slight pencil sketch of 13 1/2-inch-high Buddha, Nov. 18, 1937.

57 *Pawling News-Chronicle*, Jan. 5, 1939; Thornburg to CSK, May 10, 1938; CSK to R. Thornburg, July 12, 1939.

58 Young to CSK, Feb. 19, 1938; CSK to Young, Feb. 22, 1938.

59 R. Thornburg to CSK, May 10, 1938; CSK to R. Thornburg, July 19, 1938.

60 *KDF*, Oct 9, 1937; CSK notes from meeting with Thornburgs, Oct. 25, 1936.

61 CSK to Fitz, Dec. 7 and 11, 1936; photos and *Washington Herald*, Jan. 4, 1937, clipping in Thornburg file, also brochures from Fitz in the Thornburg file; CSK notes on "Trip to Quaker Hill, Dec. 29, 1936"; CSK to R. Thornburg, Jan. 6, 1937. Keefe received an offer to provide mill grinding machinery from G. B. Decker of Delhi, Delaware County, Feb. 23, 1937.

62 Fitz to CSK, Mar. 8, 1937; CSK to Fitz, Apr. 22, 1937; R. Thornburg to CSK, July 9, 1939, with an invitation to both Keefes to Quaker Hill for church followed by lunch at Glenness; CSK to R. Thornburg, Oct. 17, 1940.

63 Lowell Thomas, *So Long Until Tomorrow. From Quaker Hill to Katmandu* (New York: Morrow, 1977), 97; Richard Norton Smith, *Thomas E. Dewey and His Times* (New York: Simon & Schuster, 1982), 320-322; blueprints for the 1914 house by Milton H. McGuire of New York for

Charles L. Wagner in the Keefe Archive; Dewey to CSK, Oct. 17, 1939. Correspondence between Dewey and Keefe is preserved in the Thomas E. Dewey Papers at the University of Rochester Library.

64 CSK to Dewey, received Oct. 19, 1939; Dewey to CSK, Oct. 20, 1939; Dewey to CSK, Nov. 16, 1939.

65 Smith, 323; Dewey to CSK, Nov. 28, 1939; second letter, Dewey to CSK, Nov. 28, 1939.

66 CSK to Dewey, Feb. 21, 1940; Lillian Rosse, Dewey's secretary, to CSK, Feb. 26, 1940; CSK to Dewey, Apr. 24, 1941; Dewey to CSK, July 9, 1940 and Jan. 2, 1941; CSK to Dewey, Jan. 4, 1941 and Oct. 2, 1942. Beardsley was Keefe's neighbor at 288 Lucas Ave.

67 *NYT*, Mar. 4, 1941, and Nov. 5, 1943; William B. Rhoads, "New York's White Wings and the Great Saga of Sanita," *New York History*, April 1999, 170–184.

68 Rhoads, *Ulster County*, 71; Rhoads, *Kingston*, 85–87.

69 *KDF*, Oct. 9, 1937, and Dec. 13, 1957.

70 *KDF*, June 2, 1933, Jan. 13 and Dec. 16, 1936, June 2 and Oct. 29, 1937; CSK's Arnold notes, Oct. 11, 1937; CSK to Mr. Schmidt, Sept. 22, 1937.

71 CSK's undated typed description of "Residence of Mr. Charles L. Arnold."

72 *KDF*, Aug. 8, 2003.

73 Author's phone interview with Letha A. Gedney, Jan. 24, 1985.

74 *KDF*, Oct. 9, 1937, and June 12, 1948; *Pic. Rev.* to CSK, Nov. 9, 1934.

75 *KDF*, May 1, 1917, Oct. 20, 1928, May 20, 1936, Dec. 19, 1967. Gina Wouters and Andrea Gollin, eds., *Robert Winthrop Chanler: Discovering the Fantastic* (New York: Monacelli Press, 2016), 224. The portrait was given to the Woodstock Artists Association by his widow, Carol Downer.

76 *Brooklyn Daily Eagle*, Jan. 26, 1931. In 1982, as a widow, Carol Downer showed the portrait to the author and his wife, who in 2015 purchased it at a Wall Street antiques shop in Kingston.

77 *KDF*, Nov. 17, 1932, Dec. 9, 1937, May 18 and Oct. 12, 1939, Sept. 10, 1940, May 21, 1943.

78 Author's interview with Carol Downer, June 25, 1982; Carol Downer to author, Jan. 4, 1986. In thanking Mrs. Downer for our 1982 visit, I noted that, "I learned a good deal about Charles Keefe, so that he is assuming the character of a long-departed grandfather in my mind!" Author to Carol Downer, June 30, 1982. I have no memory of my own admirable grandfathers.

79 Sally and I acquired the table and sampler, suggestive of Carol Downer's taste in architecture and furnishing and her outlook on life, at the auction held after her death by JMW Auctions, Kingston, Feb. 1, 2014. We also purchased a three-piece set of Swedish pewter—two candelabra and a bowl fitted with dolphins and marked "SVENSKT/TENN/STOCKHOLM"—that suggest Carol Hallstrom Downer's family heritage. The candelabra appear on the living-room mantel in a Keefe Archive photo.

80 Marsh to author, Jan. 24, 1985; *KDF*, May 6, 1921, Apr. 19, 1922, Oct. 23, 1923, Apr. 1, 1934, Dec. 12, 1935, Oct. 15, 1943, Nov. 24, 1953, Aug. 28, 1995.

81 *KDF*, July 20, 1937, and Apr. 25, 1938.

82 Author's phone conversation with Olive Marsh, 1985.

83 *KDF*, June 17, 1958.

84 *KDF*, Apr. 24, 1913; Laidlaw to CSK, Feb. 19, 1941, and CSK to Laidlaw, Feb. 27, 1941. According to Wikipedia, "nigger in the woodpile" means "some fact of considerable importance that is not disclosed" and was widely used in literature and films in the 1920s and 30s.

85 *KDF*, Jan. 8, 1917.

86 Author's interview with Don Kent, George Kent's son, Jan. 16, 1985. In 2017 Don Kent was still owner of the house and store. In the Keefe Archive are ten blueprint sheets from the Historic American Buildings Survey of the "Dumond House," Apr. 1934, no delineator identified, although images from the Library of Congress now identify A. Schrowang as delineator for nine drawings and M. S. Teller for the tenth, of hardware details.

87 Morehouse to CSK, May 24, 1938; *KDF*, Apr. 21, 1945.

88 *KDF*, May 20, 1938; Morehouse to CSK, May 24, 1938.

89 *NYT*, Aug. 1, 1937; *KDF*, Oct. 9, 1937.

90 CSK to Thomas, Oct. 17, 1937, Thomas Papers, Marist College; *KDF*, May 6, 1957.

91 *KDF*, Sept. 7, 1940, Nov. 18, 1941, Aug. 8, 1947, and May 6, 1967.

92 *KDF*, Apr. 22, 1941. In 2017 the house stands with altered exterior at 220 Orchard St.

93 *KDF*, Aug. 18, 1936, June 23, 1937. CSK pencil notes, "Burhans," Oct. 11, 1938, and typed "Explanation of Sketches for a Proposed Convalescent Sanitarium, Ulster County, N.Y.," to Burhans, Nov. 22, 1938.

94 CSK notes, correspondence, and drawings, Jan. 29, 1938, to May 9, 1939; Evers, *Woodstock: History of an American Town* (Woodstock: Overlook Press, 1987), 609; *KDF*, June 8, 1940. Hay Meadows had formerly belonged to Alfred de Liagre who, in 1921, had had its stone house "restored" by Myron Teller. Rhoads, *Ulster County*, 307.

Chapter Six

1 CSK to Forbes, Dec. 29, 1924; Forbes to CSK, Dec. 30, 1924.

2 Douglass Shand Tucci, *Ralph Adams Cram* (Amherst: University of Massachusetts Press, 2005) discusses Boston's homosexual milieu c. 1900, of which he believes architect Cram was a part, but I am unaware of a comparable study of gay culture among New York architects of Keefe's time.

3 Three-fold circular from *House Beautiful* to "Dear Sir," May 16, 1924; Ruth Wendell to CSK, Dec. 26, 1923; CSK to Wendell, Jan. 7, 1924.

4 Flynn to CSK, n.d.; CSK to Flynn, Dec. 13, 1923 and Mar. 17, 1924.

5 CSK to Editor, *Am. Arch.*, Mar. 17, 1925; Crocker to CSK, Mar. 18, 1925.

6 Naoma L. Dalzell, Assistant Editor, *The Small Home*, to CSK, Jan. 20, 1932; CSK to "Andy" drafting a reply to Dalzell, [1932]; CSK to Dalzell, May 27, 1932.

7 Lisa D. Schrenk, Introduction, *Your Future Home* (Washington: American Institute of Architects Press, 1992), v-xx.

8 Also 7 from Minnesota, 5 from Illinois, 4 from Kansas, Maine, Michigan, Missouri, and Texas, 3 from Delaware and Maryland, 2 from Nebraska, New Hampshire, North Carolina, North Dakota, Oklahoma, Tennessee, and Washington, D.C., and 1 from Colorado, Florida, Idaho, Iowa, Mississippi, Oregon, Rhode Island, South Carolina, Washington, West Virginia, Wyoming, British Columbia, and Saskatchewan.

9 Pencil draft, "1933. Letter A. June Pictorial. Farrell Cottage." Keefe revised the form letter in a pencil draft, "Letter X. Tried this—1st used May 25, 1933," where two sets of plans and details were offered for $25.

10 Response to Keefe, Nov. 9, 1934, probably written by Frank M. Walsh, who lightheartedly proposed that Keefe was "going to get the next Walsh job. Mrs. W. was saying last night she wished you could design a house for us and have her favorite Swedish contractor build it." There is no further record of Keefe designing for the Walshes.

11 Harry M. Crooks to *Pic. Rev.*, May 13, 1933; Harvey A. Carey to *Pic. Rev.*, May 13, 1933; Carey to CSK, May 22 and 25, 1933; Miss Anna M. Hubard to CSK, June 26 and August 25, 1933; CSK to Hubard, Sept. 1, 1933.

12 J. F. Raulston to *Pic. Rev.*, Apr. 30, 1933; CSK to R. A. Emnet, Aug. 25, 1933; Miller to *Pic. Rev.*, May 11, 1933; CSK to Miller, May 17, 1933; Murdock to CSK, Nov. 16, 1933.

13 Rieger to *Pic.l Rev.*, Oct. 16, 1933; e.g., John M. Borowsky of Bridgeport, Conn., to *Pic. Rev.*, July 9, 1933.

14 Poindexter to *Pic. Rev.*, May 10, 1933; CSK to Poindexter, May 16, 1933. Poindexter belonged to the D.A.R. Hic-A-Sha-Ba-Ha Chapter DAR Register records, library. msstate.edu.

15 MaPearle Williams to *Pic. Rev.*, Oct. 31, 1933; CSK to Williams, Nov. 20, 1933.

16 Price to CSK, June 16 and 28, 1933; CSK to Price, June 23, 1933.

17 Hulbert to CSK, Sept. 19, 1933; CSK to Hulbert, Sept. 26, 1933.

18 CSK to Miss Thurston, June 13, 1933.

19 CSK to Janet Wise, Sept. 12, 1933. This was in response to a letter from the Wises in an envelope postmarked Sept. 9, 1933. Keefe did not ordinarily keep such envelopes, but he did in this case, probably because it bore two stamps depicting the Federal Building at the Chicago Century of Progress exhibition.

20 Wise to CSK, Sept. 25, 1933; CSK to James Wise, Sept. 27, 1933.

21 Metcalf to *Pic. Rev.*, Oct. 10, 1933; CSK to Metcalf, Oct. 30, 1933; Metcalf to CSK, Oct. 31, 1933. A photo of Metcalf and his family with a Santa Claus in front of their house at 602 Ash St., Brockton, on Dec. 20, 1955, is in the Bauman Collection at Stonehill College, facebook.com/BaumanCollection.

22 CSK to Kenneth Reid, editor, *Pencil Points*, May 29, 1939; Charles Magruder, Associate Editor, *Pencil Points*, to CSK, June 8, 1939.

23 The reference to "button hole makers" was then commonly a degrading term for Jewish tailors and garment workers. Christopher M. Sterba, *Good Americans: Italian and Jewish Immigrants during the First World War* (Oxford University Press, 2003), 110.

24 CSK to Chappell, Jan. 28, 1930.

25 Chappell to CSK, Feb. 7, 1930.

26 CSK interview, *Your Home*, Dec. 1930, 10.

27 Cunningham to CSK, July 17, 1933.

28 James S. Taylor to CSK, June 19, 1934; CSK to Taylor, Feb. 4, 1935.

29 CSK to Editor, *Arch. Forum*, Dec. 14, 1938.

30 Myers to CSK, Jan. 4, 1939; Myers's obituary, *NYT*, Sept. 20, 1947.

31 The October 1939 visit was made with Grace and two of his Vermont relatives, the Misses Agnes and Dorothy Keefe. *KDF*, Oct. 28, 1939.

32 *Arch. Forum*, Feb. 1939, 30, 54.

33 Schaeffer to CSK, Feb. 11, 1939.

34 CSK to Schaeffer, Feb. 24, 1939. This may be the only "damn" to appear in surviving Keefe papers.

35 Taylor to CSK, Nov. 4, 1940; CSK to Taylor, Nov. 7, 1940.

36 CSK to Dewey, Apr. 27, 1943.

37 Roosevelt to "Dear Friend," Nov. 4, 1944.

38 *KDF*, Feb. 1, 1940.

39 *KDF*, Dec. 4, 1940; Sept. 16, 1941; Oct. 9, 1942.

Chapter Seven

1 Cecil D. Elliott, *The American Architect from the Colonial Era to the Present* (Jefferson, N.C.: McFarland, 2003), 157; CSK to Taylor, Mar. 25, 1942.

2 *NYT* and *Boston Globe*, Nov. 6, 1961; *KDF*, July 22, 1944; Kingston Directory, 1944.

3 CSK to Dewey, Apr. 27, 1943.

4 *KDF*, June 16, 1943.

5 *KDF*, May 13, 1920, Sept. 8, 1945, Nov. 21, 1946, Aug. 22, 1951, Sept. 20, 1960.

6 *KDF*, Aug. 24, 1951.

7 *KDF*, July 17, 1969.

8 Peter Carey, current owner of Norton's Hebron home, e-mail to author, Dec. 2014, and author's conversations with Carey on a visit to Hebron, Sept. 13–15, 2016.

9 CSK to Thomas, June 18, 1946, Thomas Papers, Marist College; *Pawling-Patterson News-Chronicle*, Feb. 20 and Sept. 18, 1947.

10 CSK to Thomas, July 10, 1946, Thomas Papers, Marist College; *NYT*, Dec. 3, 1945, and Nov. 7, 1944; William Baehr of the Franklin D. Roosevelt Presidential Library e-mail to author, Nov. 3, 2016.

11 CSK to A. M. Schmidt, Mar. 4, 1946; CSK to Lumb, May 9, 1946; CSK to Teller, Mar. 4, 1946; Teller to CSK, Mar. 12, 1946. Morehouse was a member of the **Hurley Reformed Church** (*KDF*, July 5, 1950) and may have been responsible for Keefe making sketches for an outdoor sign for the church in December 1945.

12 CSK to A.M. Schmidt, Mar. 4, 1946.

13 *KDF*, July 20, 1946; author's conversation with Don Kent, Jan. 16, 1985.

14 William B. Rhoads, "The Germantown Parsonage in 1946: Architect Charles S. Keefe and Clients Edward and Friedl Ekert," *Hudson Valley Vernacular Architecture Newsletter*, July 2012, 6–9. Note that the illustrations are incorrectly captioned.

Correspondence between Grace Keefe and the Ekerts is held by the Germantown History Department of the Town of Germantown, which maintains the parsonage.

15 Date of death in Wiltwyck Cemetery records, checked Nov. 21, 2014; *NYT*, July 20, 1946; *KDF*, July 19 and 22, 1946.

16 CSK to Norton, Dec. 13, 1927; CSK to Oldrin, Jan. 22, 1930.

17 *KDF*, Dec. 27, 1917. One of the physicians treating Keefe was Dr. Edwin C. Fassett, who in 1935 would have Keefe design alterations to his home in Kingston.

18 *KDF*, July 25, 1936; CSK to Quick, Oct. 1, 1940.

19 *KDF*, July 23, 1946.

20 *KDF*, Aug. 15, 1969; CSK to Mother (Mattie), Dec. 13, 1937; F. A. Fitchel of John Swenson Granite Co. to CSK, Apr. 2, 1927; Swenson Granite Co. to CSK, Aug. 31, 1927. In November 1942 Keefe designed another family monument at Wiltwyck (section Laurel 8), a modest white marble slab inscribed with a caduceus, for his uncle, Christopher Fleming Keefe, M.D. (Aug. 13, 1854–Apr. 2, 1942).

21 Byrne Brothers on Broadway in Kingston was responsible for two of these markers: bill to Mrs. Charles Keefe, Dec. 10, 1927; copy of Grace Keefe's will given author by Donna Keefe. Wiltwyck Cemetery indicates, Nov. 21, 2014, that only a family member with deed to the lot can add a monument. Admirers of architect Harvey Ellis were able to place a marker over his grave in Syracuse long after his death: Henry H. Kuehn, *Their Final Place* (author, 2014), 19. This book pictures some 200 monuments of American architects.

22 *KDF*, Oct. 9, 1937.

23 *KDF*, Dec. 9, 1955; Grace Keefe to Thomas, July 24, 1946, and to Florence and Eugene Morehouse, July 25, 1946.

24 *KDF*, Jan. 10 and Dec. 12, 1941. O'Connor's copy of Newcomb's *Colonial and Federal House* is in the author's collection.

25 Grace Keefe to Thomas, Aug. 1, 1952, Lowell Thomas Papers, Marist College.

26 Author's conversation with Donna Keefe, Nov. 28, 1984.

27 *American Architects Directory*, 1956, 586; *Pictorial Review* staffer to CSK, Nov. 9, 1934.

28 CSK to Hopkins, Jan. 9, 1911.

Index

Numbers in *italics* indicate illustrations.

Acknowledgments

First and foremost is Sally M. Rhoads, my wife, cheerleader, and companion on countless historical adventures. Jane Kellar, Director of the Friends of Historic Kingston, welcomed the addition of the bulky Keefe Archive to FHK's collections and has offered continuous support for the creation of this book. Also helpful at FHK: Dr. Peter Roberts and the late Ray Caddy. Frank Futral is preparing a Keefe exhibit to open at FHK in 2018. Michael Lynch has made important additions to the Keefe Archive in the form of Keefe snapshots and periodical publications of Keefe's work. Joseph E. Hoffman has also contributed to the Archive.

Very early in my study of Keefe, his niece, the late Donna Keefe, provided invaluable memories of the family. At the same time, the late T. Jay Rifenbary, son of Kingston contractor Jay Rifenbary, was eager to share his knowledge of his father's work with Keefe and of several Kingston clients.

The late Edwin Tetlow provided encouragement by publishing my "Charles S. Keefe, 1876–1946, Kingston Architect," in *Ulster County Gazette*, Feb. 1986. Earlier the Preservation League of New York State published my "Charles S. Keefe, Colonial Revivalist" in its *Newsletter*, Sept.-Oct. 1985.

Visits to Keefe sites in Hebron and Darien were informative and pleasurable thanks to Peter Carey in Hebron and Ken Reiss in Darien. Sandra Perna and her late husband, Joseph Perna, welcomed me to their home, the Charles and Grace Keefe house, which they have proudly preserved. Janet Pinkham graciously allowed two strangers from New York to inspect her home, the Rice house in Pittsfield. Jim Hunt, Don Kent, and Will Thomas—owners of other Keefe properties—have also been welcoming, as has John Mhiripiri, Director of the Anthology Film Archives.

I am grateful for the assistance of: Rich Flynn, New Jersey State Botanical Garden; Germantown Historian Marguerite Riter; Richard Coons and Alvin W. Sheffer, Germantown History Department; John Ansley and Nancy Decker, Marist College; Karl Kabelac, University of Rochester; Linda Parent, Town Clerk, Richmond, Vt.; Dorset (Vt.) Historical Society; Interlibrary Loan office, SUNY New Paltz; Carol Johnson, Haviland-Heidgerd Historical Collection, Elting Memorial Library; and the Kingston Library (for city directories and for microfilm of Kingston newspapers before they were searchable via fultonhistory.com).

I am also indebted to the late Mary Jane and Richard Ordway (for introducing me to Carol Downer), Townley Sharp (for researching Keefe's Hurley clients), Robert Witkowski (for volunteering to clean the Keefe monuments in Wiltwyck Cemetery to prepare for Peter Roberts's photos), Thayer Hope Iaccaci (for speaking to me about her grandfather, E. Hope Norton, and her mother, Hope Norton Iaccaci), and Hugh Reynolds (for assistance with the American Legion Building). Jill Danilich directed me to St. Mary Cemetery in Richmond with the monuments of Keefe's grandparents. Scott Davies provided information about the Keefe house at 291 Washington Avenue.

This book has benefited from the considerable talents of Steve Hoare (my longtime editor and publisher), Abigail Sturges (designer), Ruth Elwell (indexer), and Gerard Burgher (Artcraft Photoworks).

Dedication

This book is dedicated to members of my family, first to my dear wife Sally and our daughters Sarah and Anne, son-in-law Jay, and our grandchildren Michael, Alyssa, Camilla, Nathanael, Samuel, and Laurel, as well as my brother Henry and sister-in-law Charley Ann, who have in their several ways created a happy environment for the writer.

It is also dedicated to the memory of my grandfathers, Dr. William S. Bertolet and the Rev. Henry S. Rhoads, professional men of Keefe's generation, and of their wives, Mary Bertolet and Sudie Rhoads, all of whom lived exemplary lives without attaining even the modest place in history occupied by the Keefes. However, unlike the Keefes and fortunately for the author, the Bertolets and Rhoadses did have children, notably my late parents, Mary Bertolet Rhoads and Paul Henry Rhoads, who were always supportive of me and my endeavors. Their oldest son, my late brother John, whose great interests were history and medicine, should also be remembered here.

The Author

William Rhoads is a professor emeritus of Art History at SUNY New Paltz. A native of Harrisburg, Pennsylvania, he studied architectural history at Princeton University where he wrote his doctoral dissertation on the Colonial Revival. He has published widely on the Colonial Revival, Franklin Roosevelt's art and architectural interests, and the architecture of the Hudson Valley. He is the author of *Kingston, New York: The Architectural History & Guide* (Black Dome Press, 2003) and *Ulster County, New York: The Architectural History & Guide* (Black Dome Press, 2011).